A CARRIER BAG OF REGENERATIVE DESIGN SCORES

DESIGN METHODS AND MEDIA FOR REGENERATIVE ARCHITECTURE

STUDIO AS BOOK
NO. 09

SCHOOL OF ARCHITECTURE + CITIES
UNIVERSITY OF WESTMINSTER

SERIES INTRODUCTION

Studio as Book is a series of publications that tender the extraordinary creative work undertaken in the School of Architecture + Cities design studios – in detail. Each book in the series covers the work of a single design studio, either undergraduate or graduate, and sometimes both, over the course of at least two years. Its objectives are:

- To record, archive, and present the pedagogical programme and creative student outputs of a design studio.
- To position the work of a design studio within a broader intellectual, scientific or aesthetic field.
- To advance the design driven research being undertaken in the School's design studios.
- To provide a reference for future iterations and variations of a design studio.

Compressing the creative output of a multi-year design studio into a single volume, using a pre-designed book template is no easy undertaking, and it is necessarily selective. At the same time, it provides a consistent, sure platform for the wide range of approaches to the discipline of teaching architectural design which characterise the school.

Each Studio as Book has been peer-reviewed on the basis of a proposal submitted by the studio's tutors to an editorial committee. In addition to studio briefs and student work, each book includes content that draws out the studio's research and pedagogical agenda. The format that this takes varies from book to book – reflective essays by tutors or past students, interviews, theoretical essays from parallel fields, and so forth.

I wish to acknowledge the contribution of the following in bringing this project to fruition: Lindsay Bremner, Director of Research and Knowledge Exchange, who was the driving force behind the series when it was launched in 2016; Mark Boyce, author of Sizes May Vary, A workbook for graphic design (Lawrence King, 2008) – and the designer of Studio as Book; Filip Visnjic and Mirna Pedalo, who have given the books a presence on OpenStudiowWestminster: http://www.openstudiowestminster.org/studio-as-book/; and the design tutors and students who have given of their time and energy to collate and edit the books into this unique series.

Harry Charrington
Former Head of the School of Architecture + Cities
University of Westminster

A CARRIER BAG OF REGENERATIVE DESIGN SCORES

DESIGN METHODS AND MEDIA FOR REGENERATIVE ARCHITECTURE

DS.3(2): 2022-2024, DS.2(4): 2018-2022

EDITED BY ERIC GUIBERT

WITH CONTRIBUTIONS BY ANTHONY POWIS, WILL MCLEAN, AND BRUCE IRWIN

STUDIO AS BOOK
NO. 09

SCHOOL OF ARCHITECTURE + CITIES
UNIVERSITY OF WESTMINSTER

PREFACE

This edition of studio-as-book is a reflection on the regenerative pedagogy and design methods used in B.A. Design Studios DS.3(2) & DS.2(4) tutored by Eric Guibert, Anthony Powis, Michael Spooner, Bruce Irwin, and Christopher Daniel between 2018 and 2024.

The book is conceived as a CARRIER BAG holding the ten REGENERATIVE DESIGN SCORES that have been developed in the studio and a collection of essays. We conceive of scores as methods open for interpretation, the opposite of a rigidly defined protocol. Each score is illustrated by key examples produced by students over the years.

The aim of the studio over these six years was to investigate what is now called regenerative architecture and the overlap between building and landscape architecture. We have been speculating on what such a design might be, how it may be created, and the pedagogies that support the learning of its design processes and philosophies.

The development of our skills and community has taken place during a period when this approach was nascent in the architectural fields, and we hope that this synthesis of our methods will contribute to its growth and help students, teachers, and practitioners alike.

ERIC GUIBERT

Eric Guibert is a gardener-architect, researcher, and teacher, practising at the boundaries between building and landscape architectures. He investigates regenerative architectures that host more equal relationships between other-than-humans and humans, and design methods that nurture the regeneration of all forms of life and negotiate the inevitable tensions between multispecies communities.

He is a senior lecturer at the University of Westminster, London, where he created the architectural design studio Architectural Animism 7 years ago. He is also a lecturer at the Bartlett, UCL, London, in the Master's in Landscape Architecture, where he leads a design studio and a theory Seminar on Feral Landscapes.

Taking a modern animist position, he researches meaningful ways of giving a voice to other-than-human lives. The mixed-methods approach is rooted in an embodied practice unfolding in a 3-hectare property in his native rural France, where the landscape has been co-created with its ecosystems since 2005. This experience is in dialogue with a mixture of academic and literary writings combined with artistic methods (photography, drawing, diagramming...), including speculative letters written as if the authors were other-than-human beings, such as soils and trees.

CONTENTS

PREFACE — 004

INTRODUCTION

A REGENERATIVE DESIGN STUDIO — 008
Eric Guibert

INTERLUDE 1 — 020
The Council for Ecosystem Restoration, *Kacper Sehnke*

REGENERATIVE PEDAGOGY — 032
Eric Guibert

INTERLUDE 2 — 044
Ritual Rewilding, *Finola Simpson*

POUCHES

POUCH 1 — 050
Regenerative Practise Methods, *Anthony Powis*

POUCH 2 — 058
Human Nature in Nature, *Will Mclean*

POUCH 3 — 062
The Ecotone Page, *Bruce Irwin*

INTERLUDE 3 — 070
The Unseen Labyrinth, *"There's Something in the Walls," Benjamin Grafham*

SCORES

SCORE 1 — 084
Ecological Sections

SCORE 2 — 102
Panarchic Mapping

SCORE 3 — 120
Ontopological Material Models

SCORE 4   138
Visual Speculative Fabulations

SCORE 5   152
Inhabited Plans

SCORE 6   164
Temporal Drawings

SCORE 7   178
Book and Drawings

SCORE 8   194
Collective Masterplans

SCORE 9   200
Ecotone Building Envelopes

SCORE 10   216
Narratives, Containers and Confections

INTERLUDE 4   222
Emi's (Cosmic) Archipelago, *Melody Akanji*

CONCLUSION

TEN REGENERATIVE DESIGN PRINCIPLES   234
Eric Guibert

ACKNOWLEDGEMENTS   238

LIST OF PROJECTS   242

STUDIO STUDENTS   272

INTRODUCTION
A REGENERATIVE DESIGN STUDIO

Eric Guibert

Architectural Animism design studio study trip at the Knepp rewilding project in October 2021

Constructing a building or a landscape is always destructive. It involves substantial felling of what is already present on site, cutting plants and digging the soil, as well as in the 'reciprocal landscapes' where materials are extracted elsewhere [1]. This largest of all human activities creates massive scars through the world, dystopian barren landscapes, deforested; the construction industry is also the largest emitter of carbon in the atmosphere, leading to climate change. The act of building destroys biodiversity and changes our climate.

And yet, not all destruction is negative. A degree of disturbance is necessary to energise the ecological dynamics that lead to resilience, the capacity of ecosystems to adapt to change [2]. All life disturbs its environment, as trees grow they shade areas and thus kill plants originally growing at their feet that require full sun, wild boar rout the soil and kill plants; disturbances, as long as they are not applied in overly large quantities, or too often, are beneficial; they create spaces for other species, restart ecological processes of re-organisation.

Decaying matter becomes the nutrition and habitat. Healthy ecosystems are never static. Change, as long as it is neither overly intense nor frequent, is beneficial to the complex systemic shifts of life.

Balanced disturbance and decay are good. But how do you define the right amount while designing architecture, and what should replace what has been removed to improve the conditions for systemic and biological life? How do you balance the needs of other-than-human and human beings and communities? Regenerative construction will remain a disturbance, but one that is designed to nurture biological and cultural diversity, and a new form of abundance, probably more intangible and relational.

A wave of regenerative design thinking has spread over architectural culture over the last 4 years, at least in British academic architectural culture. Most seem to agree on the need to improve our fragile social-ecological systems as we create architecture. There has been earlier research in regenerative design, but more focused on

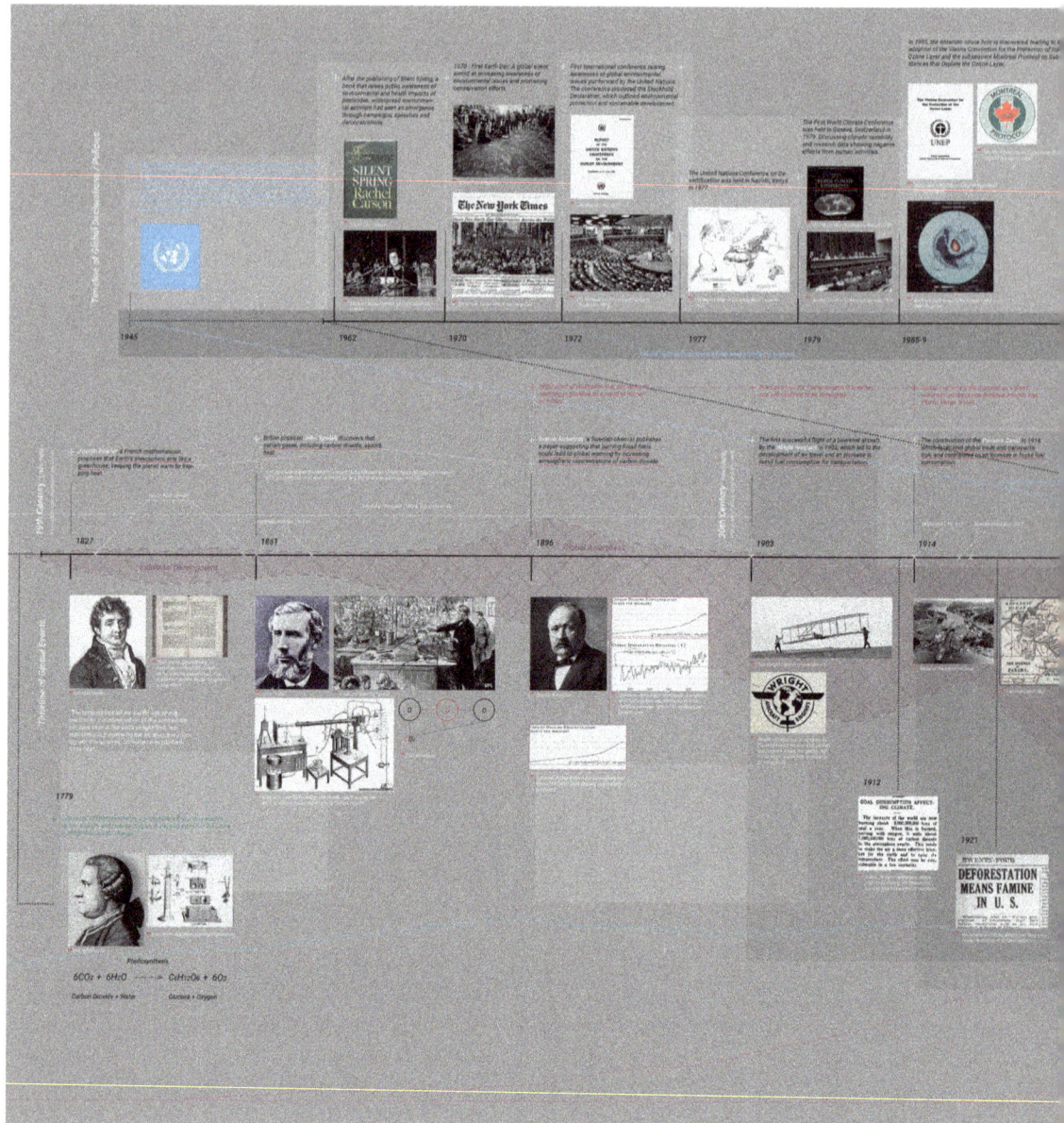

landscape and master planning, community facilitation, horticulture and agriculture.

There have been many experiments, and yet both the central questions of what regenerative architecture may be and which design and making processes help us to design it remain elusive. This book attempts to clarify the latter, and proposes some key principles by reflecting on 6 years of the Architectural Animism Design Studio located in the Bachelor course in Architecture at the University of Westminster. It began in 2018, at a time when the word regenerative design had been coined but was not yet applied to the field of architecture.

BUILDINGS ARE ECOSYSTEMS, NOT MACHINES, AND MORE THAN BIOLOGICAL BEINGS

There is a strong tradition in architecture since LeCorbusier to conceive of architecture and buildings as machines resolving and delivering defined problems and goals, and as static symbolic objects to enjoy as sculptures, detached from the natural environments that it nonetheless impacts. This rigid and mechanistic way of conceiving the built and grown architectural fields, as well as others in society, has had severe destructive repercussions, such as climate

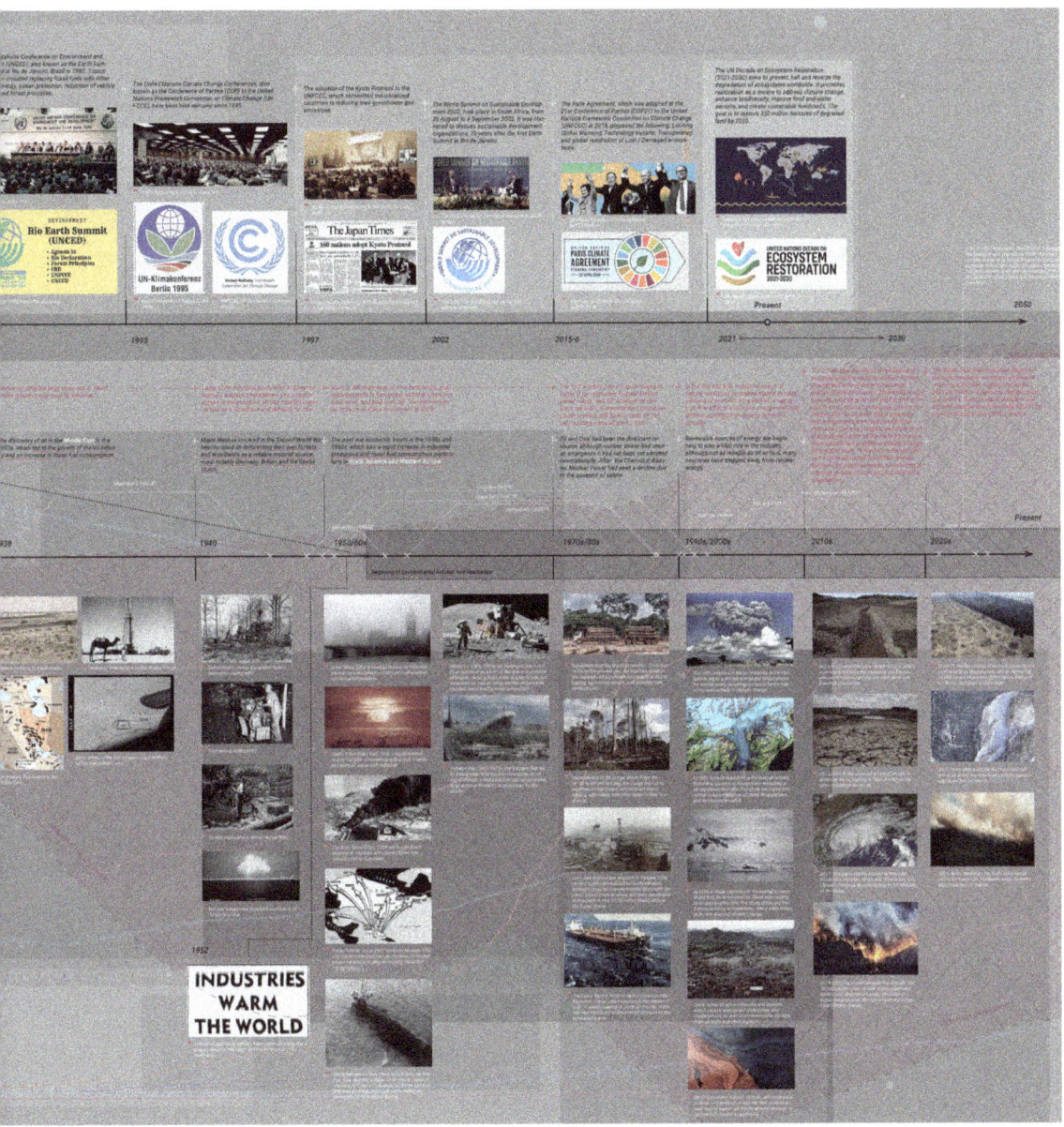

change and the 7th mass extinction of species.

In the fields of built and grown architectures, from the 1990s onwards, the paradigm of sustainable design aimed to limit the destructive quality of development to a minimum, primarily by focusing on reducing embodied and operational carbon emissions. It is only last year that concerns about the mass extinction of species have entered mainstream architectural practice through the concept of Biodiversity Net Gain.

The sustainability paradigm has been embraced, but has only managed to reduce our destructive capacity at best, or has often been co-opted into green-washing projects

Geopolitical timeline of global events related to resource exploitation, environmental activism, and regenerative policy development of The Council for Ecosystem Restoration
Kacper Sehnke

that conceal their harm. Its focus on mechanistic solutions, whether the machine is made of inert or living material, has failed to make our presence a positive contribution.

My position is that this is due to the fact that our society, including most sustainable approaches, is systemically blind; we are blind to systems and destroy them constantly, inadvertently, as well as carelessly. In large part because systems are primarily made of relations and flows that are intangible and difficult to perceive in a visually obsessed society. Objects and beings in these systems are important, of course, but primarily for how they act as knots connecting the lines of dynamic flows more than cogwheels with single, defined purposes in a static machine.

In the last decades, despite some awareness of a few key issues, the destruction has continued, and many of the ecosystems we depend on are in desperate need of recovery [3]; we urgently need to nurture their regeneration and use construction to do so by re-imagining what buildings are and their relations within these systems.

To do this, we probably need to change our metaphor; regenerative buildings are more than machines; they are living systems that are both spatial, as a mosaic of habitats for other-than-humans and humans, like a tree hosts a multitude of biological beings (insects, birds, mammals, moss, climbing plants, ferns…), and living beings through which flows of energy, information, and matter flow. These ecosystems are nested within larger systems that they impact and interact with. Like biological systems, they grow and decay, using and releasing matter as they do. Humans are similarly both a mosaic of habitats (for bacteria in our gut and on our skin) and a biological system. We need to shift from architecture as a machine and object to architecture as a mosaic of habitats and systems that are inhabited, always evolving, and deeply connected to their surroundings.

The new paradigm of regenerative design aims to resolve this issue. From humans as destructors, through over disturbance and the application of too much control, towards humans as positive contributors to the health and resilience of ecosystems, including their capacity to provide for all living beings.

The challenge at hand for the teaching and design of architecture today is that this paradigm is in its infancy. Many questions remain unanswered. What kind of tools, media, and methods are useful to design regenerative architecture? How can we transform existing modes of representation to nurture ecosystemic life? What is regenerative architure?

REGENERATIVE DESIGN HISTORIES

A SHORT HISTORY OF REGENERATIVE DESIGN

Regenerative design has a long history; before the modern era, out of necessity, humans had to live regeneratively in order to sustain the production of food, energy, and material. Animistic hunter-gatherer cultures had techniques and principles to avoid excessive foraging and hunting [4] [5]. Their lives fully engaged with that of the ecosystem they belong to also led to a personal connection, a grounded form of spirituality, and a subjective understanding of these systems. Pre-industrial agriculture also developed systems to ensure long-term productivity. These traditional forms of ecological knowledge of ecosystem and species behaviour were embodied and local, unscientific in our modern sense, yet technical and pragmatically effective.

It is only in the late 18th century, with the rise of modern industrial construction and agriculture and mechanical and chemical approaches, that the gradual destruction of ecosystems above and below ground and water began, which has exponentially increased to this day.

In the West, after the discovery of the imminent climatic and biodiversity [6] catastrophes in the 1960s, a first period of rediscovery of ecological design and making principles begins in the early 70s, with the work of the Australian ecologists Bill Mollison and David Holmgren in their concept of 'permaculture' [7], an ecological food production system. A similar method for rice production had already been developed in Japan in the late 1940s by Masanobu Fukuoka through his 'natural farming' system [8].

Such ecological thinking eventually reaches the fields of grown and built environments, first informally in the hippie and new-age culture of the late 60s as found in Stewart Brand's Whole Earth Catalogue (published regularly between 1968 to 1971, and sporadically until 1998), which covered much early systemic and cybernetic thinking.

In the second half of the 70s, this thinking reached architectural academia with the landscape architecture course developed by the Californian Professor John T. Lyle from 1976, which led to the creation of the Lyle Centre for Regenerative Studies [9] (only opened in 1994). In parallel, for the architectural field, the concept of 'pattern language' was being developed by the California-based and British-born architect Christopher Alexander [10]; it revealed the design processes inherent to life and vernacular building traditions, and redefined them for use in modern society. This concept will prove highly influential in various fields dealing with dynamically evolving complex systems such as information technology. John Lyle seems to have coined

Studio exhibition at the *OPEN Summer show in June 2024*,
School of Architecture and Cities, University of Westminster

the term 'regenerative design' in the 1980s [11].

A second wave of regenerative design development occurred in the 1990s with the creation of Schumacher College in Devon, UK, in 1991, which focuses on ecological and social regeneration and holistic approaches. Stewart Brand, the American writer, environmentalist, and editor of The Whole Earth Catalogue, writes two key books that we reference regularly during this decade: *How Buildings Learn* on the constant evolution of buildings over their lifespan and *The Clock of the Long Now* on the importance of a longer time frame vision [12]. In the mid-1990s, Regenesis [13], to my knowledge, the first consultancy supporting regenerative development and design, was created.

In 2016, Daniel Christian Wahl wrote one of the key references for regenerative thinking: Designing Regenerative Cultures [14].

Although all of these deal with questions of regenerative environmental design at architectural and regional scales, only one is an architect.

As far as I can tell, it is surprisingly late, only in 2018 that the term 'regenerative' is directly applied to building architecture [15] in my PhD, which was the foundation for the creation of this Architectural Animism academic design studio later in the same year. Later on in 2021, Michael Pawlyn and Sarah Ichioka published Flourish, which was instrumental in the adoption of the term 'regenerative' in the built environment field as the next paradigm after sustainability [16].

ECOLOGICAL PHILOSOPHIES

The development of ecological and regenerative approaches to design was supported by a parallel creation of philosophical and theoretical concepts that conceive of the world as non-linear, unpredictable, and dynamically changing. These can be found in ecofeminism (from the second half of 1970s), the foundational writings of Gilles Deleuze and Felix Guattari in Thousand Plateaux (1980) and their concept of 'assemblages', new-materialism (second half of 1990s), cosmopolitics (late 1990s), and ontopolitics (mid to late 1990s). These will be mentioned in the book where relevant.

KEY REGENERATIVE APPROACHES

Regenerative architectures use a combination of approaches to regenerate the three ecologies defined by Felix Guattari: environmental (biodiversity, climate…), societal, and personal (health, wellbeing…). Fundamentally, Guattari conceives of these layers as indissociable and constantly co-evolving; ecosystems evolve, human communities and selves also, changing in correspondence with the others.

A number of key architectural approaches have developed in response to these ecologies:

- *Architectures as a mosaic of ecosystems – Buildings and landscapes are designed as mosaics of ecosystems hosting diverse human and other-than-human inhabitants. This is at different scales, from masterplan as nature recovery frameworks, to building envelopes, to the micro ecosystems of construction. They provide ecosystem services as other ecosystems do. Humans are gardeners.*
- *Construction as disturbance – the act of building is seen as a mode of beneficial disturbance that helps the regeneration of ecosystems in a similar way to scything for meadow ecosystems. Humans are ecosystem engineers.*
- *Circular biomimicry – buildings are conceived as systemic beings that use waste or renewable matter (timber, clay, water, buildings…), and energy (sunlight, wood…) from their surroundings, and that decompose back into the land at the end of their life to be recycled again, a concept now called circularity. By doing so, they contribute to ecosystems in similar ways to biological beings. Architects can be seen as gods creating new cyborg species.*
- *Architecture as social practice – architecture is a social practice that regenerates the human communities and individuals involved.*
- *Ecophilia and biophilia – meaning and identity are gained from the integration of ecosystems and species in architecture*

THE ARCHITECTURAL ANIMISM DESIGN STUDIO

A STUDIO DEVELOPING IN PARALLEL TO THE REGENERATIVE ARCHITECTURE CONCEPT

The regenerative architecture context is very recent, and has been evolving in parallel to this studio, which was created in September 2018 at the University of Westminster in London. The first 4 years of the studio were in the second year, and the last three have been in the third year of the Bachelor in Architecture.

When we began the design studio 7 years ago to investigate architectural design processes that improve existing ecosystems, the term "regenerative" was not stabilised yet. I had previously been researching through my practice how to design with the creative emergence of ecosystems, and connected back to the concept of

Studio exhibition at the *OPEN Summer show in June 2023*,
School of Architecture and Cities, University of Westminster

nature by Freya Matthews and used the word 'regenerative' in relation to the work of the regenerative consultancy Regenesis [17].

In our first three years of teaching, we used each year a different approach to assess their respective merit: permaculture as a set of principle for both production and social dynamics, living systems design knowledge, and the metaphor of fermentation, an emergent process involving multiple species, grounded in place (at least in its low tech version).

In parallel, my own research has been investigating the concept of rewilding and other regenerative landscape practices, leading to the definition of 'feral landscapes'. During the second phase of the studio, the following three years, we have focused on designing architectures that support such processes in different contexts: rural, peri-urban, and densely urban.

RESEARCH AND PEDAGOGICAL APPROACHES

From the start, we had the key pedagogical elements that have continued evolving to this day:

- *A scaffolding of methods that were later called scores, each introduces a key concept*
- *A timetable of events with different degrees of communality: small group tutorials, student pecha kucha presentations to the studio, charettes, reviews…*
- *Encouraging the broadest possible range of regenerative approaches by building on each student's interests, subjectivity, personal history and background to test the broadest range of regenerative approaches*
- *An aim of avoiding a studio style by having a broad church approach to architectural languages*
- *An aim of the studio is to be regenerative for the students – i.e. allowing and nurturing them to emerge as resilient socialised individuals*
- *The combination and interaction between hand and digitally made media. Non-conscious (intuitive) and conscious cognition (rational)*

We will describe this in detail in the following chapter.

REGENERATIVE RESEARCH

INVESTIGATING REGENERATIVE ARCHITECTURAL DESIGN

Although the aim of regenerative architecture seems obvious, it was unclear how it might work, especially in dense urban centres.

The studio aimed to investigate both what kind of architectures would appear from such an approach, and which design methods were necessary. It was decided from the beginning to eschew a particular formal style; we wished for the students to test the broadest range possible of styles to see which would be the most ecological, or whether style matters.

This book reflects on the regenerative architectural design tools and processes that we have developed over 6 years in order to understand and develop them further, as well as speculate on potential alternatives or next steps. The aim is to integrate this knowledge into the following years of the studio, which will both take the studio into the next phase and afford a more conscious and hopefully freer use of the scores. It is also hoped that these media may be useful for other educational purposes, as well as practice.

The contribution of this book is to explicitly provide a set of scores (methods) and a pedagogical framework. Our work has learned from many sources that will be mentioned throughout the book, but to our knowledge, no one has yet collated and analysed them together as a pedagogical scaffolding.

There are 3 primary lines of enquiry:

- *How can we design regeneratively? Which media do we need to think systemically? How do existing media need to be adapted?*
- *Which concepts are engaged with through these media?*
- *Which architectures nurture the simultaneous regeneration of the three enmeshed ecological layers* [18]*: environmental (ecosystems, biodiversity, climate…), societal (politics, communities, economy…), and personal (wellbeing, meaning, aesthetics…)?*

REFLECTIVE METHODOLOGY

Although a selection of the students' projects is available in an appendix, the core of the book will be an enquiry in the design methods themselves. The central method is a series of methodological biographies, in a similar sense to the 'material biographies' used by Jane Hutton in Reciprocal Landscapes [19]. We will follow the development of each of the key methods to reveal what inspired them, how and why they evolved within the studio over 6 years, how they work, and what these journeys reveal of regenerative architectural design. This methodology also shares similarities with the research through reflective practice methodology used for my PhD, a form of Action Research, where the ongoing development of the work is reflected on to inform further development.

SCORES

The central pedagogy is through the introduction of scores; these are open methods. Each score is a medium that affords the designer's regenerative thinking around a particular principle(s). (Throughout the book, we will capitalise the names of scores). For example:

- *ECOLOGICAL SECTIONS afford systemic and circular thinking,*
- *Through PANARCHIC MAPPING are thought the multiple nested scales of the project that interact with each other,*
- *GRAPHIC SPECULATIVE FABULATIONS support worlding practices, the imagination of alternative ways of living and the architectures that foster them.*

Following Lawrence Halprin, we prefer the word 'score' to method, as these are not definite protocols [20]. They are defined enough to afford the thinking of a specific conceptual layer, efficiently, while open enough to allow for a multitude of interpretations.

These tools are diverse as thinking systemically is dealing with complex systems that engage with different layers of knowledge and ontologies: time and dynamic change, multiple relationships and scales, construction and inhabitation… The studio drawings and models mix multiple modes as useful, from the handmade to the digitally designed and fabricated.

The medium is the concept. A medium is not neutral, it is not only a representation of a message, it is also a way of understanding and designing our world and architecture. Applying a score is thinking through a specific understanding of architecture and looking at the world and architecture in a particular way.

The theorist of media Marshall MacLuhan's famous aphorism 'the medium is the message' conveys how a medium shapes our perception and interaction with the world [21]. More than the content, it is the medium that has greatest effect on society. For example, print leads to linear thinking and individualism.

Similarly a medium makes the designer, as well as the viewer, think in a particular way, forces us to deal with a particular concept, or theme, or way of seeing; a timeline forces us to think of rhythms, evolution, change; a section showing all inhabitation within and around the building forces us to think systemically and conceive of the broad range of relationships the architecture negotiates.

These scores are not fixed, they have and will evolve each time they are used, and their order will change. Regenerative architectural design requires shifts in ontology, epistemology, and methodology; we need to tweak our conceptions of what architecture is, what we need to think about and design, and how we design it.

In terms of the development of our methods, it is an evolution, a layering and tweaking of existing media, more than a revolution. Most of the scores are not entirely new, as some systemic aspects are already, partially, and implicitly present in traditional architectural design methods. For example, mapping, environmental design sections, the use of colour to express intangible qualities in plans, drawing inhabitation… Nonetheless, each medium is transformed so that it can be effective at thinking and communicating systemic qualities, the relationships between processes, inhabitation and form, time and change…

A CARRIER BAG OF SCORES

Inspired by Ursula Leguin, we conceive of this Studio as Book as a 'carrier bag' [22] of these regenerative design scores, a light and easy-to-carry container for what we have gathered and gardened so far, adaptable tools that others can freely pick from to use in different fields and situations, as well as add to.

We have begun with this description of the design studio and its context and follow with the pedagogical framework, the way the scores work together.

3 POUCHES OF REGENERATIVE METHODS USED IN RELATED FIELDS

After these introductory chapters, the first part of the book is an extra pouch of scores from different fields written by some of our community of practice. Anthony Powis, who taught with me for the first 3 years (2018-21), writes about the methods used by regenerative practitioners. Will McLean, who leads the technical module in 3rd year, discusses the work of the studio from the technical angle. Bruce Irwin, who also taught in the studio (2022-23), reflects on the role of drawn inhabitation in the drawings of the studio by bringing it in parallel with the "monsters" drawn on the edges of medieval and Renaissance maps.

10 SCORES

The second part of the book are the scores used in our studio. Each chapter is conceived as a biography of one score – methods – followed by a few examples created by students.

The story covers the precedents that inspired it, how the process and media was originally designed, how it evolved overtime, key aspects to be aware of, and what this reveals of regenerative design. It will summarise the key regenerative concept that the score allows us to think and design with. It is followed by a few students examples to illustrate how they work and the diversity of approaches within the same medium.

4 INTERLUDES

Spread through the book are four interludes, each composed of a VISUAL SPECULATIVE FABULATION, a visual narrative that conveys the essence of the project and summarises its various layers. Kacper Sehnke's is a narrative combining a journey through the building and the building's evolution over decades as it decays back into the soil. Finola Simpson's describes the funeral and grieving ritual of human bodies composting into soil. Ben Grafham's takes us through the labyrinthine world of the secretive organisation concealed within the public facing lobbyist face of the same institution. Lastly, Melody Akanji's narratives weaves her family animistic culture with a journey through a series of ecosystemic houses.

10 PRINCIPLES

The book ends with a list of 10 principles succinctly summarised; they are concepts that echo through the book listed to act as prompts, or reminders, that may serve as guides.

HOW TO READ THE CARRIER BAG

Each chapter introduces both a key regenerative concept or theme and the medium that is used to conceive and design with it.

The chapters in the carrier bag and its pouch are conceived to be read in any order; nonetheless, we have ordered them in a succession that helps the linear reading inherent to the book form. We begin with the pouches from related fields to give some context, before delving into our studio scores, roughly ordered in the chronology of their appearance most years. But the scores tend to be adapted and evolve through the design process, so most are used multiple times through the year in increasing levels of complexity.

It is important to highlight that this should not be understood as a definite set of methods to be used in a specific order; they are only those that have been most useful so far, or in the case of a few, that we see as having the most potential in the future.

We hope that you may pick the score that seems useful to you at a point in time, and encourage you to feel free to transform them to your needs, and to add more scores to the bag.

We would be grateful if you could let us know about these additions. The development of regenerative design will be a collective affair that will benefit from the generous sharing of knowledge. The carrier bag will remain open for the addition of more scores.

Endnotes

(1) Jane Hutton, Reciprocal Landscapes: Stories of Material Movements (Routledge, 2020)
(2) Fikret Berkes, Johan Colding, and Carl Folke, Navigating Social-Ecological Systems (Cambridge University Press, 2003) p.352-383
(3) 'The Living Planet Report 2024 highlights the average change in observed population sizes of 5,495 vertebrate species. It shows a decline of 73% between 1970 and 2020.' in Living Planet Report: A System in Peril (World Wide Fund for Nature, 2024) https://livingplanet.panda.org/en-GB/ [accessed on 03-08-2025]
(4) David Abram, The spell of the sensuous: Perception and language in a more-than-human world (Vintage Books, Random House, 1996)
(5) Graham Harvey, Animism: Respecting the Living World, 2nd edn (C. Hurst & Co., 2005)
(6) Rachel Carson, Silent Spring, 1st edn (Houghton Mifflin, 1962)
(7) Bill Mollison & David Holmgren, Permaculture One: A Perennial Agriculture for Human Settlement, (Tagari Publication, 1990) first edition published in 1978.
(8) Masanobu Fukuoka, Mu I: The God Revolution (1947) this was only published in Japanese; this first text will be followed by many including the better known: Masanobu Fukuoka, The One Straw Revolution (Rodale Press, 1978) translation in English of the 1975 Japanese original.
(9) https://www.cpp.edu/env/lyle/about/history.shtml [accessed on 13-01-2025]
(10) Christopher Alexander, A Pattern Language: Towns, Buildings, Construction (Oxford University Press, 1977)
(11) John T. Lyle, Regenerative Design for Sustainable Development (Wiley & Sons, 1994)
(12) Stewart Brand, How Buildings Learn: What Happens After They're Built (Viking, 1997 second edition, first 1994). Stewart Brand, The Clock of the Long Now: Time and Responsibility (Basic Books, 1999)
(13) The Regenesis group was created in 1995. Their approach is described in Pamela Mang & Ben Haggard, Regenerative Development and Design: A Framework for Evolving Sustainability (Wiley, 2016).
(14) Daniel C. Wahl, Designing Regenerative Cultures (Triarchy Press, 2016)
(15) Eric Guibert, The Gardener Architect: Designing with the emergent Natures of Places (doctoral thesis at the Faculty of Architecture, KU Leuven, Brussels Guibert, 2018). (2025) https://lirias.kuleuven.be/retrieve/510314 [accessed on 12-08-2025]
(16) Michael Pawlyn and Sarah Ichioka, Flourish: Design Paradigms for Our Planetary Emergency (Triarchy Press, 2021)
(17) Guibert, The Gardener Architect
(18) Félix Guattari, Les Trois Écologies (Galilé, 1989)
(19) Hutton, Reciprocal Landscapes
(20) Lawrence Halprin, RSVP Cycles: Processes in the Human Environments (George Brazilier, 1969) p.1.
(21) Marshall MacLuhan, Understanding Media: The Extensions of Man
(22) Ursula Leguin, The Carrier Bag Theory of Fiction, (Cosmogenesis, 2024), the essay was first published in 1989. I originally thought of 'box' but the metaphor seemed overly square, tidy, difficult to carry and impermeable.

THE COUNCIL FOR ECOSYSTEM RESTORATION

INTERLUDE 1

KACPER SEHNKE

Arrival at the Regenerative Parliament

View from the public walkways

Interior view of the Parliament Chamber

View from the raised platform within the Parliament Chamber, showing natural overgrowth

Breaking ground: restoration of the tennis court landscape *(above)*
Merging boundaries: forest landscape encroaching and blending with the site *(below)*

View from 2050: an overgrown and decayed monument reflecting human impact on the natural world *(above)*
Becoming a feeding ground: embracing natural nutrient cycles on site *(right)*

FRAMEWORK
REGENERATIVE PEDAGOGY

Eric Guibert

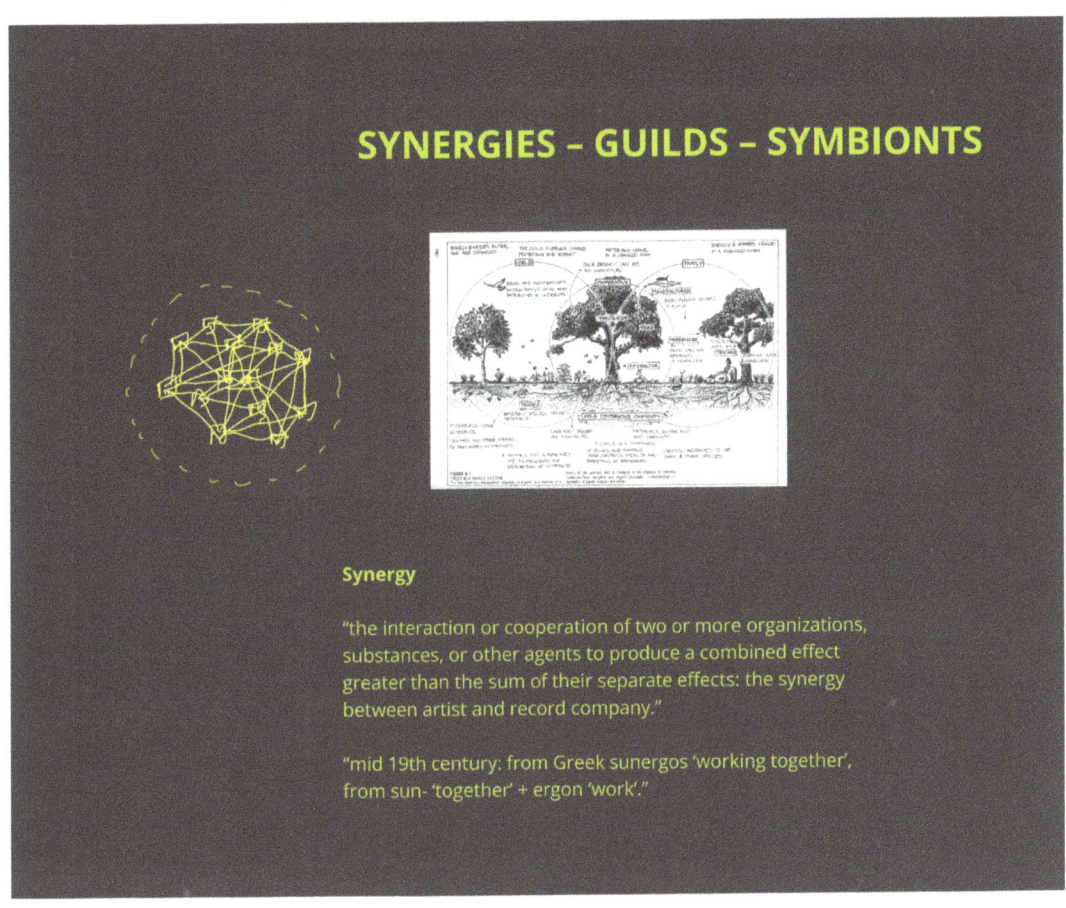

Segment of the digital board introducing the studio explaining the concepts of synergies, guilds, and symbionts (Eric Guibert)

This book is on both regenerative design and regenerative pedagogy. It is focused on the scores and media that are used to design regeneratively, but to understand how these unfold, the overall regenerative pedagogical strategy and framework of events need to be explained first. It is based on and fits within the design studio model as it functions at the University of Westminster BA. This model is tweaked towards a regenerative approach to both design and learning. In particular, our central aim is to nurture the development of student resilience, ownership, and critical thinking, both as future architects and as citizens.

This means avoiding the increasing contemporary tendency towards placing the teacher/tutor as the primary source of the knowledge of a defined curriculum handed down to the student, and at times of the design studio of a tutor as the designer of students' projects. Our central concern is to create a safe environment and framework that energises and supports students to lead their personal journey.

It also means that we aim to balance the industry's desire for skilled workers – often understood as a capacity to produce drawings and digital models – with a capacity for critical design judgement.

This framework and environment are still in development, and probably always will be, as the cohorts differ, the academic sector is constantly restructuring due to the lack of resources, and as we develop our understanding, yet some patterns have appeared. The central question that we repeatedly as ourselves, as we are sure others do, is how much freedom and how much, or little, scaffolding affords the most agency, creativity, and productivity of students each year. Too much control and direction leads to student passivity, too little leads to a lack of learning and productivity.

Who we all are

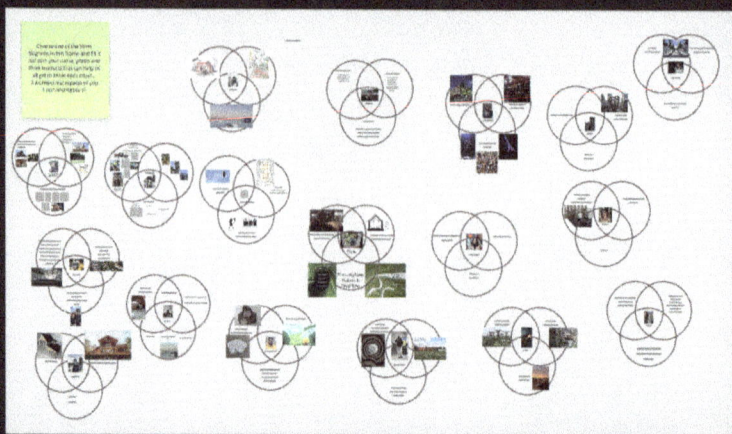

INFORMATION

GROUPS

PRESENTATION

STUDIO RHYTHM

Some ecological principles

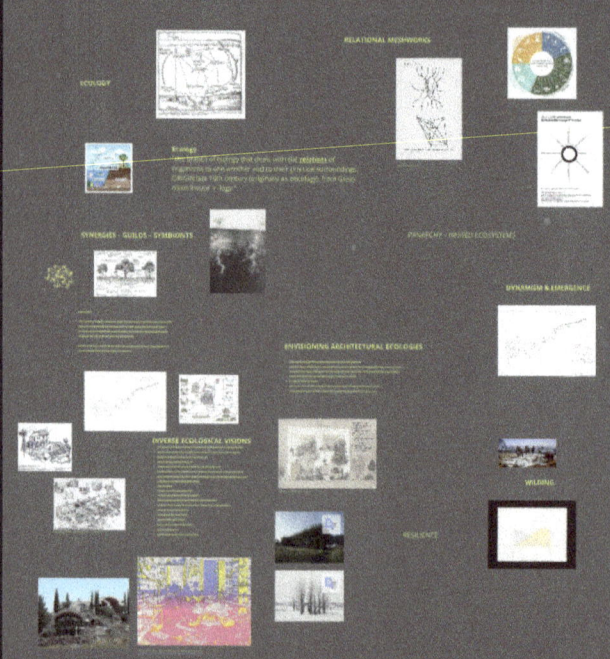

TIMETABLE

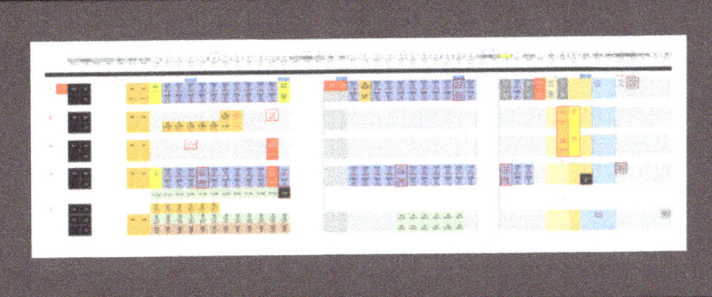

RITUAL THEORIES & PRACTICES

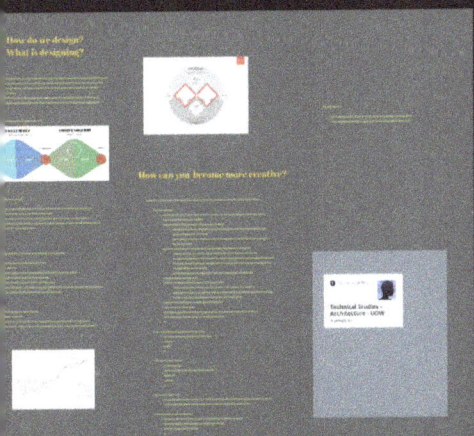

The entire digital board introducing the studio during the first week of teaching.
Eric Guibert

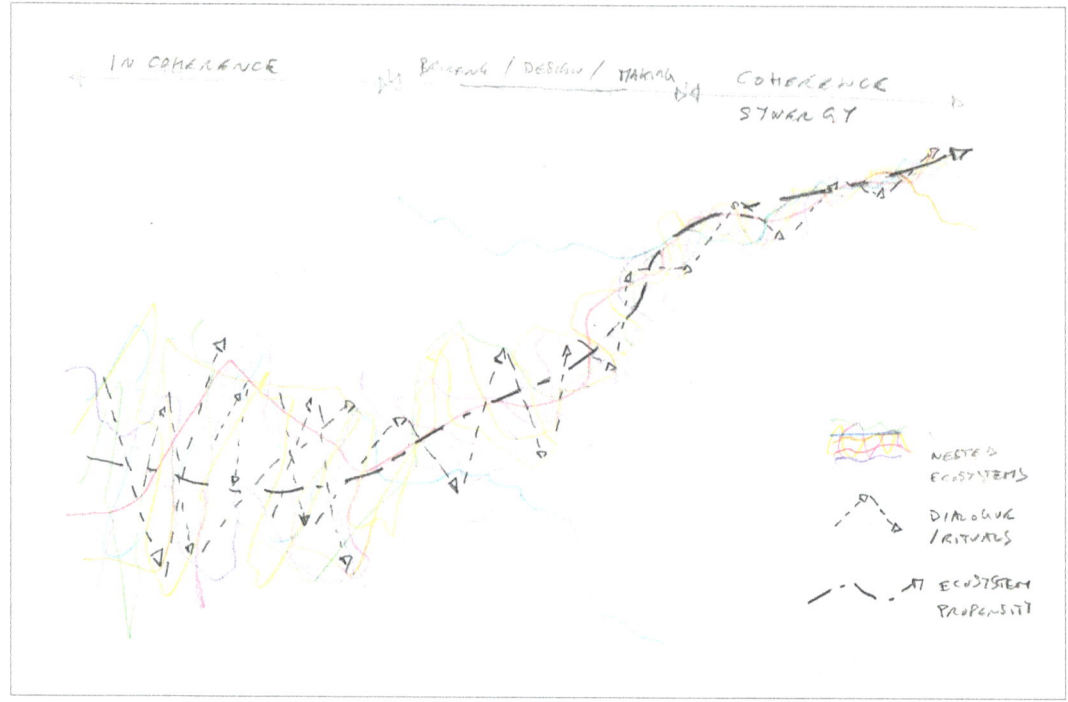

ECOLOGICAL AND REGENERATIVE PEDAGOGIES

In the UK, the community connected to Schumacher College has written extensively about 'regenerative learning' [1] and 'educational systems based upon an ecological paradigm' [2]. Central to their thinking is the concept that learning should include three layers of education, 'of the head, [...] of the heart, and [...] of the hand' [3], or 'seeing, knowing, and doing' [4], and a focus on 'the "body-mind-environment" interactions [as they] play a fundamental role in cognition' [5]. They also conceive of education as an 'agent of change' [6] towards a regenerative/ecological society.

From these texts, we can outline a number of shared principles relevant to regenerative architectural education, including the tension around one of them in relation to university education [7].

- 'RELATIONAL WORLDVIEW' – Regenerative education needs to be 'transformative'. It should nurture a paradigm shift from 'the dominant mechanistic and reductionist view of reality' that has shaped contemporary education to a grounded 'ecological or relational worldview' [8], a 'contextual relationism' [9] based on a 'cyclical economy' [10].
- 'ECOLITERACY' – Students should learn the key principles found in ecology, systemic design, complex systems theory such as: emergence, synergy,

(above) Diagram explaining how the diverse student projects emerge in dialogue with each other within the studio through the year. They are all different yet deal with a similar range of questions, and learn from each other.
It was originally drawn by Eric Guibert for his PhD to convey how an architect can design with a complex system, such as an ecosystem, overtime by nurturing a degree of coherence defined as a direction that adapts to the behaviour of the community.

(opposite, top) Overview of Project 10 years after its construction
Communal Meadery
George Darlington

(opposite, bottom) Mixed media assemblage visualising the devices monitoring ecosystems.
A Systems Directorate
Dawoud Sohail

panarchy, 'the planet is a self-regulating system', 'life is self-generating', 'diversity assures resilience', waste is a resource, 'nature sustains life by creating and nurturing communities' [11].
- EMPATHY – The teaching, learning, and design should be based on empathy and ethics: as a designer towards the communities and ecosystems you are designing for, as a teacher towards each learner's special quality [...] and help to nurture it and enhance it' [12]. This requires an openness of the mind and time to perceive the specific qualities of a place or person.
- EXPERIENTIAL AND GROUNDED – This education

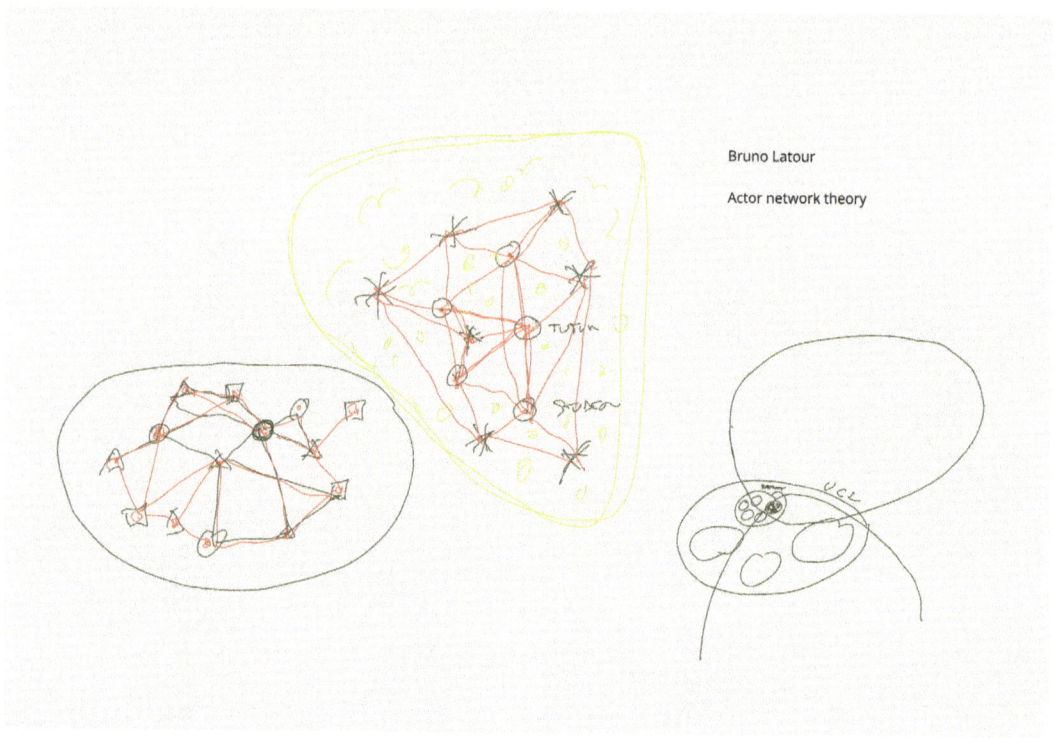

Diagrams conveying the flow of knowledge inside a well enmeshed design studio community. This is used in the first month of each year to explain that there are more opportunities for learning and support from the other students than the tutors. The diagram to the right explains that this is also valid at the larger scale of community of practice within the course, school, and beyond. (Eric Guibert)

should be experiential and grounded, based on making (often gardening), with your body, with your hands, in a specific place with its human and other-than-human communities. Iterative and project-based.
- A PERSONAL JOURNEY WITHIN COMMUNITIES – Education is 'a journey of exploration [taking place in] a community of learners' [13], the group of students is a 'living system' that is part of a larger 'community of practice' [14].
- ETHICAL WORLDING – It should include ethical and worlding forms of creativity, the imagination of scenarios for the future, 'to discover right ways to relate to the world and find meaningful means of living in the world' [15]
- INTERDISCIPLINARY & COLLABORATIVE – working with multiple fields and/ortypes of knowledge towards a shared purpose

As will be seen throughout the following description of our pedagogical strategy and the scores themselves, our teaching is in line with all of these categories. The aspect that we don't yet fulfil as much as we wish is that of an EXPERIENTIAL & GROUNDED learning. Our studio encourages making by hand as much as possible, and the teaching is very much based around the experience of a community of practice, but we encounter limits to teaching in an actual ground. We have tried a number of times in the past to create a garden that the multiple cohorts of the studio would create over time, by coming back to it a few times each year. This has been without success, as a suitable piece of land on campus tends to be allocated for future uses. There is a limit to what can be achieved professionally within an academic setting, both in terms of skills and capacity and the academic year timeframe.

The central challenge to establishing this elsewhere is triple. Primarily, it is due to the scarcity of land in the dense capital. The second is our focus on the overlap between building and landscape architectures, and the scales of enquiry needed for this to take place. There are a number of live projects that do create architectures, but these are designed and constructed as a group and focus on the building scale and construction. Most are not fully embedded in place, but some do, such as the few projects in Cody Dock in London realised by Maria Kramer's studio in our school. Lastly, there is a resistance from architectural academic structures, especially within Bachelor courses, to working in fully grounded ways; it requires unusual situations, and a great deal of energy and time, to successfully set up.

What we have realised over time is that such focus on construction and making is not appropriate for our studio as we think across scales, especially between the landscape and regional scales, and beyond.

The M.Arch at Central Saint Martin, which started after our studio in 2020, is, to my knowledge, the only architectural course in the UK where students are fully working individually from within a community for their main project, and on larger scales [16]. This was created by Melanie Dodd when the course was first set up, and maybe this foresight allowed for a gradual growth of partners for placements with the number of students, probably also helped by the high profile of the school [17]. Central Saint Martin is a node in a range of regenerative and systemic teaching and research focusing on the flows of matter and their impact on the sites of extraction, including the impressive MA Regenerative Design [18], the Living Systems Lab Research Group [19], and the work of Professor Carole Collet; these are more focused on product design.

The contribution that our studio has made is on the pedagogies and methods that support the learning of regenerative architectural design at Bachelor level. This brings the question of how to integrate systemic and holistic thinking in the learning of the foundational skills as required by the RIBA, such as the basics of architectural design, representation, critical design thinking, and technology.

THE REGENERATIVE POTENTIAL OF THE STUDIO SYSTEM

In opposition to this challenge, the common framework of design studio teaching welcomes regenerative approaches as it welcomes diversity and is decentralised. Most regenerative pedagogues point out that it is key to 'maintain human diversity, cultural diversity, and diversity of talents through decentralised, democratic, human-scale, and personalised systems of schooling' [20]. Successful studio systems nurture a broad diversity of architectural approaches as each studio is able to define a specific agenda, usually based on a philosophy or sense of purpose. This evidently required the support from the head of the school (Harry Charrington), and course leader (Paolo Zaide), for which we are very thankful, but it does not necessitate a universal common position across the design modules. It is only during marking moderation that conceptual frictions are perceivable.

Although architecture is often seen as a highly top-down field, the decentralisation of the design studio system affords the beginning of a regenerative approach in a way that other academic pedagogical frameworks might not so easily foster.

NURTURING A DIVERSE REGENERATIVE COMMUNITY OF PRACTICE

From the start, the studio's regenerative approach has been applied at all scales: the project (brief and design), the studio processes and its culture, and the students both as a collective and as individuals. The studio is conceived as a learning ecosystem; the students, with us and others, form a "community of practice" investigating regenerative design and the overlap between landscape and building architectures.

The studio proposes a common regenerative question(s) each year (a collective purpose), a scaffolding of events, and shared media/scores. Each student's enquiry contributes to this discussion while being encouraged to develop a personal journey through this scaffolding.

Central to this is a belief that the most productive range of investigations and resilience comes out of the highest diversity of approaches that resonate around the focus at hand. They do not have the same answer, nor exist in the same worlds, yet these speculative journeys evolve in relation to others. This understanding was analogous to my conclusions on the way I design with ecosystems and species in my 'feral landscape' practice [21], and the diagram drawn during my PhD [22] is used to convey this.

This is achieved through nurturing a broad diversity of worldviews and philosophies, critical ambitions, briefs, concepts, formal languages, styles, modes of representation, and challenging students to develop their own voice.

DIVERSITY OF WORLDVIEWS

We have increasingly, over the years, introduced moments of disturbance to nurture an increase in diversity. Students are encouraged to follow their intrinsic drive through the choice of their brief, guided by a few parameters to ensure they meet requirements and investigate the studio core question(s) of the year. They typically also choose their site, often from a selected range.

This nurturing of the emergence of diversity requires many qualities in the teaching: championing difference between students, aiming to avoid an understanding that there is a studio style, or a single approach to these questions, giving them usable freedom made possible by the safety and focus of a strong scaffolding. And it also demands students to take responsibility for the rigour, commitment, and leadership of their own project. Encouraging the students to develop their personal library of references and precedents, including some we might not favour or share the values of.

This is done by giving permission to students to do things that may seem strange, occasionally imperfect, at times downright messy, to celebrate them when this contributes to architectural creativity. It is also present in phrases we often use to describe a task in an open way: "of your choice", "a range of scales", "made simply but with care".

We increase this diversity by bringing specific recommendations, as many do, with the BOOK & DRAWING score, which specifically aims towards diversifying the range of ecological ontologies and worldviews in the studio each year.

Students naturally tend to develop in different directions, which reminds one of Gregory Bateson's concept of 'schismogenesis' that explains how neighbouring societies may develop their culture in contrast to each other [23].

THE INTUITIVE HAND WORKING WITH THE RATIONAL DIGITAL

Diversity also comes from a strengthening of intuition in students' work through a celebration of the hand-drawn and hand-made. The hand opens the intuitive creativity of students. The hand reveals inner worlds, especially through VISUAL SPECULATIVE FABULATIONS; it reveals personal philosophies, which, once made visible, can be discussed.

The students find it stressful to show their hand drawings nowadays, probably because it is telling, but mostly through a lack of confidence resulting from the lack of embodied drawing practice, and because the increasing dominance of digital means of production leads to an expectation of perfection, even though this quality is often lifeless and meaningless. Encouragement builds their confidence gradually, and shows personal qualities they can build on, and how this feeds a personal imagination.

Another benefit of intuition is its 'nonconscious' capacity in dealing with complexity. Our conscious mind is explicit, but it can only cope with a limited range of factors and is slow [24]. Our students, of course, also use digital means, but we encourage them to shift between the more positivist media (CAD...) and the more intuitive designerly modes of thinking, the latter being given more prevalence in the earlier stages. This leads to design taking place in the widest possible 'cognitive assemblage' [25], formed of the body and its memory, with matter, digital equipment, and other technical tools present.

SYNERGY

The concept of synergy – the effect of two or more elements working together being larger than the sum of their individual effects – is central to any ecological architecture and introduced from the very beginning of the year. This is both what the projects aim to do, working in synergy with their contexts and nurturing synergies within, and how the studio should function. If all aim to work in synergy with each other, everyone gains more than they contribute.

NURTURING THE SYNERGY OF THE STUDIO BY CHOREOGRAPHING ITS COMMUNITIES WITH MORE OR LESS PUBLIC EVENTS

We encourage collective help and the taking over of the studio space as a place to work (although, regrettably, there isn't enough space for all). This is done by explaining and celebrating how the group comes together, how special and rare this is, and how the connections they make during the year will help them in the future.

Central to this is what Tim Ingold calls 'meshworks', or Donna Haraway calls 'cats-cradle', an understanding of the world as enmeshed ecosystems and valuing these complex webs of relations. This understanding radically changes the tutor-student relation, as well as the student-student relation. Each relation is an opportunity for the exchange of knowledge and data. The more we cherish equal relationships, the more we can all progress. A resilient student is both independent and enmeshed.

Concretely, this means avoiding any one-on-one learning that reinforces the tutor(s) as provider of defined knowledge or definite judgment. In our studio, students are always developing in relation to groups of students and others. These vary in scale, from the most usual and small collective learning of the small group tutorials (three students). These groups are defined by the students and seem to follow a combination of who they would like to discuss projects with and personal sympathies. In them, the work is looked at generally as pin-downs. We have a rigorous timing system aiming to allocate equal time regardless of level, and allowing them to organise the rest of the day at university freely.

The following scale of exchange is medium group discussions (6 to 9 students), during which we discuss particular scores, how they work, how they help the development and refinement of the design, how it feels to use them, or have broader theoretical and architectural discussions. These generally unfold around artefacts placed on a large table, or a shared text.

We also use regular studio-wide collective events. One is the fairly common visits to buildings, landscapes, and exhibitions, including the study trip, to discuss architecture in situ. Others are based on a Pecha Kucha system with either on-screen slides or pin-up presentations. Despite the anxiety-inducing quality of public speaking, most students love this as it allows them to see how others' narratives and designs grow, and gradually find confidence and a voice through the year.

This prepares them for the larger events of the reviews commonly used in architectural education, connecting the studio ecosystem to the outside, within and without the school.

The rhythm between more private and more public forms of exchange has changed over the years. From the typical small group tutorial and crits, to a rhythm that shifts back and forth between different scales of events. Experiencing this range, from private groups to public events and back, is essential to give them the experience that they learn as much, if not more, from each other than from us.

Some students struggle with this shift to being an active learner and collective pedagogies. This is often related to either psychological or personal difficulties, and/or a lack of independence at home. Students regularly comment during feedback how much they learn from seeing each other's work, the energy and inspiration that seeing the creativity of others developing gives, and how productive this makes them.

REGENERATIVE ACTIVE DESIGNERS

For this synergy to occur, it is necessary for students to be active, independent learners. They are given freedom, but with this comes the responsibility of the ownership of one's own journey and choices, including rigour...

In the early weeks of the year, three key aspects of an active architectural learner are presented. Firstly, the cybernetic concept that 'design is a conversation held primarily with the self' [26], the studio, and others, through a medium (as we will see a diversity of media), and that its success is in the focus on this conversation and the number of back and forth.

Secondly, by using the 'double diamond' diagram of a design process [27], design quality comes from the breadth of precedents and references, as well as the breadth of methods used. If the double diamond of a process is flat, the project will be bland and one-dimensional. Creating breadth in the process is primarily the role of the student, their curiosity in seeking precedents through direct physical experience, as well as books or other disseminations, and the amount of iteration.

The concept of flow developed by the psychologist Mihály Csíkszentmihályi is another central concept in the studio [28]. It is based on the principle that the designer balances the degree of complexity in a task with her/his level of skills in order to be in a state of energised creative productivity, a state of flow; the aim is to avoid both the boredom of not being challenged and the anxiety of doing something too complex. This is helped by the shared framework of scores, but ultimately is dependent on personal management, and especially regular work and trials.

Through all events, a focus on asking questions and roundtable discussions to gain the opinions of the students embodies the democratisation of thought through the group. The questions guide the students to discuss the necessary areas to cover, but leave openness to their interpretation. We are not always successful at this, but we constantly strive towards it. Sometimes our instinct to give a solution steps in, but often it is the result of insufficient time. For regenerative discussion to occur, a tutorial needs to be 30 minutes minimum per student each week; this is in serious jeopardy currently in British architectural academia.

The last discussion of the year is a moment of feedback, after all marking is done, just before the opening of the summer show exhibition, during which they are asked two questions:

1. What have you enjoyed most and found most useful in the year, and why?
2. What should be improved, why and how?

During the year, passive students shift to being active learners as they gain confidence. Regenerative pedagogy is equally about fostering this shift to be resilient, confident, creative, socialised, and productive beings, instead of machines producing mindlessly on command.

It is worth mentioning a slight danger of this way of working; occasionally the collective confidence leads to the group undervaluing a central requirement and no longer listening to our advice; for example, the importance of drawing plans and sections early so that they have time to refine them through iteration. But confidence with some hiccups is more important than more refined passive work in a student's future.

REGENERATIVE PEDAGOGICAL SCAFFOLDING

The support of these personal journeys is a strong scaffolding formed by weekly scores (methods) and events that introduce concepts and ways of designing with them, in a collective learning environment, where both students and tutors learn. At the beginning of each semester, more in the first project than the second, the scores are collective – all students apply them at the same time to learn from each other. Later on, the scores are personal and defined at tutorials.

A few moments are worth noting. In our very first meeting as a studio, key regenerative concepts, the pedagogical framework, and the key scores used are introduced, both to understand the design process and the studio culture. This is followed by a quick workshop where students present to each other and us why they have chosen to study architecture and our studio, and share something personal about them.

The scaffolding is communicated through virtual boards (Miro) where descriptions of them, examples, and the work of the students are shared.

THE STRENGTH AND THE DEGREE OF OPENNESS OF THE SCAFFOLDING

We have always been hesitating on how extensive the scaffolding should be, veering between little scaffolding to allow students emergence, and realising that when insufficient Bachelor students spend too much time thinking about what to do rather than doing it, and do not tend to learn the tools that allow them to design regeneratively, in part because those are not used by the other studios they have experienced. At the opposite end, an overly rigid and tight framework leads to passive students and limits their speculations and the range of positions. The scaffolding needs to be strong, but open.

Our conclusion is that, at least for BA students, the first semester should be highly structured, as well as the beginning of the main project, in order for students to learn these new ontologies, the skills to use media in a regenerative way, and reach the complexity necessary.

Synchronicity of experience between students often helps; students performing these scores, at least for the first time, at the same time, enhances cross-fertilisation between students; the studio learns as a group. Limiting the number of factors leads to both increased productivity and more daring creativity. Narrowing the breadth of the possible leads to more creative, deeper and more refined outcomes.

THE OPENNESS OF THE SCORES

This strong scaffolding is composed of scores, methods that are not protocols, that are open, creative, and intuitive. Diversity is also dependent on the openness of the scores themselves. Over time, our descriptions of each score have evolved towards a widening of the range of possible performances of the scores, the range of media that can be used, as will be described in the later chapters.

The quantity of work is a factor that we need to be careful of. We often will ask students to produce a few things as part of one score, but we should be careful not to create too much work. Openness of interpretation requires some slack.

AMBITIOUS, BEAUTIFUL, AND MADE WITH CARE

For a score to be open, the description needs to give a sense that any outcome is possible. This is usually reinforced by showing multiple contrasting precedents.

The danger is that a single example is copied mindlessly by most students; scores used as protocols with fixed outputs neither leads to personal enquiry nor creativity; they are ineffective when overly defined.

A certain level of quality is necessary, as otherwise the outputs tend to be overly messy pieces that are difficult to include in their portfolio without much post-production. I often use the words: "ambitious", "beautiful", "drawn, or made, with care" to set an aspiration and level of quality. When commenting on them, we aim to make clear the separation between a process that is useful for the design development and the level of care with which it is made, so that they don't end up thinking what they chose to do is wrong. This distinction is key to personal development. Taking the risk of trying a personal approach takes the courage of going into the unknown and opening one's creativity and judgement to others. Generosity and precision of feedback is essential to create an atmosphere that welcomes enquiry. Overly critical feedback leads to students copying examples mechanically, and this limits their own speculation and the diversity across the studio.

ECHOING SCORES…

Over time, some of the scores have begun to recur and echo through the year. They begin as relatively simple and gradually increase in complexity. This is in part to nurture the sense of flow and help limit the anxiety of dealing with more data than can be processed at once; the iterative process gives time for the gradual learning of new skills.

Time is also needed for the radical, transformative, and philosophical shifts that take place during the year. And most importantly, as the iterations are gradually shown to others, within and outside of the studio, students gain confidence in their value and role in relation to other scores. They are also inspired and challenged by the work of others, to speculate further, and synthesise. The repetition leads to skill development, paradigm change, ambition, and psychological strength to emerge together.

Many of the upcoming score descriptions will describe these rhythms.

CONSTELLATIONS OF SCORES

Initially, students use the scores separately; each medium makes the designer think about their architecture in a particular way, but over the months, they work as multimodal constellations. The systemic knowledge of one spreads in the others, the mesh of connections densifies through the year, and the design of the building develops, together with the scenarios of various inhabitations, at different spatial and temporal scales.

As we will see with the last score of CONTAINERS,

CONFECTIONS & NARRATIVES, students eventually organise them as assemblages, which are conveyed through narratives.

Endnotes

(1) Satish Kumar & Lorna Howarth editors, Regenerative Learning: Nurturing People and Caring for the Planet (Global Resilience Publishing, 2022)
(2) Stephen Sterling, Learning and Sustainability in Dangerous Times: The Stephen Sterling Reader (Agenda Publishing, 2024)
(3) Satish Kumar, 'The True Meaning of Education: Schools and Universities can become part of the Solution Rather than the Problem', in Satish Kumar & Lorna Howarth (eds), Regenerative Learning: Nurturing People and Caring for the Planet (Global Resilience Publishing, 2022) 57. Satish Kumar is the key founder of Schumacher College.
(4) Stephen Sterling, ibid. p.7. This is his 'Triang Model', 'based on the three dimensions of paradigm/ worldview being ethos, (the perceptual, affective, belief and imaginal dimension), eidos (the cognitive dimension of ideas and concepts), and praxis (the conative and practical dimension of reflective intention and action). This theory of paradigm applies at any level, from individual, to organizational to societal.'
(5) Donal Gray, 'The Synergy of Arts and Sciences: We must change our way of thinking for Education that is Future fit', in Satish Kumar & Lorna Howarth (eds), Regenerative Learning: Nurturing People and Caring for the Planet (Global Resilience Publishing, 2022) 138
(6) Sterling, Learning and Sustainability in Dangerous Times, 12
(7) There is a diversity of viewpoints of course in these texts, in particular as the book Regenerative Learning covers all forms of education from the earliest age to tertiary. There is no space here for an in depth description, or for a full literature review and critical analysis.
(8) Sterling, Learning and Sustainability in Dangerous Times, 2
(9) Sterling, Learning and Sustainability in Dangerous Times, 6
(10) Kumar, 'The True Meaning of Education', 62
(11) Fritjof Capra, 'Ecoliteracy and the Dance of Cooperation: We need to teach our Students and our Political and Corporate Leaders the Fundamental Facts of Life', in Satish Kumar & Lorna Howarth (eds), Regenerative Learning: Nurturing People and Caring for the Planet (Global Resilience Publishing, 2022) 89-95
(12) Kumar, 'The True Meaning of Education', 56
(13) Kumar, 'The True Meaning of Education', 56
(14) Lauren E. Clare, 'From Conquest to Participation: Reimagining Education as a living System within a Community of Practice', in Satish Kumar & Lorna Howarth (eds), Regenerative Learning: Nurturing People and Caring for the Planet (Global Resilience Publishing, 2022) 313
(15) Kumar, 'The True Meaning of Education' 56.
(16) https://www.arts.ac.uk/subjects/architecture-spatial-and-interior-design/postgraduate/march-architecture-csm#course-summary [accessed on 04-08-2025]
(17) This is based from an informal, and late night, discussion with Melanie Dodd at the Milan Triennale opening in April 2025.
(18) https://www.arts.ac.uk/subjects/textiles-and-materials/postgraduate/ma-regenerative-design-csm#course-summary [accessed on 06-08-2025]
(19) https://www.arts.ac.uk/colleges/central-saint-martins/research-at-csm/-and-living-systems-lab-research-group [accessed on 06-08-2025]
(20) Kumar, 'The True Meaning of Education', 56
(21) Eric Guibert, 'Co-creating with Feral Landscapes: Delineating a useful definition and ontology of (re)wilding for the architectural fields', in Mo Michelsen, Sophia Meeres, Ben Stringer (eds) Rescaling the Rural (ORO Editions/AR+D (Applied Research + Design Publishing), 2025). The proceedings of the AlterRurality – Rescaling the Rural conference, in Aarhus, 20-23 May 2022
(22) Eric Guibert, The Gardener Architect: Designing with the emergent Natures of Places (doctoral thesis at the Faculty of Architecture, KU Leuven, Brussels Guibert, 2018). (2025) https://lirias.kuleuven.be/rotrievc/510314 [accessed on 12-08-2025]
(23) This is quoted in David Graeber and David Wengrow, The Dawn of Everything: A New History of Humanity (Penguin Books, 2022)
(24) Katherine Hayles, Unthought: The Power of the Cognitive Nonconscious (The University of Chicago Press 2017)
(25) Hayles, Unthought
(26) Ranulph Glanville, A (Cybernetic) Musing: Design and Cybernetics (Cybernetics and Human Knowing, Vol. 16, nos. 3-4, 2009) 175-186
(27) This diagram was designed at the Design Council https://www.designcouncil.org.uk/our-resources/the-double-diamond/ [accessed on 06-08-2025], but was much inspired by another diagram by Bela H. Banathy's. See Benjamin, P. Taylor, The Double Diamond as an example of some challenges of attribution in the history of ideas (Chosen Path blog, 2021) https://chosen-path.org/2021/05/05/the-double-diamond-as-an-example-of-some-challenges-of-attribution-in-the-history-of-ideas/ [accessed on 06-08-2025]
(28) David Robson, The flow state: the science of the elusive creative mindset that can improve your life (The Guardian, 20-07-2024) https://www.theguardian.com/science/article/2024/jul/20/flow-state-science-creativity-psychology-focus [accessed on 06-08-2025]

RITUAL REWILDING

INTERLUDE 2

FINOLA SIMPSON

THE RITUAL OF DEATH AND DECOMPOSITION STORYBOARD

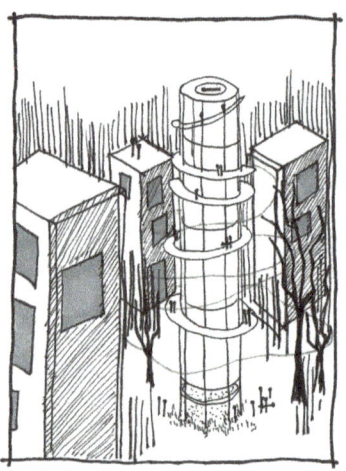

PART 1

POUCHES

REGENERATIVE PRACTICE METHODS

ANTHONY POWIS, SHEFFIELD SCHOOL OF ARCHITECTURE AND LANDSCAPE

In recent years, the language of regenerative practice has dramatically usurped that of sustainability – first within ecology, and more recently in design. Just as Charles Jencks pinpointed the death of Modernism in the demolition of the Pruitt–Igoe housing projects in 1972, multiple authors have now proposed the award of the highest-ever BREEAM sustainability rating to Foster + Partners' new Bloomberg HQ in 2017 (along with the RIBA Stirling Prize the following year) as the final death knell for the corporate capture of sustainability. [1]

Sustainability – still the dominant concept in global environmental discourse – was an obvious sort of reaction to have in the face of a radically changing climate: a yearning to keep things as they were, to preserve an imagined state of innocence in the face of what the Victorian art critic John Ruskin called 'the foul storm' of industrialisation. [2] When the term 'global warming' was introduced in the 1970s, indicating a permanent and directional change in climate, 'sustainability' emerged as its opposite and counterpart. It represented not only a defensive positioning towards the coming threats of climate change, but one which largely assumed the continuation of the foundations that had led to climate breakdown in the first place.

Whilst it is vital to acknowledge the vast amount of good work that is done under the auspices of sustainability, it is also reasonable to critique its roots in an objective and detached conception of the relationship between humans and nature. In this view, humans operate on, rather than in the earth, and in largely predictable and measurable ways. Just as we have manipulated climate thus far, so we can continue to manipulate it in whichever way we would like! Sustainability, frequently described as the employment of technological add-ons to reduce harm (primarily in terms of greenhouse gas emissions via reducing energy use and waste), in fact encompasses a myriad of more active and interventionist approaches, from geoengineering to population control.

OK, OK, I know: you know all this; you have already moved on from sustainability; why is it important to critique it over and over? Because all the emphasis on technological tinkering masks the political and structural roots of climate breakdown: the racist, colonial, and patriarchal ways of thinking and acting that are fundamental to the modern world. [3] Cloaking all of this by narrowing climate to a technical problem to be solved by technical means, sustainability enforces a restrictive view of what climate breakdown is, and the methods with which we should approach it. This is what allowed sustainability, and by extension the ways in which architecture and design engage with climate, to become so narrow and apolitical.

It follows, then, that if the concept of regenerative design is to hold any water, it must remain expansive, challenging, and resistant to such mainstream capture – not simply allow its unchallenging aspects to win over those that are more errant and abrasive. How? If the concept of sustainability implants certain approaches, methods, and assumptions within design thinking – the teleological trojan horses of solutionism, technocracy, and band-aiding – then moving towards a regenerative design framework means interrogating the methods that characterise this new paradigm. One aspect of regenerative design which its proponents are quick to mention is that it is about fundamental ways of thinking, not just instrumental formulas:

we believe that the necessary changes lie primarily in cultural, rather than technological, transformation [...] essential to the evolution from "sustainable" to "regenerative" design and development. [4]

In Decolonising Methodologies, Linda Tuhiwai Smith articulates 'Twenty-five Indigenous Projects' – approaches 'currently being pursued by indigenous communities' that consciously depart from dominant western modes of knowledge production. She foregrounds methodology 'because it frames the questions being asked, determines the set of instruments and methods to be employed and shapes the analyses.' In such a way, I will attempt briefly here to define some key tenets of regenerative practice methods. Real world examples are included to support the articulation of each method. Each [PRACTICE] also refers to an entry on the website *architectureisclimate.net*. Go there to learn more.

The tropical forest garden in Devon by the European forest garden specialist Martin Crawford. Tropical fruits and vegetables are growing in an unheated glasshouse. *(photograph by Anthony Powis)*

SUPPORT STRUCTURES

Meaning renewal or rebirth, regenerative practice is rooted in ecology. As such, the focus moves from the architectural object to systems, infrastructures, and networks which enable and support growth: beginnings and possibilities rather than something that is 'finished' at the point it is put out into the world. This is an idea that should not be at all strange to architects. Florian Beigel famously described the work of his Architecture Research Unit as 'designing the rug, but not necessarily the picnic'. [5] That is, architecture is the background – even if it commonly mistakes itself to be the foreground.

Architecture still has much to learn from regenerative approaches in ecology. [Regenerative Agriculture] is a system focused on rebuilding the capacity of soils and typically involves minimal or no tillage, eliminating bare soil through cover cropping, utilising diverse planting, and avoiding chemical treatments. These are methods that are about slowing down and allowing carefully-selected organic processes to do the work of restoration, rather than overworking the land beyond its capacity combined with quick fixes to try and restore it to productivity. The particular focus on regenerating soils as part of an intergenerational project of land repair is just a starting point: the earth care principles regenerate wider systems such as water and nitrogen cycles, as well as provide carbon storage, and the methods are similar to those found in broader socio-ecological approaches such as permaculture.

Caring for soil requires working at a different pace, which is not solely centred around human demand and economic pressures. [6] In Martin Crawford's [Forest Gardens], its seemingly overgrown nature provides bountiful food crops by using a horticultural technique known as companion planting, whereby species are planted near each other that have mutually beneficial impacts such as natural pest resilience, fertilisation, or nitrogen fixing. Companion planting encourages plants to follow natural cycles of growth and decay, and fertilises the earth with natural compost rather than cutting and removing so-called 'waste' material. Although the garden needs to be harvested by hand (its geometry isn't suited to large-scale machinery), Crawford claims it produces more food per hectare than the equivalent factory farm and requires less labour, because agroforestry works with, rather than against, the land, stewarding nature's emergent capabilities within a regenerative cycle. [7] Crawford's experiments in forest gardening demonstrate ways of working with complex systems, as well as a form of land management founded on stewardship and regeneration, rather than exploitation and depletion. They introduce a more resilient set of ecological-economic relations, working through the interrelationship of labour, natural systems, and economics.

So far, so clear. It is when these ecological principles are translated into other fields – architecture and design, but also economics and politics, that things become shaky. The metaphorical content of such principles smooths over their more disruptive aspects, or ecological concepts are misused to naturalise discrimination. [Sweet Water Foundation] (SWF), working in Chicago's South Side, confront the discourse of 'blighted' neighbourhoods, 'rotting' houses, and 'decaying' communities by focussing on building capacity as an alternative to maintaining dependency on municipal services that have long since left them behind. SWF seeks forms of collective healing and re-growth in socially and ecologically exhausted spaces. Its ecologically-driven approach to neighbourhood transformation, based upon building collective infrastructures and shared support systems, seems to directly confront the rhetoric of blight on its own terms, by asking: how can we "create safe and inspiring spaces and curate healthy, intergenerational communities that transform the ecology of once-blighted neighborhoods?". [8] Co-founder Emmanuel Pratt makes the question – what is or is not valued – central to SWF's work, which operates through art, architecture, agriculture, education, and culture to redefine what is valuable beyond the norms of the market.

The idea of support structures – seemingly agreeable and unchallenging enough – is confrontational to more patriarchal modes of design because it shifts values from foreground to background, from architectural object to generative network, and necessarily embraces uncertain outcomes and complexity over the imposition of order. [9]

MESHWORKS

How big is a regenerative network? The concept draws on the relationality and response-ability of ecosystems as an example for the relationality of other networks. If an identifying feature of modernity is its project of separating issues so as to better control them, [10] then a defining feature of regenerative practice is both restoring and making new connections: exploring the complex networks that both feed and emerge from one's own practice.

These connections can be further understood in terms of Tim Ingold's proposed distinction between a 'network' and his preferred term, 'meshwork'. [11] A network is a collection of points: connected but rigid, each part of the network remains separate and distinct, performing its own function in a limited, modernist sense. A meshwork on the other hand is a complex of intersecting lines which overlap, knot, and fuse in different ways – individual elements are transformed in the process and retain loose edges that allow for new influences and associations. Seeing architecture as part of a meshwork, then, is about engaging (with)in a process of infinite transformation.

[Constructive Land] – a programme led by design and research practice Material Cultures in collaboration with Forestry England – does this both practically and beautifully, exploring alternatives to standardised building materials from monocultural plantations by engaging with the larger construction system to investigate possibilities beyond established industrial practices. The project begins to reimagine the relationship between buildings, landscapes, and materials – in the first instance by critically reconnecting material components with their impact on the landscape, and then by combining nonstandard species with new ways of building and new forms of agriculture and forestry management to test alternatives. It suggests that linking with other industries, and thinking through all the connected elements of construction, might enable more holistic and resource-conscious decision-making to benefit social infrastructures and climates alike. In this way, Constructive Land aims to develop alternative regenerative material cultures through a combination of practical and material exploration, with contextual and strategic research into the relations between material, land, and building systems.

Social and professional networks, as well, seek to overturn the isolation of elements of the building industry from one another. [Climate Movements] such as the Architects Climate Action Network and [Architectural Unions] such as the United Voices of the World Section of Architectural Workers and The Architecture Lobby operate both within and beyond traditional professional structures in agile, democratic, and interdisciplinary ways to constructively rethinking architects' daily work and their role within wider cultural transformations relating to energy and climate. Others such as the [Zöop] model of cooperative governance – developed by ecologists, philosophers, artists, entrepreneurs and lawyers at the Nieuwe Instituut in Rotterdam – suggest ways of involving the more-than-human in decision-making frameworks.

Meshworks are challenging because they undo a fundamental aspect of capitalist thought: the separation of elements into disconnected parts. Undoing isolation, mending and reconnecting, or simply acknowledging, celebrating, and nurturing the connections that are already there is a powerful method of regenerative practice.

ALLOCHRONIC FUTURES

At the core of the concept sustainability is a contradictory approach to time that consists both of a sense of timelessness – necessary to the idea of keeping the climate in a constant state, and maintaining a political, economic, and social status quo – alongside a constant promise of a new kind of future that exists just around the corner. In combining these, sustainability neatly eliminates the possibility of alternative futures: the future is always both distant and the same. Regenerative practice is less concerned with distant futures, but more so the search for 'an absent, but perhaps possible, other present'. [12] It shares much with repair and recovery in trying to resurrect something that is already there, but dormant or supressed. It is an important contrast to the dominant discourse within ecological politics where an emphasis on the future makes forgetting the past easier. Instead, regenerative practice means working in an allochronic temporality where all possible scenarios exist at once, and 'whether the future is now or the past is the future really depends on the actions taken today'. [13]

Two long-term urban projects – the city of Zurich's [Bachkonzept] and SCAPE's [Living Breakwaters] project in New York – could be said to embody this concept of working backwards to uncover alternative presents. Zurich's Bachkonzept or river daylighting policy, first introduced in the 1980s, involves the practice of reclaiming urban waterways through a variety of initiatives such as waterfront revitalisation, greenways and parks, public access to beaches and waterways, and urban fishing/boating. By simply separating sewerage channels from urban rivers and uncovering, deculverting, or 'daylighting' freshwater streams as part of biodiverse urban landscapes, Bachkonzept creates and rebuilds relationships between people and their environment, encouraging a greater appreciation of urban ecosystems. [14] Representative of a wider movement towards urban nature, what sets it apart is both its longevity and the fact that it has the potential to make holistic and long-term change to a country's attitude to waterways, both infrastructurally and culturally. Similarly, New York's Living Breakwaters – a programme of coastal infrastructure developed by landscape architects SCAPE in response to Hurricane Sandy and the increasing threat of storm surges and flooding – looks back to recent histories of inhabiting the coastline, in particular how combinations of human activity, plant life, and marine fauna created a complex coastal-protection system. The resulting project combines an ecological infrastructure of regenerative reefs with community and educational programmes to develop a model for how to co-inhabit cities in the face of climate breakdown. It understands urban infrastructures as spatially, socially, and ecologically inter-dependent – and proposes multiple contexts for these relations to come together.

An allochronic reading of climate is crucial to addressing its complex and non-linear temporality. Moving on from terms like emergency and crisis, which are both apocalyptic and imply the existence of a solution, responses to climate breakdown cannot be simply about trying to change the future. The climate crisis challenges the temporal dimensions and limits of architectural projects understood as creating the 'new' out of the 'old'. This in turn demands that regenerative practice engages with the present, rather than the future, as a space of possibility – a subtle but important distinction.

RECLAMATION AND REDISTRIBUTION

Alongside and within making support structures, rebuilding relations, and reimagining the present, a crucial aspect of regenerative practice must be the redistribution of both control and capacity, including the reclamation of rights. Regenerative practice is also about undoing infrastructures of exploitation – what Alberto Escobar calls 'the structures of unsustainability that hold in place the contemporary, so-called modern world'. [15] Groups such as [The Red Deal] and in North America and [Movimento Dos Trabalhadores Rurais Sem Terra] in Brazil represent the interests of landless, poor, and Indigenous people – using education, direct action, and media to achieve land reform. [Black Dirt Farm Collective] confront the problem of land rights and racial segregation by combining a focus on food sovereignty with a larger project to achieve self-determination and solidarity. In such work, the transition from an extractive to a regenerative economy is inseparable from one that undoes societal and racial injustices belonging to an extractive industrial system. The redistribution of rights and capacity is crucial to the project of ecological and social regeneration.

Redistribution of control is also a key aspect of movements to open-source making, design, and especially repair of everyday objects. [Tzoumakers] – an open-source agricultural community of farmers and researchers in the mountainous region of Tzoumerka in Northern Greece who collaboratively design and build practical solutions and tools – and the [Distributed Design Platform] – a European network of design and educational programmes, "fab labs" and maker spaces, cultural-sector organisations and industry bodies – are based on the wresting of control away from distant centres of production and back into the hands of people. All of these also share a fundamental emphasis on redistributing knowledge from something made and held by the powerful to something that is shared, such as in the work of [The Southern Collective], a network of researchers whose notion of 'postnormal' knowledge production is aimed at democratising and creating frameworks for more distributed, democratic, and diverse research culture.

CONCLUSION

These four methods are the beginnings of a definition of what 'regenerative' might need to mean if it is to genuinely change the way we think about and do 'design'. Regenerative design is often referred to as a process of simply mimicking the natural form and structure of ecosystems. In its worst form this might mean biomimicry and other aesthetic imitations of nature. A more sophisticated view beyond the aesthetic to forms of organisation found in more-than-human systems. But whilst regenerative practice may well involve reducing some of the constructed distance between humans and nature, it should not be understood in terms of getting closer to, communing with, or understanding nature without mediation. It should certainly not be imagined as some supposed return to the purity of natural systems. As Donna Haraway remarks on the difficultly of such adventures, 'Efforts to travel into "nature" become tourist excursions that remind the voyager of the price of such displacements-one pays to see fun-house reflections of oneself'. [16]

On the contrary, whilst these methods imitate, are analogous to, or are inspired by the way ecosystems function, regenerative practice cannot simply be about mimicking nature. There it only ever becomes a metaphor. Rather, regenerating means fully engaging with the world in all its unnatural complexity, good and bad, and imagining other ways of living in it.

ANTHONY POWIS

Anthony Powis is currently Lecturer in Architecture and Climate at the University of Sheffield. He was previously Post-Doctoral Research Fellow at Central Saint Martins on the project Architecture is Climate . His PhD as part of the project Monsoon Assemblages was from the University of Westminster, where he also taught design studio from 2015 to 2021.

Endnotes

(1) Barnabas Calder, Architecture: From Prehistory to Climate Emergency (Pelican, 2021), p. 169; Sarah Ichioka and Michael Pawlyn, Flourish: Design Paradigms for Our Planetary Emergency (Triarchy Press, 2021), pp. 7–8.

(2) John Ruskin, The Eagle's Nest: Ten Lectures on the Relation of Natural Science to Art (1872). Although recent work in both environmental history and social science has shown that the idea of a stable climate is a relatively recent invention. See e.g. Jean-Baptiste Fressoz and Fabien Locher, Chaos in the Heavens: The Forgotten History of Climate Change (Verso, 2024); Nigel Clark, Inhuman Nature: Sociable Life on a Dynamic Planet (Sage, 2011).

(3) See 'Foundations' in Architecture is Climate <https://architectureisclimate.net/foundations/>.

(4) Ichioka and Pawlyn, Flourish: Design Paradigms for Our Planetary Emergency, p. 2.

(5) Daniel Rosbottom, 'Florian Beigel Obituary', Art and Design, The Guardian, 13 September 2018 <https://www.theguardian.com/artanddesign/2018/sep/13/florian-beigel-obituary> [accessed 26 June 2024].

(6) Maria Puig de la Bellacasa, 'Making Time for Soil: Technoscientific Futurity and the Pace of Care', Social Studies of Science, 45.5 (2015), pp. 691–716, doi:10.1177/0306312715599851.\\uc0\\u8216{}Making Time for Soil: Technoscientific Futurity and the Pace of Care\\uc0\\u8217{}, {\\i{}Social Studies of Science}, 45.5 (2015

(7) Martin Crawford and Joanna Brown, Creating a Forest Garden: Working with Nature to Grow Edible Crops (Green Books, 2022).

(8) Architecture Foundation, '100 Day Studio: Emmanuel Pratt – Sweet Water Foundation', YouTube, 26 Aug 2020 <https://www.youtube.com/watch?v=QwirmoNeRiQ> [accessed 28 June 2023].

(9) For a direct translation of this concept into architecture, see N.J. Habraken, Supports: An Alternative to Mass Housing (Architectural Press, 1972).

(10) See 'Separating' in Architecture is Climate <https://architectureisclimate.net/foundations/>

(11) Tim Ingold, Lines: A Brief History (Routledge, 2007).

(12) Donna Haraway, 'The Promises of Monsters: A Regenerative Politics for Inappropriate/d Others', in Cultural Studies, ed. by Lawrence Grossberg, Cary Nelson, and Paula A. Treichler (Routledge, 1992), pp. 295–336 (p. 295).

(13) Ytasha Womack, Afrofuturism: The World of Black Sci-Fi and Fantasy Culture (Chicago Review Press, 2013), p. 174.

(14) Fritz Conradin and Reinhard Buchli, 'The Zurich Stream Daylighting Program', in Handbook of Regenerative Landscape Design, ed. by Robert L. France (CRC Press, 2008).

(15) Arturo Escobar, Designs for the Pluriverse: Radical Interdependence, Autonomy, and the Making of Worlds (Duke University Press, 2018), p. 1.

(16) Haraway, 'The Promises of Monsters: A Regenerative Politics for Inappropriate/d Others'.

HUMAN NATURE IN NATURE

WILL MCLEAN, UNIVERSITY OF WESTMINSTER

"We now know, perhaps for the first time in history, how to go to wounded places and heal them; how to stabilize carbon in the atmosphere and park it (or sequester) it into the earth's soils...the list goes on. Of what we can't do, I don't think there is a single problem facing humanity for which there is not a practical, useful and immediate solution." [1] John Todd

When a design studio is established, it is always interesting to see how the interests and design ambitions of the studio tutors are reflected and made manifest through the drawings and models of student projects. With the case of the Design Studio DS[3]2 and previously DS[2]4 led by Eric Guibert we can see the clear evolution of a design methodology borne out of Eric's lead role as both 'architect and gardener'. The choice of language here is very deliberate and inciteful and whereas Eric might have described himself as 'architect and ecologist' or 'architect and environmentalist' he eschews these more general and perhaps larger thematic descriptors and uses the more precise and perhaps more evocative subtitle of gardener. A gardener seems a useful descriptor and perhaps embodies the art of design as a key component in a way that perhaps a horticulturalist does not.

The studio has evolved over several years and naturally reflects the contributions of different teaching partners. In its current format with Eric working with Christopher Daniel the studio has established a particular confidence which is both evolved and reflective of the contemporary actuality of climate change, (re)wilding and an increasingly sustainable and regenerative approach to architecture. The approach of the studio has also evolved in its approach to the design and communication tools used, in particular, the successful use of the 'Ecological Section Drawing' – both longitudinal (long) and transverse (cross). For the long sections, Eric's use of the word 'score' is a useful shorthand for students to delineate a series of designed moments or foci across an inhabited or re-inhabited landscape. The use of 'score' also indicates the fourth dimension of time which is both the immediate movement across and through a site as well as seasonality. The transverse, short or cross section has a different job and allows the student designers to pinpoint constructional and material approaches and ask what these designs are made of and how do they work structurally. The cross section also allows for a more detailed examination of how the projects touch the earth which seems especially pertinent given the studio themes and sites. The cross-section drawing can also serve as a useful diagram indicating passive design measures, such as orientation, building overhangs, thermal mass and insulative strategies. Like the long section, time can also be alluded to, with indicative high and low water levels, changing seasonal sun angles and an exploration of the climatic envelope as variously bio-receptive skin, carapace, hedge or tree.

The projects of the studio are increasingly a melding of nature and architecture, and parallels might be drawn to the works of Rudolf and Steiner and his Goetheanum campus in Dornach near Basel. Whilst the work of the studio might not share the idiosyncratic and recognisable geometric forms of Steiner's architecture, the close examination of the surfaces, fine geometry and relationship to nature share much with the all-encompassing anthroposophical approach of Steiner. However, there are other dynamics at play here and as much as the design projects and the 'ecological section' celebrate biodiversity and the possibilities of the synthesis of humankind and nature in a new architecture, how important is the interplay between them? Writing in Eero Saarinen: Shaping the Future, Reinhold Martin describes the interesting design development of the Deere and Company Administrative Centre, Moline Illinois 1957-63. Designed for the makers of John Deere tractors and other agricultural machinery, the building was to embody a Midwest farmers robustness and simultaneously appear to have grown out of its farmland location. Eero Saarinen and job architect John Dinkerloo were instrumental in the siting of the new HQ in a rural location with "built-in scenery" [2] that would provide a sympathetic rural panorama. The architects then decided to use Cor-Ten steel (the first structural use of the material), a steel alloy that oxidises (or rusts) to provide a protective coating and that does not need painting. The structural frame and deep brise soleil façade is made from a busy matrix of large Cor-Ten steel sections that resemble a forest-like structure and whose colour, like that of the trees will change over time.

One of the earliest ECOLOGICAL SECTIONS in our studio based on a synergy between an aquaponic system and a restaurant. Aquaponic is a food production system that uses the nutrients created by fish to grow vegetables. Waste from the restaurant is used to feed the fish.

Grow.Kill.Eat.Repeat, Aquaponics and the Architecture of Self-Sustaining Ecologies
Daniel Berende

The whole project is predicated on the new headquarters building working in harmony with the existing natural woodland setting, however, a more detailed survey of the site required the removal of trees affected by Dutch elm disease and so an extensive landscaping project by Sasaki, Walker and Associates was undertaken. Martin explains "…both Saarinen and the Deere Leadership encouraged the impression that the building's Cor-Ten steel exterior was designed to harmonize with a nature that was, in a sense, a priori–already there, original, authentic…But there is ample evidence that the reverse is also the case: that the supposedly natural setting (including the trees) was designed to harmonize with the steel façade." (3)

> "Wilderness maintains a slight but tenacious toe-hold there, side by side with a mix of industrial uses, from recycling, through light engineering and construction, to warehousing, wholesale storage and distribution." (4) William Mann

In William Mann's essay Bastard Countryside: The Mixed Landscape of London's River Lea, he explores another relationship between nature and the human built in his study of the light industrial landscape of the Lea Valley. He explains that "…the vestigial landscape of the lower Lea is almost invariably to be found in or around areas of industry. For it seems there that there is a curious symbiosis existing between industry and wilderness." (5) This 'curious symbiosis' is in some part related to changes of industrial usage (less heavy and polluting industry), but it might also be that zoned industrial use has a managed edge (building, carpark or building plot) whereas nature need not understand these arbitrary boundaries. Witness the successful growth of the Buddlea along railway viaducts, and building parapets throughout London, which is now neatly celebrated in Rachel Whiteread's sculpture Tree of Life (2012), where cast and gilded Buddlea (or Hackney Weed) are transposed onto the Whitechapel Art Gallery façade. It is in this territory of 'curious symbiosis' that Eric's design studio works, creatively exploring the interplay of architectural intervention and site.

To circle back to the opening quote of this essay and to add a useful reference to Eric's brilliantly named Carrier Bag of Regenerative Scores, the ideas and approaches of ecologist John Todd continue to provide both hope and technological solutions for ecological regeneration. For over 50 years Dr John Todd has pioneered ecological design. He established the New Alchemy Institute on Cape Cod in 1969 with his wife Nancy Jack where they researched closed loop farming and food production. It was Todd's work with hydroponics that led to the development of the first Eco-Machine® in 1986. Todd explains, "An Eco-Machine® is a technology that combines civil engineering and ecological life. They can be designed

to grow foods, they can be designed to treat waste, they can be designed to purify water, they can be designed to repair damaged environments ... and in some instances, they can be designed to also provide fuels." [6] The Eco-Machine® consists of a series of tanks and ponds and growing substrates and environments that contain all of the five (or six) kingdoms of life which might include microscopic algae, fungi, bacteria, protozoa, snails, fish and zooplankton. Through biomimicry (engineered systems inspired by nature), Todd has designed natural processes for the removal of industrial waste such as oils and other toxic contaminants from water courses, as well as create (non-chemical) sewage and waste treatment plants. The Eco-Machine® is a complex, but importantly, visible system that also functions as a teaching tool for schools and universities. Todd explains that "...all an ecological designer is, is someone who uses the strategies of an eco-system like a lake or a pond, or a marsh or a salt-marsh, or a wood, to carry out the work of society." [7]

Like the work of John Todd, the work of the design studio led by Eric might be understood in similar terms, with students creating new architecture(s) that live symbiotically with nature and explore the boundaries of architecture, horticulture and arboriculture. The students are encouraged to work as ecological designers with similar regards to structure and place. The students are also asked to usefully reimagine both the construction and material make-up of their new architecture and be precise in the specification of native hardwoods or engineered timber, and the upcycled and recycled substrates of the new and emerging circular economy of building.
In the manner of a good gardener, seasonality must be understood, and the robustness and frailty of materials (like plants) must be acknowledged for their utility and delight.

Ecological section of *Wildswimming Haven*
Christian Thunik

The entire building is designed as a mosaic of aquatic ecosystems that purifiy water.

WILL MCLEAN

Dr Will McLean is a Reader in Regenerative Structures & Materials at the School of Architecture and Cities at the University of Westminster where he lectures and leads technology teaching across the school. McLean writes about architecture and technology, and he has co-authored six books with colleague Pete Silver including Structural Engineering for Architects: A Handbook, Air Structures, Environmental Design Sourcebook and Sustainable & Regenerative Materials for Architecture: A Source Book, which was published by Laurence King in January 2025. In 2008 he established Bibliotheque McLean, publishing new titles including Sabbioneta: Cryptic City by James Madge, Quik Build: Adam Kalkin's ABC of Container Architecture, and Building with Air, the first English language book on the work of Italian architect and construction innovator Dante Bini.

Endnotes

(1) Healing Earth: A Diversity of Solutions (interview with Dr John Todd). Sustainable World Radio. 07.10.2019
(2) Martin, Reinhold. (2006). 'What is a Material?'. Eero Saarinen: Shaping the Future. Newhaven: Yale University Press. pp. 70
(3) Ibid pp.72
(4) https://www.wwmarchitects.co.uk/site/assets/files/1/bastard_countryside_wwm.pdf
(5) Ibid
(6) Ibid
(7) Ibid

THE ECOTONE PAGE
DRAWING NEAR THE EDGE OF THE PAGE

BRUCE IRWIN

Finding the woodland rave – *Anthropic Tropism* – **Benjamin Leathes**

SURVEYING THE ECOTONE

'A drawing is simply a line going for a walk.' Paul Klee

My aim is to ponder architectural drawing in the context of some recent visionary design investigations by Architectural Animism. Because the proposals exist in a speculative and risky future, they seek to develop a regenerative and ecological design process, and the tools needed to see and create within it. This project is both cartographic and visionary – it speaks as much about the future landscapes as ways to inhabit those foreseen places.

So, this paper examines drawing as a visionary and cartographic act — imagining both future landscapes and our potential inhabitation of them. I will explore some thoughts on mapping as a speculative architectural device because maps are a seemingly elastic, accessible, and ancient category of drawing used specifically for spatial reasoning and description of a relatively analogue and visual order.

To this end, I will describe some uses, construction, and readings of an Inhabited Plan, the Ecotone Section drawing, and finally will consider Graphic Speculative Fabulations, as a means of dreaming (aloud) on paper.

But first it is important to discuss one or two points of vocabulary, and to offer these as keys for interpretation – Ecotone & Score. I do not intend to elaborate widely here, just to set out what is meant by these terms here as they are grounding for Architectural Animism.

ECOTONE

Ecotone names a boundary or transition between two ecologies or two adjacent ecological communities. The word combines two roots – ecology and 'tone', from Greek *tonos*, meaning tension. Examples of an ecotone might include a boundary or transition from forest to prairie or from an estuary to the sea. It might be broad and clearly visible, or slight and elusive.

In this context the term is understood to offer a fertile transitional space, a space of mingling and coexistence and creation. It may reference natural ecologies and natural systems, boundaries between human, animal, plant, and insect, but might apply to unrestricted spaces of imaginative thought and exploration, such as a piece of paper or the strong (paper) fold between the second and

Approaching the research facility of *The Silvaesium*,
Benjamin Leathes

third dimensions. And it certainly pertains to the tension between a visible and visitable and walkable site and a drawing that contemplates a hypothetical, future place tethered loosely to that location.

SCORE

The teacher and landscape architect Lawrence Halprin used the term *score* to suggest an open, adjustable, and collaborative category of endeavor. Halprin borrowed

Map by Gutiérrez, Diego, and Hieronymus Cock
Americae Sive Qvartae Orbis Partis Nova Et Exactissima Descriptio
(Lessing J. Rosenwald Collection, drawn in Antwerp: s.n, 1562)

the word from music, probably developing it out of his collaborative spatial work with Anna Halprin, his partner, a renowned modern choreographer and dancer. His concept of the 'score' introduces open-ended, collaborative design — interpreted here as a guiding principle for drawing in imaginative spaces. A musical or dance score must be reinterpreted at each performance, and especially over lengths of time, inevitably there is a collaboration between performer and composer or choreographer at each performance.

A designer stepping into the ecotone (page, score) might act with similar open intent – straddling, tracing, following, eliding, sliding on the mud. Perhaps rather than named and collected species of an investigation, the surveyor or draughtsperson will discern atmospheric, blurry, abundant scores, like immersive and flittering probability fields.

A designer stepping into the ecotone (page, score) might act with similar open intent – straddling, tracing, following, eliding, sliding on the mud. Perhaps rather than named and collected species of an investigation, the surveyor or draughtsperson will discern atmospheric, blurry, abundant scores, like immersive and flittering probability fields.

Score may offer potential rather than fixity, but strategically, also favours collaboration over authority or final word. The page is an invitation, a provocation.

THE PLEASURES OF DRAWING MAPS

Architects draw to survey or record a place or condition. A sketch may attempt to tease out possibilities in material and connection. A sketch may reproduce, with rapid evolutions. Architects draw to propose, communicate, or instruct - Lutyens described a working drawing as a letter to a builder (via Forty). Drawings also embody, record, and remind us of the process that is design.

And drawings enable architects to consider problems that relate to space, use, material, time, weather, climate, change and movement - visually and to scale (usually). The drawing is both a place or space of thought and a record of the thought, and - if beautiful and rich in construction lines, erasures, and overlays- a record of the thinking hand/mind itself.

Drawings can also be collaborative, sometimes having the hand of many draughts people. A single drawing (digital or analogue) may be worked over by many hands and it inevitably refers to other drawings, some of these entanglements unknown to the reader. A drawing is for *both* the drawing and for the reading.

GRAFTING

Mapping deploys familiar graphic techniques of adjacency, line weight and type, scale, and formal mimicry in describing territories, but also uses a collage element that I will call *grafting*, also is a technique of sectional investigation. Grafting requires the suspension, to a degree, of conventions of realism in plan representation, but in context can also become invisible or unremarkable.

I borrow grafting from horticulture, where it means to place a portion of one plant into the body of another in such a way that the resulting plant combines desired traits of one or the other or both. Grape vines, fruit trees, and modern roses are familiar instances of the use of grafting techniques.

I use it in relation to drawing because it is free of some of the associations of collage (not that there is something wrong with a good collage!), and because it might help to imagine a more purposeful and specific relation between the page, the map drawn on the page, and the place mapped. Also, it has delightful vegetal implications, and suggests that the result might borrow the best of both origin plants, or that the one might be brought into the world of the other via the graft, and also because it might help to imagine a more purposeful and specific relation between the page, the map drawn on the page, and the place mapped.

> '...Those unconscionable maps no longer satisfied, and the Cartographers Guild struck a Map of the Empire whose size was that of the Empire, and which coincided point for point with it.'
> Jorge Luis Borges, *On Exactitude in Science*

"Map" (n.) is a usefully expansive category of drawing, and so "mapping" (v.) is an activity of geographers, but also of social scientists and visionaries, including architects. Mapping may be done with high-minded aims, but pleasure alone can never be ruled out. Recall, for instance, of the charred edge of a pirate's treasure map.

Most often, a map is a drawn plan representation of an area of land or space. At times it may mean a diagram of a set of systems using the language of mapping to describe relationships - to suggest a crucial rubric for understanding something. A person's face in a moment of crisis, for instance, is, in cliché, *a map of emotions*.

It is intriguing to observe when and how (quickly) maps become strange, irritating, or unnerving. A measure of the hegemony of the conventions of cultures can be tapped in the simple act of rotating the map to 'upside down', rendering the familiar uncanny. A map be folded, and even re-folded, but it must be held the right way up, indeed part of unfolding is working out which way is "up".

Grafting is also present on maps when drawn representations of geography or space are combined with any kind of non-plan drawing or that refers to an external knowledge, such as when an oblique or axonometric is overlaid onto plan view (often with mountains, cliffs), graphic insertions, external text or other reference, or overlay, scale notations, folds, un-folds, parallels and graph lines, techniques which attempt to acknowledge the spherical form of the planet, other graphic notations such as city locations, and the presence of pleasing and strange monsters at the periphery of the page.

These creatures may have been symbols of anything unknown – real distances, scale, alignments, currents, the ocean form itself – or to represent beliefs drawn from received wisdom, rumor, folklore or legend. They surely also had a commercial objective – these maps were produced for sale and so were produced for visual pleasure.

The contrast between fantastical bodies and real coastline features, forms, and real distances, paring specific knowledge and observation to projected, speculative, or imagined dangers, is provocative. It offers an interesting way into reading these drawings and a tool for exploring unknown or imagined territories and the devices within which we could inhabit them. The potential is great for regenerative design – the possibility to imagine inhabitation as a symbiosis, strange and familiar. The known and the real might even flourish with the graft of a fantastic appendage - and the scar between be worthy of material articulation.

INHABITED PLAN

An Inhabited Plan illustrates not just structure but life within space. Through layered drawing, designers meditate on use, inhabitation, time, and detail. It is different from a construction document in that it is not primarily focused on how to arrange the space so much as how to live in the space. Inhabitation is read in the detail of the spaces, the forms, the rubbed out and redrawn line, but also in the specific objects that can infer a narrative of life.

The technique is an alternative to text – preferring showing to telling. It is also a kind of designers' method-acting or the accents of Meryl Streep. The act of drawing prompts an interrogation of the detail and form of lived spaces, and so offers a potentially limitless design opportunity. And it offers multiple possible narrations of the space through the plan instead of shaping a single storyline

An inhabited plan can have a theatrical atmosphere that may obscure a clear reading of the spatial. To be convincing it requires heightened attention to all the telling details of inhabitation. The drawing will either be persuasive and immersive or off-putting or banal, or all of these at once. As Louis Kahn is said to have said, God is in the Detail.

Because drawing is a cumulative and occasionally subtractive process, the inhabited plan can also present its own, recorded time – the time it took to make or model or

Isometric render view of
The Council for Ecosystem Restoration
Kacper Sehnke

draught, and possibly the time it took to render or to print.

To return to the idea of the graft – the inhabited plan may pair elements of the construction plan with drawing techniques borrowed from film, photography, theatre design, files found online, shadow rendering software, a remembered space from some time ago to inscribe time into the drawing. The eye surveys the page, and in doing so redraws time onto the page. The drawn page also offers clues about the meaning, the direction of the proposal, which may be explored on subsequent pages. Borrowing from the traditions of aerial perspective - colour tone, intensity, and fading, and layering (overlap) can be used to suggest aspects of time related to space, construction, age, and depth of field.

A baroque density of layering (lines, inhabitation) can also lead to creative restraint and contrast. Super-saturation and de-saturation of colour, density and void, can provide a glimpse into thinking, focus, and intent. In skilled hands this can offer the potential for developing parallel narratives, co-inhabitations, day and night lives, stowaways and parasites and interlopers and good monsters within the home.

Trough coded line-weights, formal or material distinctions, tonal variation, blur, variations of scale and time and season, the bodies of the proposal bubble with life. The grafted branch may disregard the host and carry on an independent life in the interim space between layers, and from this may be discovered or imagined a wholly new form of regenerative design.

In short, I am (mostly) in favour of the *method* draughtsperson, the put-on accent, the funny hat, the baroque layers, ecotone stowaways, and stolen details and images. They offer a glimpse of the weirdness of things, of mis-use and re-use and appropriation, of collaborative and unrehearsed and breathless interaction – of improvisation on the spot, which is not easy to achieve in a drawing, which is, after all, drawn (and *printed out* downstairs). An ecotone page.

ECOTONE SECTIONS

'The hand is the cutting edge of the mind.'
Jacob Bronowski

Walking is a particularly useful setting-out practice in the construction of section drawings; you can imagine yourself tracing the first line with your feet, like shuffling through snow. Plus, the act of walking moves the blood around and stimulates thought, especially in cold weather. Walking with a companion affords an opportunity to talk, discuss, argue, and get lost, but then walking alone can be even better - so that you can talk to yourself. If you don't want to be seen talking to yourself, walk in a remote space, or pretend you are wearing an earpiece (as if on a call), or borrow a dog – some people think it is normal to talk to dogs. Best of all, walk with a folded map of the territory where you walk, the folds themselves record both the size of the pocket the map travelled within and can mark the section lines to be paced out on the ground, if refolded with intention. So, obviously, refold the map. Once you have gotten over the fear of re-folding your map, drawing and writing on the map comes naturally.

Later, back inside, play a parlour game of *Exquisite Corpse* with your collaborators (or inner voices) for the folded map, projecting a section drawing in sections. The result is surprising, collectively built, unselfconscious, and frequently amusing or strange - composite creatures, chimera, with folds and trailing misaligned lines. The constituent parts are recalled from memory, and redrawing forces a rethink, redesign, or simply an adjustment to try to link to the hinted connection from the prior draughtsperson. Sometimes in shared studio work live drawings can behave like this – with surprising meanders to reflect another mind.

Sections need not depict existing conditions. They can be speculative — layered, altered, revisited — capturing imagined transitions and ecologies. A section drawing is frequently thought of as a drawn slice through a structure, space, landscape, or object, like an x-ray, as if the subject, the thing or place or structure already exists. But what if the section is speculative, projected, dreamed, in the works?

This is not a rare – we project and construct through section all the time, in fact. A section drawing is made, figured out, half erased, assembled, collaged, redrawn, painted behind, outlined, overdrawn, traced, and re-figured. Over and over. This time the phantom fiddler, who changes the drawing in the night, with inexplicable aims, is you. Each morning, over coffee, you reconsider your late-night stroke of genius – what were you thinking? Or maybe you were on to something. And the corpse is, indeed, exquisite. Or maybe it's your coffee talking.

If an ecotone is a "region of transition between two biological communities" – what is an Ecotone Section? The name suggests an exciting boundary place, where biologies mingle and strange hybrid conditions are conceived. Within this studio the term explores a propositional, speculative, researched, imagined, and evolving dwelling, structure, assembly shared and inhabited by people and by other creatures – animals and insects and varieties of plant. Any useful strategies are encouraged – including walking, folding, collaboration, and collage.

GRAPHIC SPECULATIVE FABULATIONS

Framing as a device for understanding and scaling the land, for making a landscape, has precedents, among these the *Claude Glass*, or *dark mirror* - a tool for viewing the land as a landscape. This handheld mirror-device, sometimes framed, or leather-bound and hinged like a cosmetic compact, was a tool to assist the aspiring artist or the aesthetically minded ambler to achieve the correct framing, tonality, and haze of aerial perspective. Tools like the Claude Glass demonstrate how framing shapes perception of landscape. Graphic Speculative Fabulations extend this to storyboarding imagined futures.

The term landscape itself derives from the language used to discuss painting and originally referred to a category of painting (i.e., portrait, still life, landscape), not to a walkable piece of the countryside. The mirror was usually darkly toned, to reduce the colour range and mimic the atmospheric light and colour of a varnished landscape painting. The glass was held in the palm of the hand, and the viewer would turn their back on the view, the landscape framed in the glass.

Graphic Speculative Fabulations are visionary and exploratory storyboards used to develop the potential outcomes of proposals about the site, over time and inside a designed narrative.

Within the storyboard framework visions of discovery, land surveys, key events, inhabitants, passersby, elements, devices pace out key narrative moments. The technique offers the potential to envision, explore, and propose a walkable line linking the present - the site as found - to a future biome, a future ecotone. Students are encouraged to expand the range of their techniques of drawing, using the framework of the storyboard as a structural connection.

Storyboard techniques structure speculative drawings over time — allowing sequencing, rhythm, and discovery within narrative design.

'...our artefacts tell more about ourselves than our confessions.'
Joseph Brodsky, *Watermark*

THE MONSTER AT THE EDGE OF THE PAGE [VERSO]

'x = rabbit'
Meret Oppenheim

The page becomes a site, a landscape, of misreading, blending realms, detour and shadow. It invites return, revision, and wandering — like a folded map revealing hidden edges and surprising adjacency.

The back of the page and the very edge have disappeared in the same way as designing buildings in section. It is the triumph of the old idea – that the front edges of the page form a window 'into' another space. What is framed within is not a surface, meticulous or careless lines and erasures and tracings, but a webcam-ish glimpse of an interior world, fully formed, if lacking mud, sounds, and smells. There is nobody back there because there is no 'back there'.

Ecological Section sketch of
Captain Charlie and the Cherry Factory
Changsoo Yoo

Perhaps the whole page could host the Ecotone (front and back), and the pleasing monsters might come over from that other side? It would be worth folding the page just to have a look around and invite them round for an 'après-printout' walk. Say it was a mishap with the water glass, or the insatiable appetite of your borrowed dog. Take a walk back there with your pencil or an atmospheric ink wash. Repair the blurry ink with pencil, carefully, or intuitively, walking a new line of thought.

BRUCE IRWIN

Bruce Irwin studied art and architecture at the Bartlett and Rhode Island School of Design and has lived and worked in New York and London. His practice combines design, writing, teaching and curating. He is a co-founder and co-director of SCAN Projects, a not-for-profit initiative that supports emerging artists. SCAN operated a project space in East London for five years, and organised exhibitions in London, Spain, and Berlin. Current projects include the restoration of a 16th building in Granada, Spain.

Visual Speculative Fabulation
For-Rest
Syafiqah Aziz

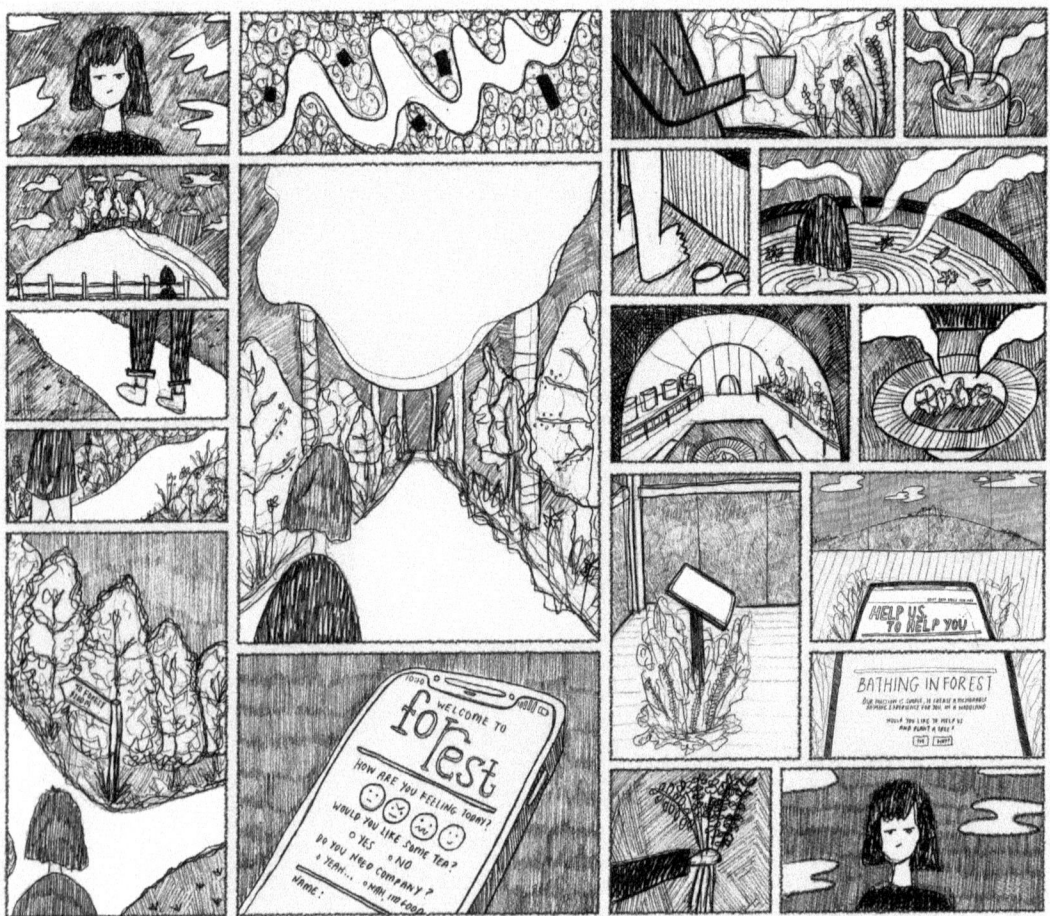

Facade Timeline
in years 0, 10, and 20
Earthly Hills: Epping Forest Centre of Ecologies and Climate Change
Farah Mazloum

THE UNSEEN LABYRINTH

INTERLUDE 3

BENJAMIN GRAFHAM

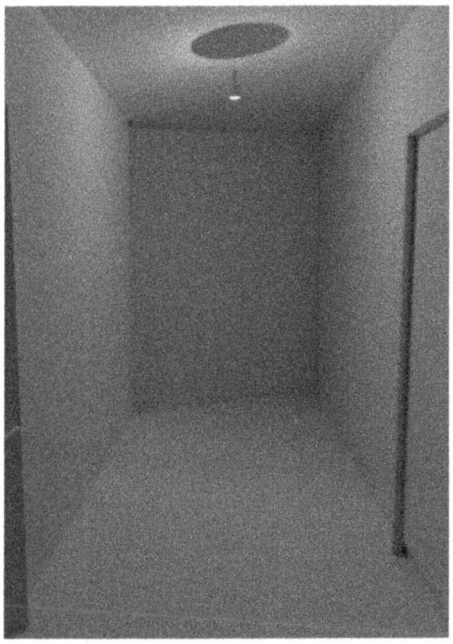

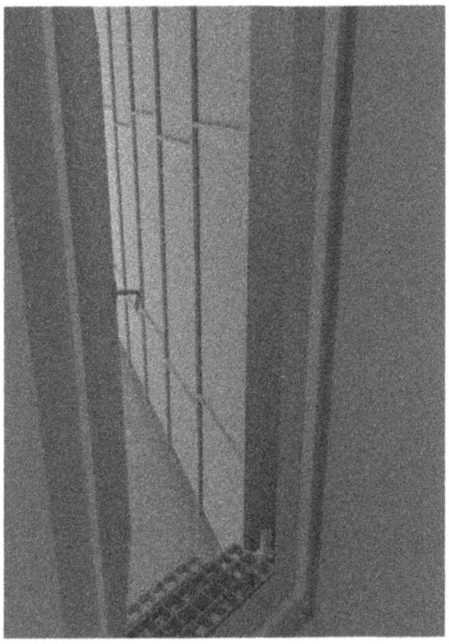

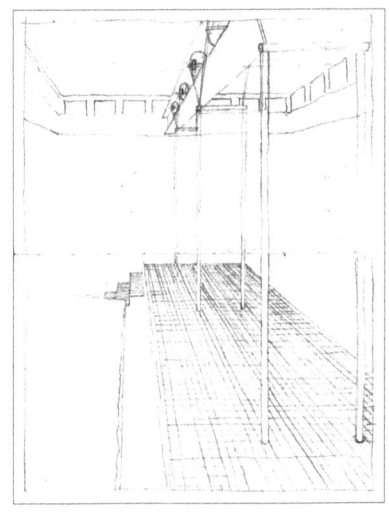

"yeah, just a quiet one tonight, as quiet as it can be with the kids around... see you monday"

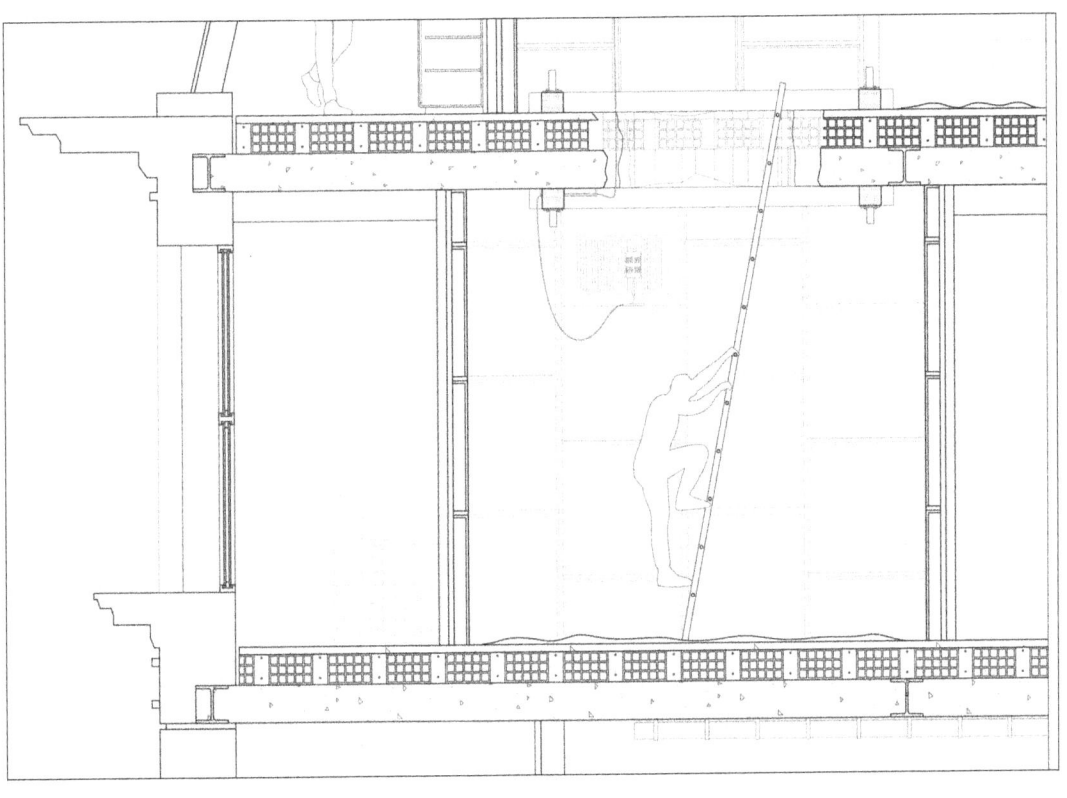

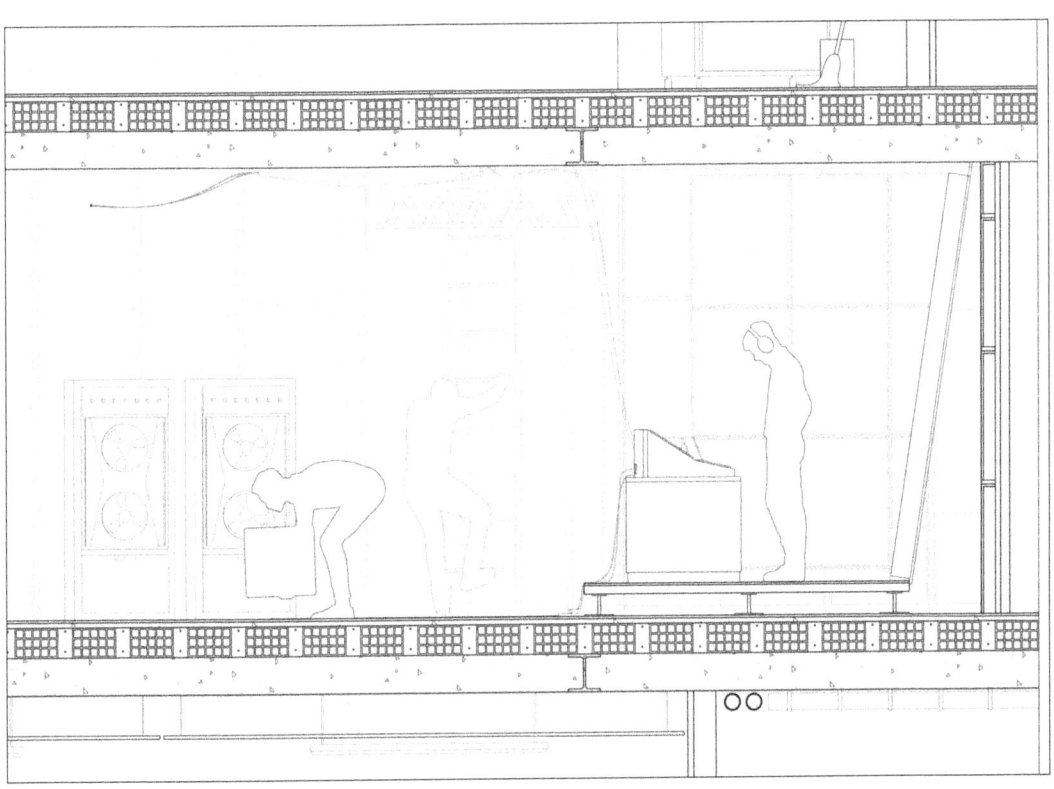

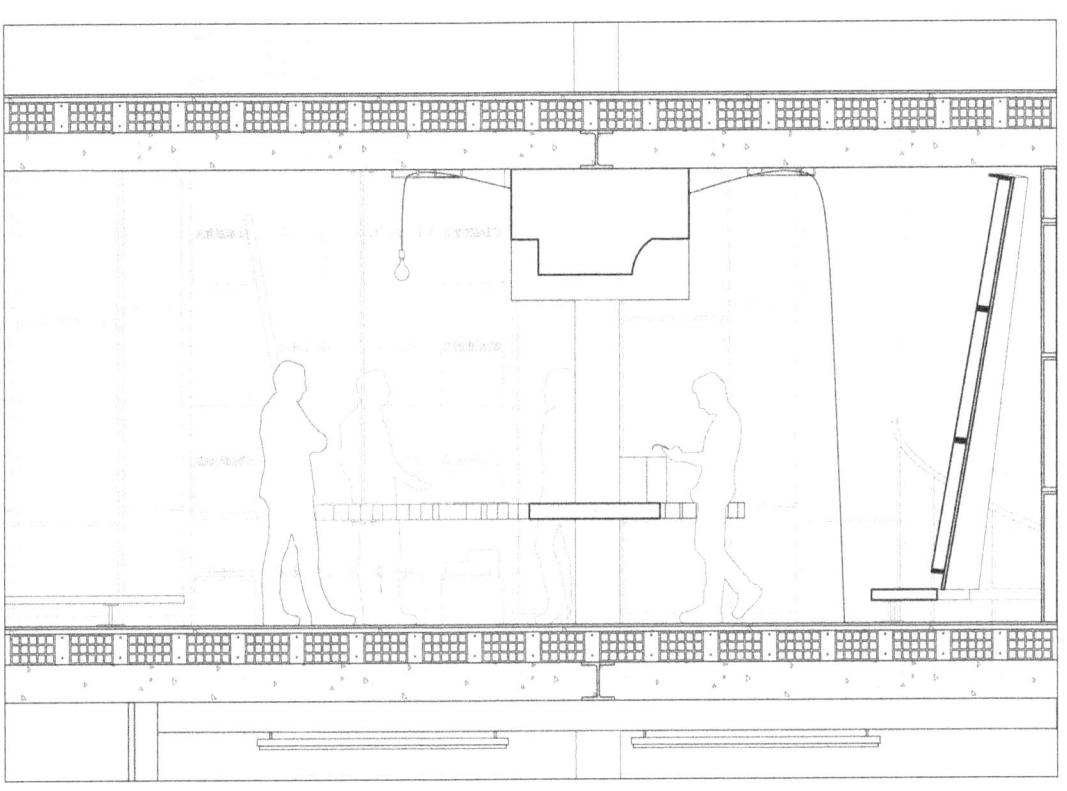

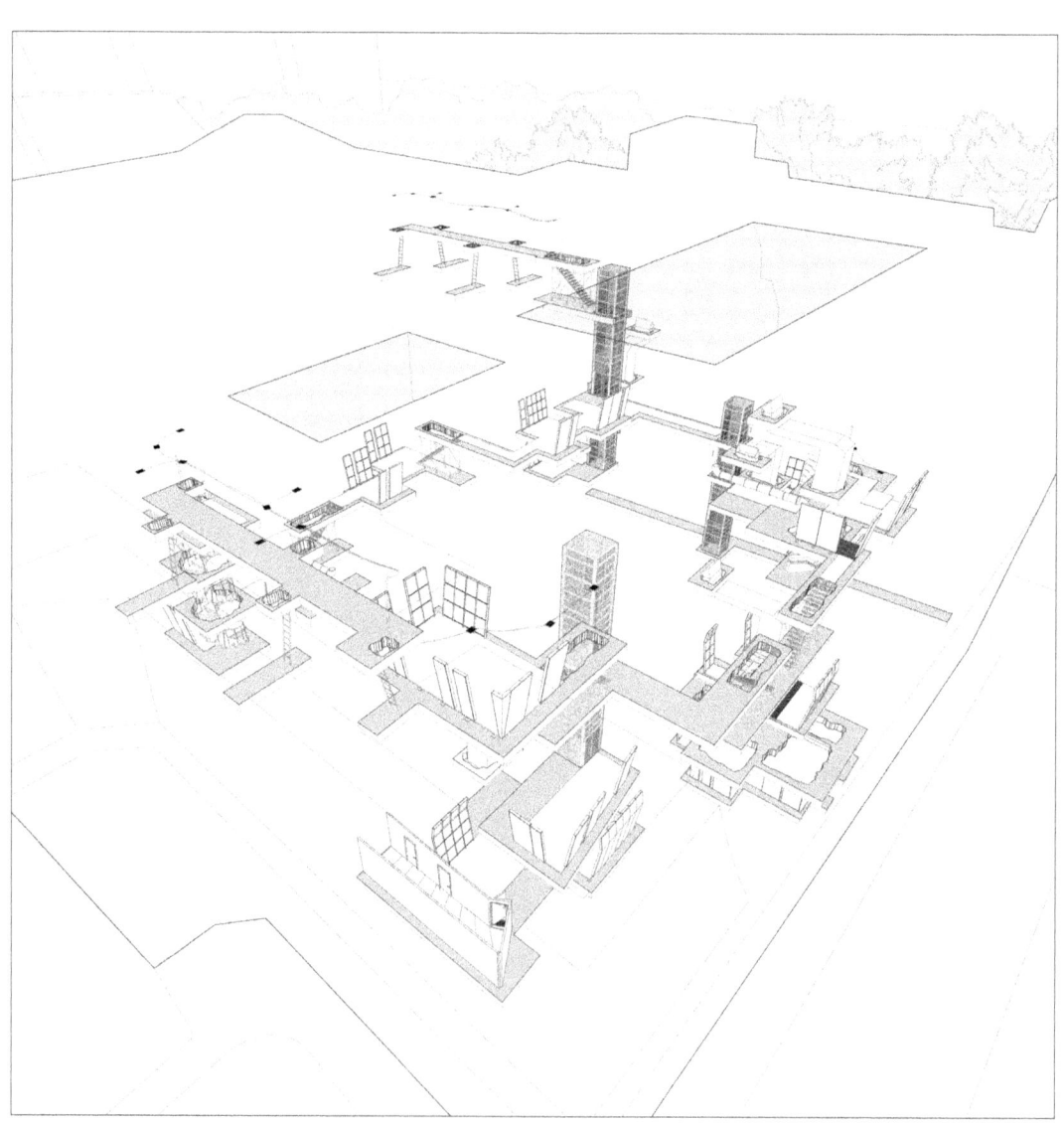

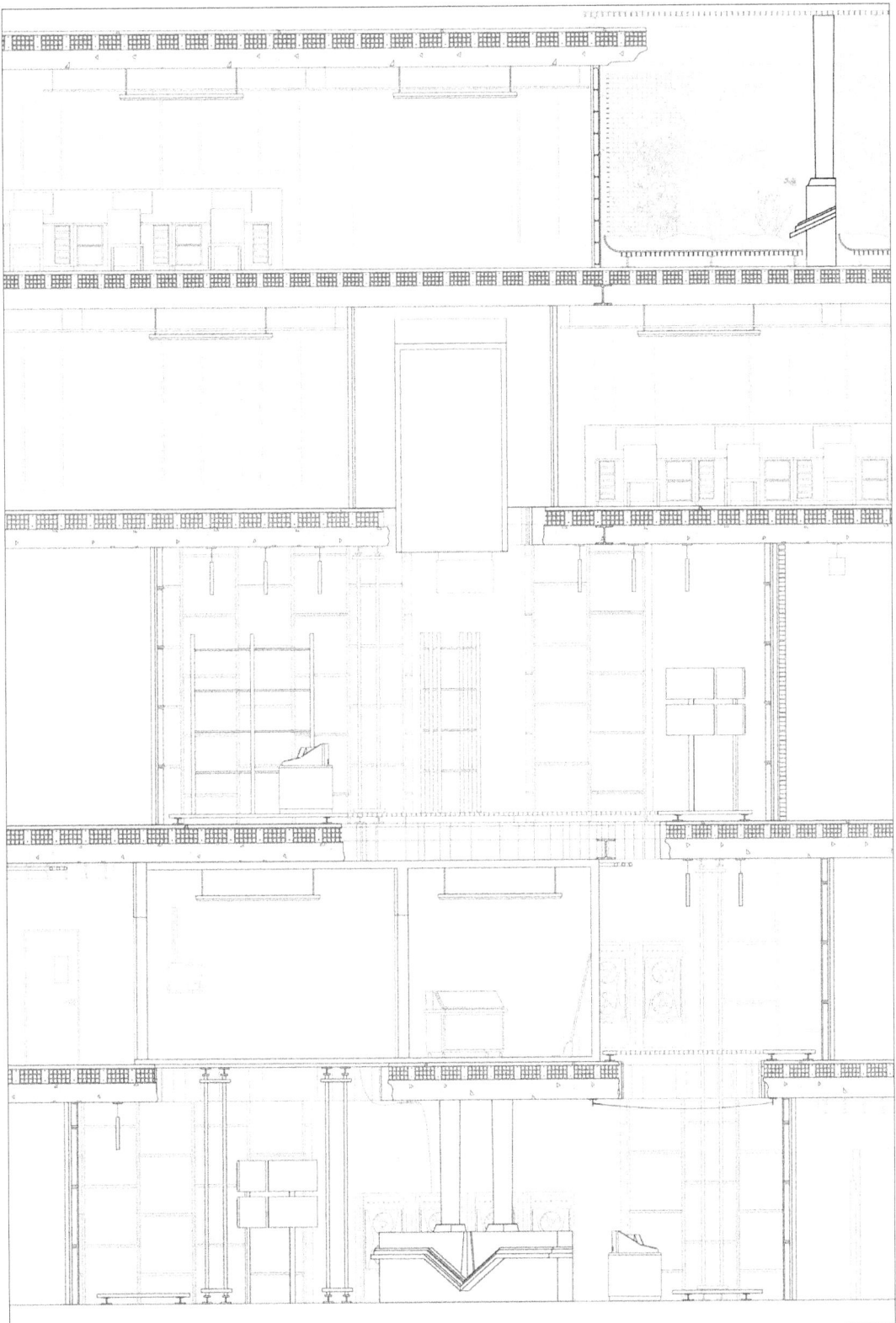

PART 2
SCORES

SCORE 1
ECOLOGICAL SECTIONS

Eric Guibert

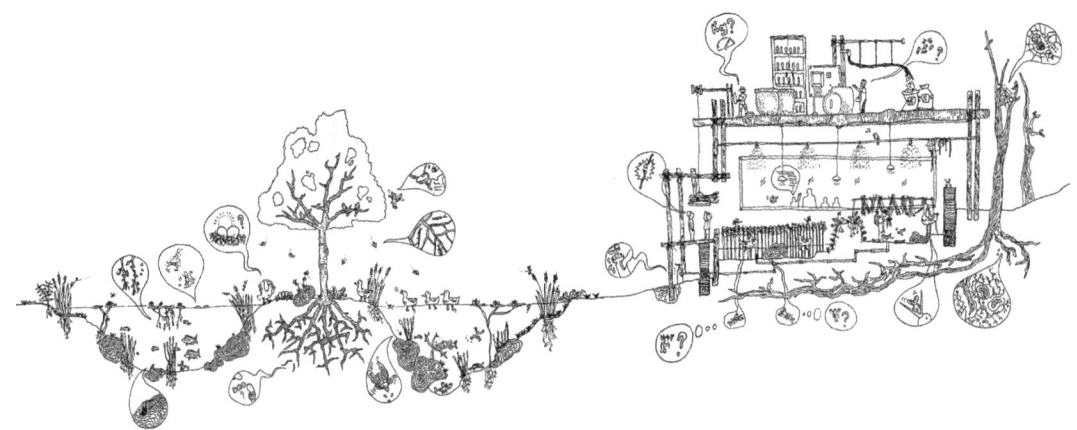

An early ECOLOGICAL SECTION sketch that was fundamental in the development of the relationships within the brief and spatial connections for the project *Captain Charlie and the Cherry Factory*
Changsoo Yoo

A key dimension of regenerative design is its systemic nature. In order to create architectures that regenerate life, you need to think of buildings and space as tools that negotiate the relationships between living beings and systems. There are two systemic dimensions: as 'meshwork' [1] of relations and flows of matter, information, and energy, and as habitats – as a mosaic of ecosystems nested within each other. Different systemic aspects and scales are thought through different scores. ECOLOGICAL SECTIONS deal with how buildings negotiate relationships and provide habitats within and near buildings.

From the first year of the studio, it was clear that a different way of drawing sections was necessary in order to think of architecture as systems. We researched ways of drawing diverse elements together: the building and its materiality, of course, but also the flows of climatic elements (sunlight, air, rain…), other animal and vegetal inhabitants, soil and geology, human inhabitation… to investigate how they can best coexist, enter into synergy.

An ecology is often best drawn as a section as it is defined by climate and gravity, the way the energy of the sun light reaches from the sky to be used by the food chain, rain fall, decaying matter falling on the ground to compost into soil, and the opposite upward growth of plants. As a result, in ecosystems, life is stratified, different species exist in different horizontal planes to make use of what they need for survival, birds fly, tree canopies grow above all to get the most sunlight, other plants grow below, some exist only in the ground… This is equally true of human activities in buildings.

The systemic is also horizontal, of course, which is defined through other scores; in INHABITED PLANS, the focus is on the mosaic of ecosystems and territories within the site; in PANARCHIC MAPPPING, the interaction between different scales of ecosystems nested within each other.

ECOLOGICAL PROCESSES

There are usually three key stages in the development of these sections that gradually increase in complexity as the project develops.

The first stage is usually a drawing of an ecological process so that students can discover some principles through something manageable and small. In the first studio epoch, this analysed the processes of the chosen brief and its synergy with the site and context. In the second rewilding period, the focus moved towards the interaction between humans, ecosystem engineer animals, and habitats, through modes of care.

This was inspired in the first year by various diagrams describing the interrelation between multiple beings, climate, soil and buildings in rural and urban ecosystems found in various permaculture books that we were focusing on then by David Holmgren and Bill Mollison, the very first books about permaculture [2] [3], and the newly published Retrosuburbia [4]. Our later inspiration for representation in recent years is the seminal work of the studio of Teresa Galí-Izard in Harvard Regenerative Empathy [5], which analyses the complex interrelations between various species and the ecosystems of the Camargue delta in Southern France.

This first sectional stage is equally about the student project development as it is about collective learning about ecological processes for the entire studio community. The students present their own processes to the group, and all gain an understanding of the multitude of processes looked at throughout the studio and the connections between them.

In terms of process, to help with rigour and complexity, we encourage students to read academic papers or book chapters on the subject, first draw a series of sketches by hand of moments in the section, which are then composed together in a single section. The most talented students have included a temporal dimension as if the section were a timeline showing a day, a year, or decades, often from left to right. This was inspired by a Beetle lifecycle temporal section found in a book by the graphic design theorist Edward Tufte, as well as 15th-century miniatures of the months drawn by the Limbourg brothers in the famous manuscript *Les Très Riches Heures du Duc de Berry* [6].

ECOLOGICAL SECTIONS

After the ecological processes, we usually shift media with an exercise in sketch and concept model making. After this, ECOLOGICAL SECTIONS are produced to develop the design by integrating the building concepts with the ecological processes looked at earlier. These also begin with sketches. And the earliest successful example of such a sketch is the hand drawing by Changsoo Yoo used on the cover, as it successfully brought together a productive landscape with buildings and inhabitation.

These are then developed in a first developed ECOLOGICAL SECTION drawn to scale and with accurate topography. After the drawing of a first draft, a workshop is organised to ad complexity and represent the system and refine the project's systemic spatial intelligence.

Sections in architecture are not new, of course, but ours represent more complexity of relations and diverse inhabitations than most. They were nonetheless inspired by a few architects. The perspectival sections used by Studio Bow Wow to represent built projects in their book *Graphic Anatomy* that combine detailed representation of materiality with inhabitation of spaces inside and out, ground condition, and, implicitly, the climatic elements.

Other references include Tom Emerson's Academic Design Studio sections in the Glasgow Atlas, 2014, at ETH Zurich [7], which show buildings, above and below ground conditions, infrastructure, foundations... And an impressive witty section by Ted Cullinan [8] that represents the building and its inhabitation with climate, and most cheekily the busy underground layers including infrastructure, historical remains, soil and animals.

Our sections combine elements of all of these, with an increased attention towards the other-than-human inhabitation.

Towards the end of the project, these sections are redrawn as large drawings, with more ambition, and sometimes adding other scores onto them, whether timelines or VISUAL SPECULATIVE FABULATIONS. These are often drawn at a 1/50 scale, although often printed at 1/100 due to their size.

Many of the first best ECOLOGICAL SECTIONS have been drawn by hand, this is in part because drawing soil and vegetation, inculding the roots, is often easier freehand. We also beleive that the act of drawing with your body connects to the memory of embodied experience of space inhabited by multiple species.

Buildings relationship with the landscape of *Communal Meadery*, *George Darlington*

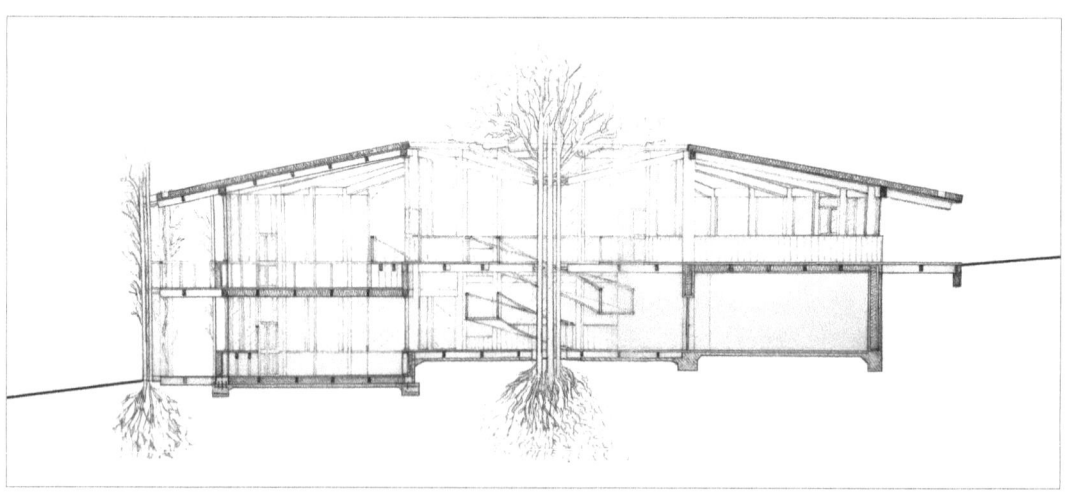

088

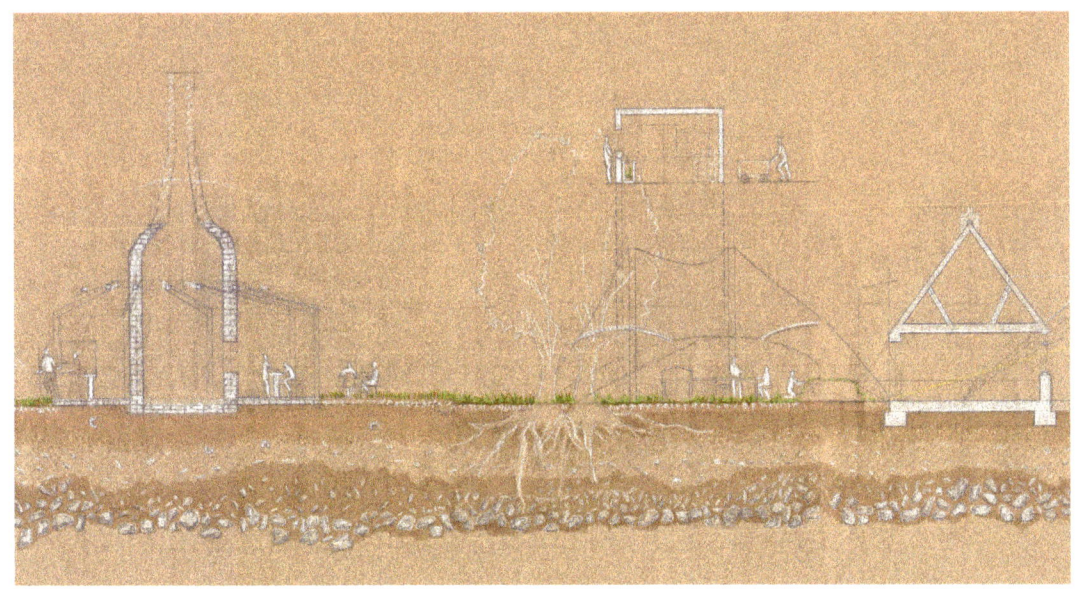

This is one of the very first ECOLOGICAL SECTIONS produced in our studio in its first year in 2019
Esther Calinawan

"SOLARPUNK" GRAPHIC LANGUAGE

All the sectional precedents mentioned above favour line drawings in black on white, generally drawn digitally in CAD. This may be in order to unify the multiple drawings drawn by different students in a publication, but it also expresses a "scientific" quality of precision and rigour, one that we perceive as modernist and in some way problematic, as it, to some degree, extracts what is represented from an empathetic relation. Although the various precedents do draw relationships in space, the visual language expresses a detachment from species and ecosystems, nature and context.

Our studio has used these cold representations at times, but has increasingly included hand-drawn elements, colourful representations in watercolour or pencil, as well as many forms of digital collages. A more recent reference is the work of French artist Fabrice Hyber [9], paintings that are generally sectional diagrams conveying ecological principles and related human experience, expressively drawn in colourful paint with a childlike exuberance.

These positive and optimistic languages can at times lean uncomfortably towards the cute for some, but this risk is worthwhile to convey empathy and care towards the other-than-human, whether vegetal or animal, as valuable agents instead of scientific objects of study. The rejection of the cute in architectural discourse often appears as a remnant of a sexist avoidance of the feminine in favour of the masculine, supposedly rational, at times violent or dystopian, whereas our future will require us embracing the relational, the empathetic, and this includes softer forms of representation. As my current co-tutor Christopher Daniel often states, we need more the utopian quality of Solarpunk than the dystopian Cyberpunk worlds.

Encouraging positive visions is political and pragmatic. We will not be able to find a path in the midst of the impending catastrophes through negative and dystopian visions of uncanny worlds, which at best communicate the disasters, and at worst, often, uncritically commodify these visions as supposedly innovative formal languages. Pragmatically, there is also a psychological dimension to this, wallowing in despair, however visually striking, will not nurture the resilience we need; we need hope to find our way through the ruins. Nonetheless, although we are primarily positive, we also nurture in our studio some darker visions of our route to ecological futures, or regenerative processes, such as Ben Grafham's project in INTERLUDE 2.

RELATIONAL SPATIAL INTELLIGENCE, OR THE BUILDING AS BACKGROUND

The qualities of these sections are unusual in another way as, although clearly drawn, the buildings often appear invisible in the middle of the profuse inhabitation represented. This expresses that the architecture's key role is to host all these processes and inhabitants and facilitate their interactions.

The systemic spatial intelligence and refinement of these drawings is often missed; their language baffles those used to the graphic exercises of abstracted plans and sections, those most celebrated in the 90s and early 00s that focused on developing complex forms through various formal drawing and model exercises detached from questions of life: climate, ecology, or even human inhabitation.

The relational language of ECOLOGICAL SECTIONS, which is also found in INHABITED PLAN, brings inhabitation to the fore. It is necessary to decentre the building traditionally conceived as the central purpose of architecture, and refocus our spatial intelligence on hosting life in all its forms, on nurturing the relations and flows that define living systems. The constructed elements as a result are primarily tools designed for the affordance of the habitats they provide to their inhabitants, and the facilitation of the exchanges between them; buildings define mosaics of ecosystems, both internal and external.

If the creativity of a project is pursued primarily in the graphic quality of the drawn building fabric, and the resulting form, and inhabitation is a secondary exercise only used to demonstrate functionality, a mechanical simplification of life, spatial relational complexity is missed.

Ecological process section of the year in the life of a bat. This is also a timeline from left to right. It was used for the project

Dwelling for a Chiropterologist
Darya Prokopets

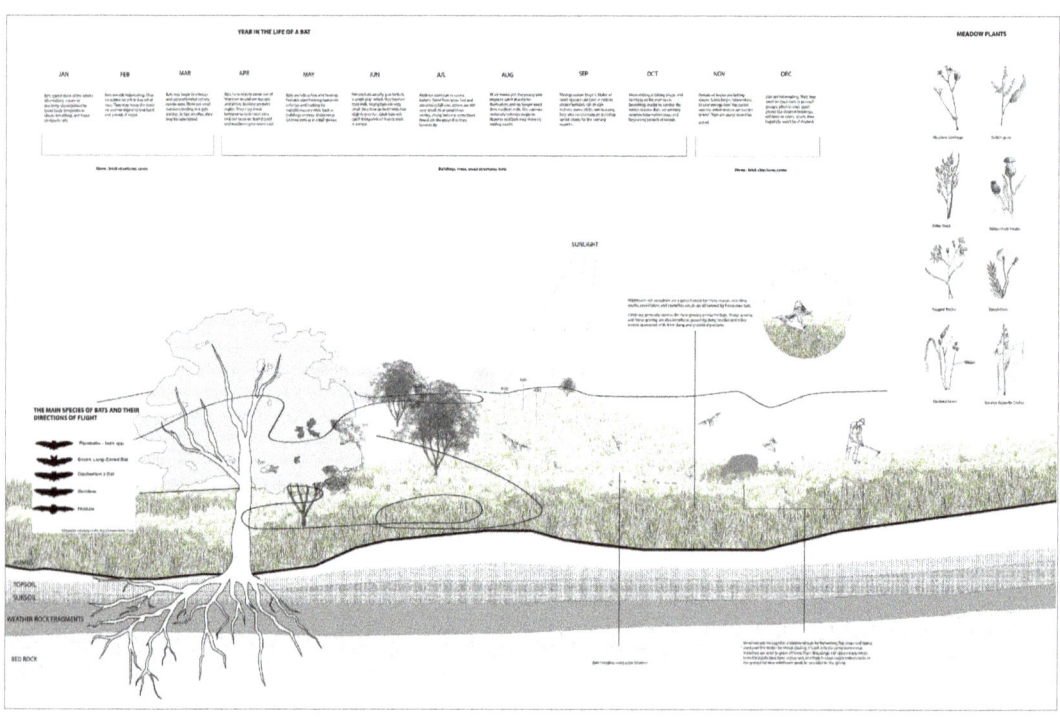

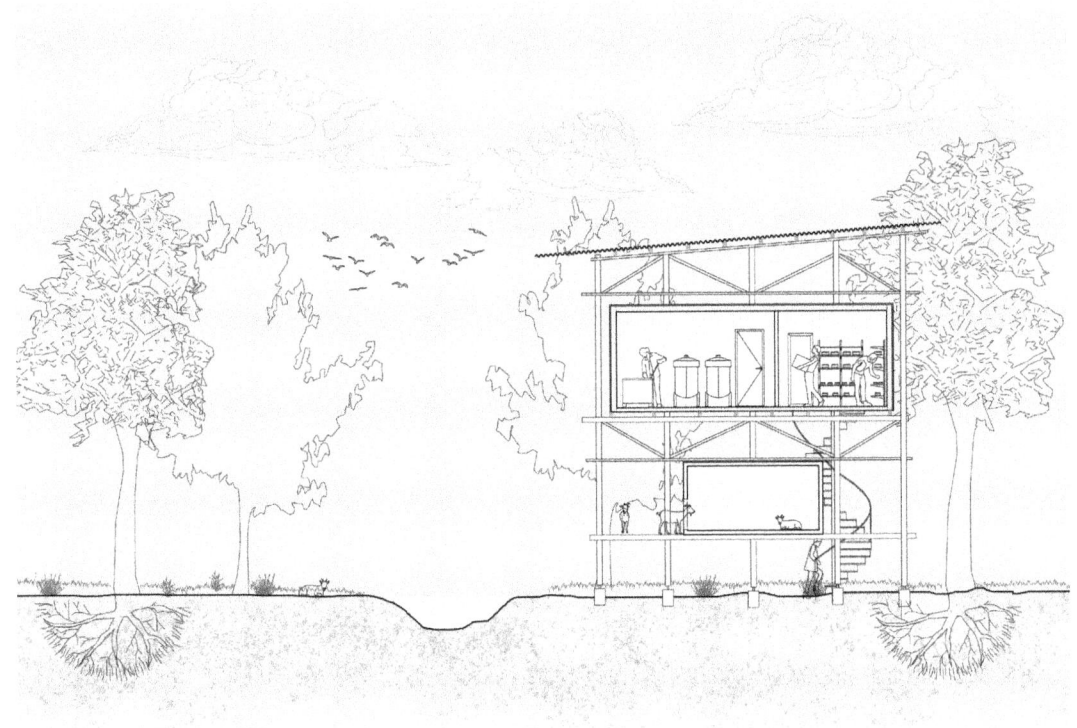

Ecological section with goat and human cheese production.

A (Raw)dical Cheese Factory
Giorgia Bresciani

Endnotes

(1) Tim Ingold, Lines: A Brief History (Routledge, 2007), p.82.
(2) Bill Mollison & David Holmgren, Permaculture One: A Perennial Agriculture for Human Settlements (Tagari Publication, 1990, first edition 1978)
(3) Bill Mollison, Permaculture. A Designers Manual (Tagari Publications, 2021, first edition 1988)
(4) David Holmgren, Retrosuburbia: The Downshifter's Guide to a Resilient Future (Melliodora Publishing, 2018)
(5) Teresa Galí-Izard, Regenerative Empathy: Complex Assemblages in a Shared Environment. Studio Report from the Fall 2018 semester at the Harvard University Graduate School of Design based on the option studio "Rhizosphere". https://issuu.com/gsdharvard/docs/regenerativeempathy
(6) For illustrations follow this link: https://en.wikipedia.org/wiki/Très_Riches_Heures_du_Duc_de_Berry
(7) Tom Emerson, section in the Glasgow Atlas (2014), created in his academic design studio at ETH Zurich, Gardens, Community Gardens... drawn by Carla Häni and Anouk Wetli. https://www.emerson.arch.ethz.ch/design-studio/glasgow
(8) Ted Cullinan, 21st Century Townhouse (Instagram, 2014). https://www.instagram.com/p/CGAexEfs_IP/?igsh=ZDNrZTY2OW0zN3hn [Accessed 16-07-2025]
(9) Although he is from the same area as my parents families, we only discovered his work at his impressive retrospective exhibition at the Fondation Cartier. Fabrice Hyber, The Valley (Publication Fondation Cartier pour l'art contemporain, 2022)

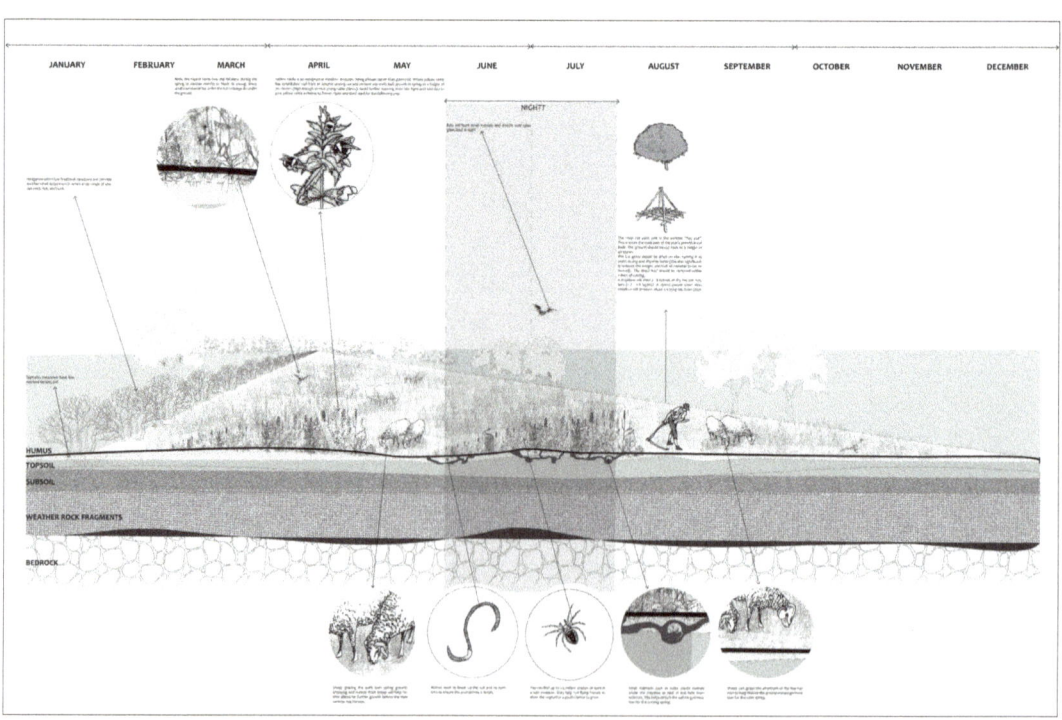

Finola Simpson's first semester project *The Purple Emperor* grew out of an impressive design process through ECOLOGICAL SECTIONS, starting with an analysis of the other-than-human and human rhythms of the meadow ecosystem in her Life Space [& time] Section that also shows yearly change from left to right. *(left image)* This was iterated into a series of hand drawn site specific sections combining the life of the purple emperor butterfly and a dwelling for a lepidopterist.
It culminated in her Storytelling Section which combines the building project, the ecosystem context, the pollarding of the willows that produces construction material and encourages the growth of foliage on which the caterpillar feeds on. The life cycle of the butterfly is also represented. *(above)*

The Purple Emperor
Finola Simpson

After her first project in the previous spread, Finola transferred the understanding of living systems, and the skill of representing these, to the more human focussed processes of accelerated decomposition of human bodies and the funeral ritual. The resulting compost is returned to the soil in a procession at the end of the four weeks process.
Perspective Section showing the composting tower in the centre, with grieving houses on either sides.

Ritual Rewilding
Finola Simpson

Benjamin Leathes, developed a project for a forest rave based on the importance of soil and plant disturbances for biodiversity. He analysed that multiple animals such as wild boar and bovids open the ground leaving bear soil where many plant and animal species can thrive. He proposes to replace the missing animals in Epping Forest with human ravers.
The project began with the Disturbance Mapping sections of the effect of the animals *(this page)*.
It then was developed in a concept that dynamically changed the location of the rave between events to spread the disturbance of humans.
The construction of infrastructural small buildings (toilets, washing facilities...) were themselves understood as disturbance creating new soil conditions of dry stone walls for other species.
Concept Ecological Section *(facing page, top)*, Gabion Ecological Section *(facing page, bottom)*.

Anthropic Tropism
Benjamin Leathes

Christian Thunik pursued his fascination for the hydrological processes in the site and its surroundings to develop a bathing building that embodies the processes of water and nutrient within a building facade and roof composed of a mosaic of aquatic ecosystems that purify water.

Ecological sketch section of
Wild swimming Haven
Christian Thunik

Yohei Yamane began his design process with an interest in saproxylic ecosystems, these are dead trees in the process of decomposition that are habitats for multiple species of insects, especially in their larvae stage, and fungi.
It reveals the materiality of architecture itself, its very structure, as an ecosystem, where species co-author space, and structural decay is
embraced as a catalyst for biodiversity.
A radical sectional cut through DeadWood Villas.

The House That Rot Built
Yamane Yohei

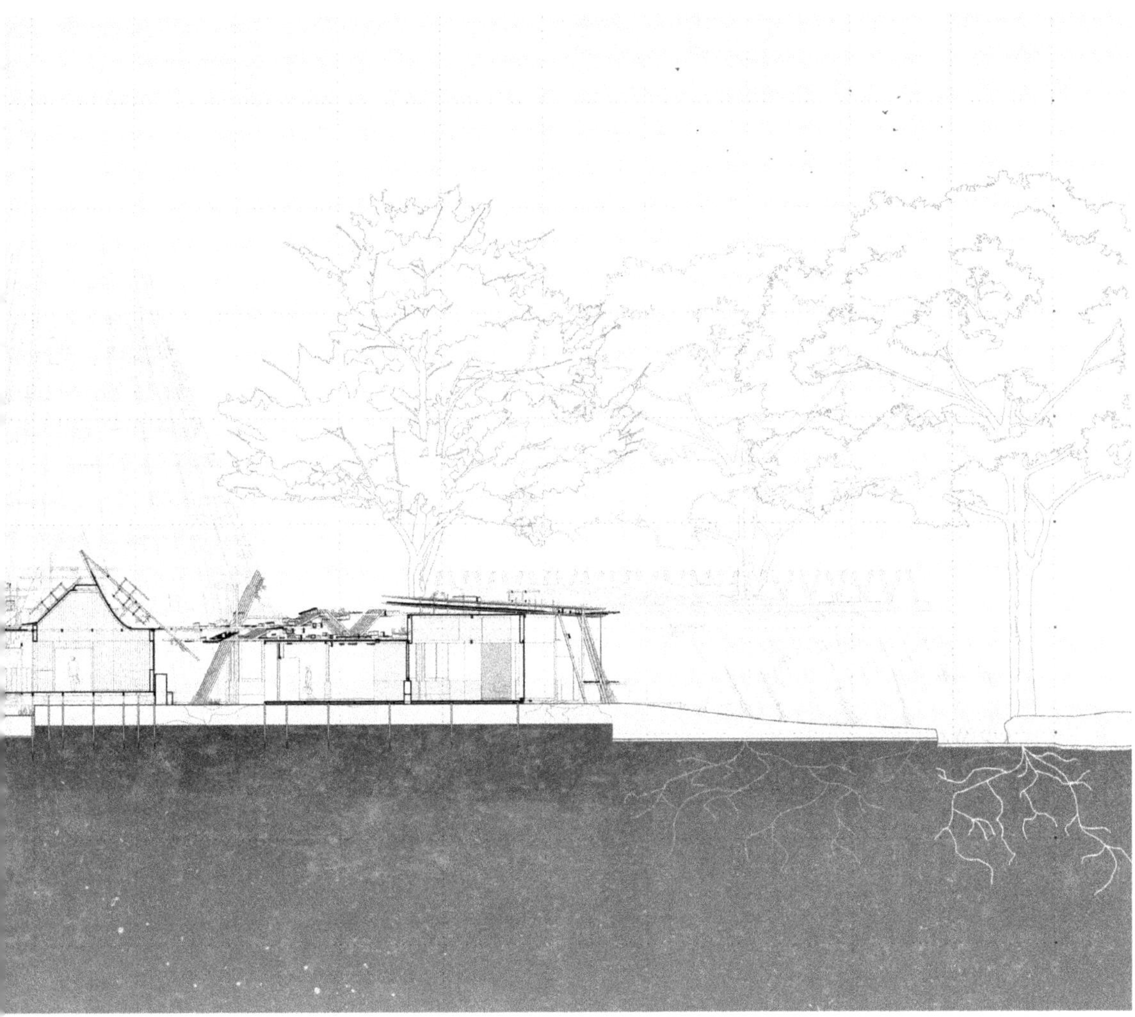

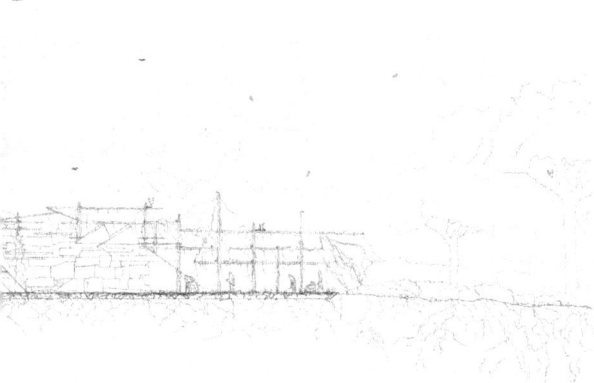

Kacper Sehnke's RIBA President Bronze Medal Winner project was based on two interventions in the existing ecological processes on site and in its surroundings. The existing tennis court finishes are broken up and the pieces rearranged to create gaps for plants forming a garden with entropic qualities.

The buildings are made re-using materials found in Epping Forest and the rubble from the suburban area. The harvesting of the timber nurtures biodiversity by pollarding the trees which creates a mosaic of varying light levels within the woodland beneficial to different species.

The project was developed through an impressive series of ECOLOGICAL SECTIONS, starting with sketches and a large hand drawn section, which was further developed in CAD for the final version.

Short Ecotone Section
of *The Council for Ecosystem Restoration*
Kacper Sehnke

SCORE 2
PANARCHIC MAPPING

Eric Guibert

Another dimension of systemic design is the understanding that ecosystems are nested inside each other and connected; a change at one scale will impact the other scales, both those that are smaller and larger than the one in focus. In the study of complex systems, the conceptual framework that analyses the interactions between nested systemic scales is called panarchy [1]. A famous example is the so-called 'butterfly effect' that showed that a micro event, such as the flap of a butterfly in one location, can cause a hurricane in another part of the world.

In architectural terms, an ecological organisation, for example, can regenerate ecosystems within its site, and this will be most effective if it contributes to a nature recovery framework of the local area, and then the region; the same organisation will also benefit ecosystems beyond through its activities, nationally or globally. Another application is the concept of 'acupuncture urbanism' [2], a small transformation in the public realms that leads to systemic regeneration. Thinking of a strategy on site in synergy with those at other scales is key for both effectiveness and economy.

Mapping is used by many architects, especially those who conceive architecture as a social practice, a way of improving the life, and increasing the agency, of local communities and individuals, a position defined by Jeremy Till as 'spatial agency' [3] [4]. Such an approach, focusing more on the intangible aspects of architecture than their form, was the focus of a previous studio also at Westminster, which Camilla Wilkinson led, where I was involved with its creation.

MAPPING WITH SYSTEMIC PURPOSE

There is a different, but not opposed, understanding of context to that which is generally understood in architecture, where context is discussed as the existing surroundings and the vernacular forms and materials, and scale, of the buildings and open spaces. Here, contexts are as much about systems, flows and exchanges as they are about form. They are also as much about the larger global and national scales relevant to the project as they are about the local.

In the Architectural Animism studio, in the first years, we have approached mapping in one of two ways, each leading to not entirely convincing results. Either students chose individually, early in the process, a specific theme(s)

An example of the careful understanding of the site reached by careful redrawing by hand.

Site plan of meadow in oil pastels of Communal Meadery
George Darlington

Hydrology - Site Analysis

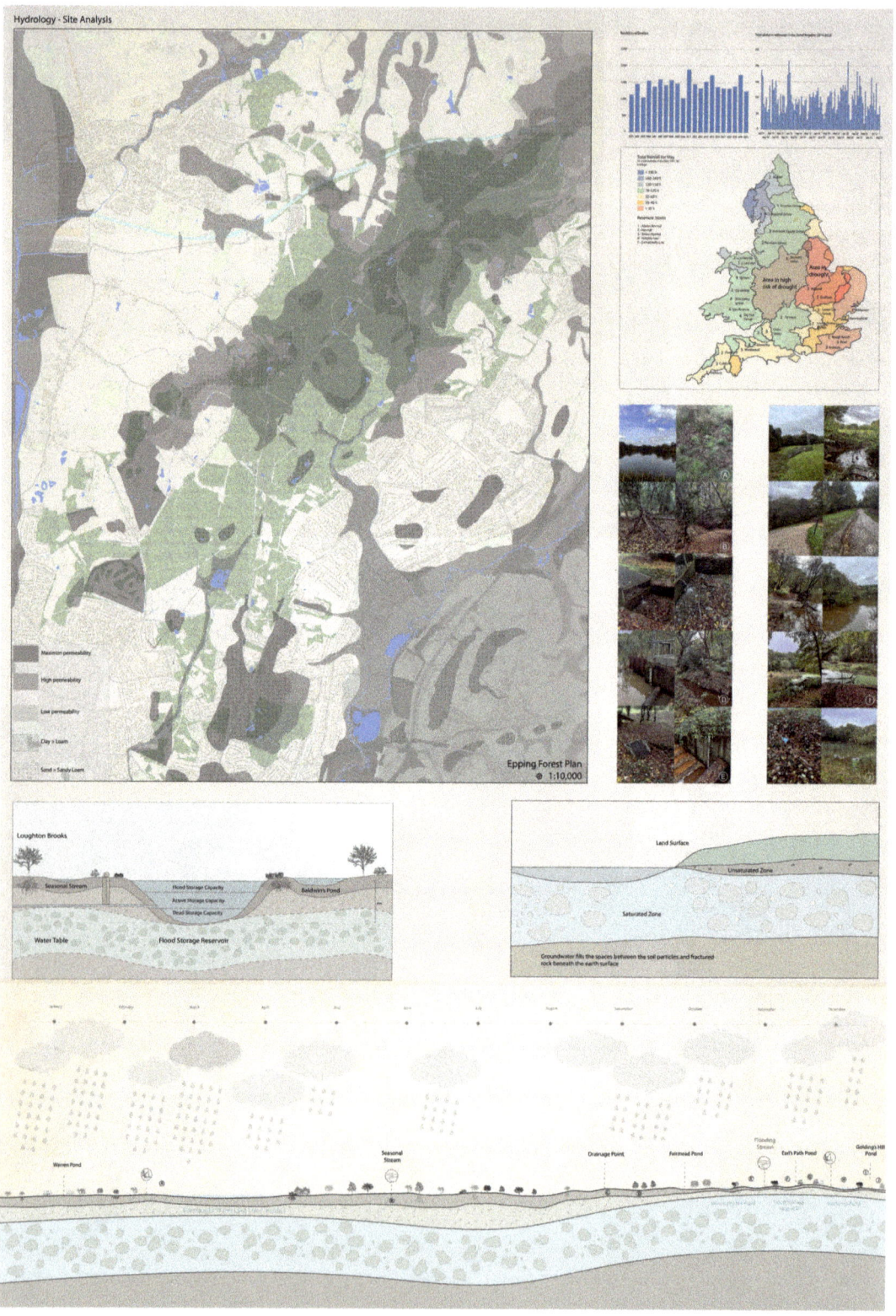

or subject(s) of focus to analyse the area that is relevant to their brief; this often led to simplistic one-dimensional analysis. Alternatively, they worked as a studio in small groups covering different layers, which covered a broad and rich range of information, but many students passively dealt with it as a tick-box exercise and failed to productively use this knowledge in their schemes.

Gradually, the two approaches have been merged into a two to three-stage process to gain the benefits of both.

ECOLOGICAL LAYERS

Although the order has sometimes changed, the first stage usually looks at the ecological layers of the site and local context: soil/geology, hydrology, climate, ecosystems, history, and human environment today. This is similar to the landscape design process developed by Ian MacHarg in his famous book *Design with Nature* [5].

Usually, the studio is organised into 6 groups of 3 students, each of which looks at one of the layers. This is a great way of developing and sharing knowledge across the studio, but it often leads some students to insufficiently engage. Each student later chooses the relevant information and redraws the maps for their project based on the digital drawings produced collectively.

This mostly takes place at two scales: a local context map and site analysis with near context. Most years, each group is asked to draw a minimum of: a map, a section, and a timeline.

PANARCHIC BRIEF MAPPING

Panarchic mapping consists of drawing three relevant maps of the brief at different scales that together represent the project's panarchy.

This is most of the time composed of:

- *a brief program drawn as a spatial diagram,*
- *its relationships with the surrounding context,*
- *and one or two larger scales usually dealing with its community of practice, organisation it collaborates or competes with, and/or where its impact is located.*

Drawing the three or four scales leads the students to think about a broad range of relationships and synergies taking place within and across these scales; the brief is contextualised and expanded to exchange with other institutions, ecosystems…

The aim is to simultaneously develop the brief and the systemic understanding of how the project effects, and is shaped by, multiple scales; how what would happen here, on this site, expressed as a spatial diagram, would change

its local surrounding, and other elements beyond, whether at the scale of London, the UK, or globally. It reveals the multiple contexts that are relevant at these scales, the communities of other institutions that may be involved, the ecosystems that may be regenerated…, hopefully leading to increased synergies.

As it forces students to develop simultaneously brief and multiple contexts, the process gains in effectiveness and relevance. Before this combination of brief and mapping, students were thinking of a limited number of factors, often factors that had a limited relevance to their brief. The panarchic mapping encourages designers to conceive what happens within the building with the effect that this has beyond its walls, to think of the impact of the brief and design and how it is shaped by its context. It is a co-evolution of brief and mapping.

As students generally have a few location options to choose from, the drawings of varied context scales are also a way to test the choice and begin analysing the site. They can propose alternatives if there is a more obvious choice, but this has rarely been necessary.

There is a similar effect of connecting scales that humans often perceive as unrelated as that brilliantly achieved in the *Factor of Ten* film made by Ray and Charles Eames (1968, remade in 1977) that begins from a picnic blanket's bird's eye view, zooms out all the way to see our entire galaxy, and zooms back in to the atomic scale. But this is done to show the coexistence and synergies between different aspects of the project and its communities, instead of the atomic and astronomic materiality of our world at different scales.

This multiscalar enquiry develops further through the design process in other scores: the massing and typology scale that integrates multiple ecosystem types in INHABITED PLANS, and the fabric of the building itself, its materiality and the circularity, in ECOTONE ENVELOPES.

GRAPHIC LANGUAGES

There are many precedents given, and we are keen that students find their own, for example, on the Act of Mapping [6] Instagram Account. We often mention the maps in Regenerative Empathy mentioned in the ECOLOGICAL SECTIONS.

Another foundational reference is the "Making Space in Dalston" map of cultural venues that the London based feminist architectural practice MUF [7] created to reveal to those not aware of the extraordinary density of micro-cultural venues in this area of London. This was used to convince the client and community that, instead of

Hydrological layer mapping of Epping Forest
Christian Thunik, Saleh Shesha, and Nikhil Shetty (opposite)

creating a new large institution, it would be more effective to nurture this thriving existing community. The exercise reveals what is invisible to many.

If the above tends to be more digital, and primarily map or plan views, they do not have to be. We also make reference to hand-drawn forms of mapping that are not necessarily maps per se. Such as many examples from the *Architectural Ethnography* exhibition at the Japan pavilion of the 16th Venice Biennale, such as the perspectives of Yukiko Suto [8]. Also, the extraordinary drawing by Adam Dant [9] of Hoxton Square, combining a central rooftop perspective framed with a border of portraits of characters using the square.

Whereas the digital drawings tend to give more precise data, or at least allow speed in working at the larger scales, those drawn by hand are more precise, empathetic, and complex at the human scale, and convey a sense of an inhabited place, of its qualities, through a located and subjective act of drawing.

DEFINING THE SCALES AND BOUNDARIES OF THE RELEVANT CONTEXTS

Reflecting on the mapping done in different years reveals that different sites and briefs lead to a different focus between smaller and larger scales. The panarchic brief mapping, with ecological layers, has been particularly effective in 2022-23 and 2023-24 at nurturing highly speculative yet relevant briefs; they have supported complex critical ambitions, understood in their multiple contexts. This may have taken the students slightly away from spending more time on site. The smaller scale may not have been analysed with as much care, in part because we only went there with them twice each year for short visits.

The most successful year in terms of close context was the 2021-22 year, when the site was near Knepp, and we spent half a day together precisely mapping and measuring the site. We are now considering that the second exercise should be done with a workshop on site, where students connect the broader information with what is experienced in situ. It is beneficial for sites to be easily reachable.

The challenge for teh designer is to define the relevant contexts of the project, the type of mapping, and their scales (whether they are maps or other media). These are the relevant systems that the project belongs to. What are the territories of engagement: whether ecosystems, territories of animals, site boundaries, spatial adjacencies, institutional networks…?

And with this lies the question of the type of boundaries and their representation. In ecosystems, they are often dynamic, thick, and porous, in contrast to human boundaries that are often static and thin, such as the site boundary line on a plan. Territories of animals, unless bound by fences, are dynamically shifting seasonally. Boundaries between ecosystems – ecotones – are equally deep, open, and move, encroaching or receding.

GRADUAL DEVELOPMENT OF A POSITION THROUGH THE MAPPING OVER THE YEAR

The focus of mapping in our studio has increasingly been on the development of a political or critical positioning that is defined through the relationships between the programme and the various contexts, especially the broader ones.

This benefits from a gradual development throughout the year. It usually begins with the collective exercise of Ecological Layers in semester 1; the data found forms a substrate for each student to develop an area of interest; the students re-use and adjust some of the drawings at the end of the same semester.

This becomes a foundation for the main project's panarchic mapping at the beginning of semester 2; Influenced by the philosophy and concepts discovered in the BOOK AS DRAWING score, which will be described later, the final panarchic mapping exercise leads to a strong position and a programme enmeshed in the relevant contexts.

Studio mapping of site ecosystems during a site visit on the edge of Southwater, near the rewilding project in the Knepp Estate, in October 2021.
Photograph of student measuring and drawing their site by Eric Guibert *(above)*

Endnotes

(1) Fikret Berkes, Johan Colding, and Carl Folke, Navigating Social-Ecological Systems (Cambridge University Press, 2003) p.18

(2) Originally developed in Barcelona by Oriol Bohigas, Manuel de Solà-Morales and Joan Busquets. Helena Casanova & Jesús Hernández, Public Space Acupuncture, https://urbannext.net/an-alternative-way-of-understanding-urban-planning/?utm_source=chatgpt.com [accessed on 16-07-2025]

(3) Jeremy Till, Architecture Depends (MIT Press, 2009)

(4) Nishwat Awan, Tatjana Schneider, Jeremy Till, Spatial Agency: Other Ways of doing Architecture (Routledge, 2011)

(5) Ian MacHarg, Design with Nature (25thn anniversary edition, 1992, 1st edition 1969)

(6) Act of Mapping Instagram account https://www.instagram.com/act.of.mapping?igsh=MTFwbzNndmcObXhtZw== [accessed on 16-07-2025]

(7) MUF, Hackney Map of Arts and Culture in Hackney, http://muf.co.uk/portfolio/making-space-in-dalston-2/ [accessed on 02-08-2025]

(8) Yukiko Suto Instagram account https://www.instagram.com/yukiko_suto?igsh=MTB5Zmo2ajZ4bG4ONg== [accessed on 16-07-2025]

(9) Adam Dant, Atelier Dant Instagram account https://www.instagram.com/atelier_dant?igsh=MWI2c3NkcnROazFzag== [accessed on 16-07-2025]

(opposite)
During one of the Covid years, students had to develop an understanding of context through redrawing the site through knowledge gathered remotely, such as in this map drawn from google map images by **Nina Busz**

Kacper Sehnke's project focused on international environmental politics through the angle of the United Nations' decade on Ecological Restoration.
He mapped the contexts at four scales. Starting from the Global (below), to the national (opposite), the London wide survey of relevant political and knowledge institutions (following spread, left-hand side), and the broader context of Epping Forest locating other potential restoration sites (following spread, right-hand side).

RIBA President Bronze Medal Winner

The Council for Ecosystem Restoration
Kacper Sehnke

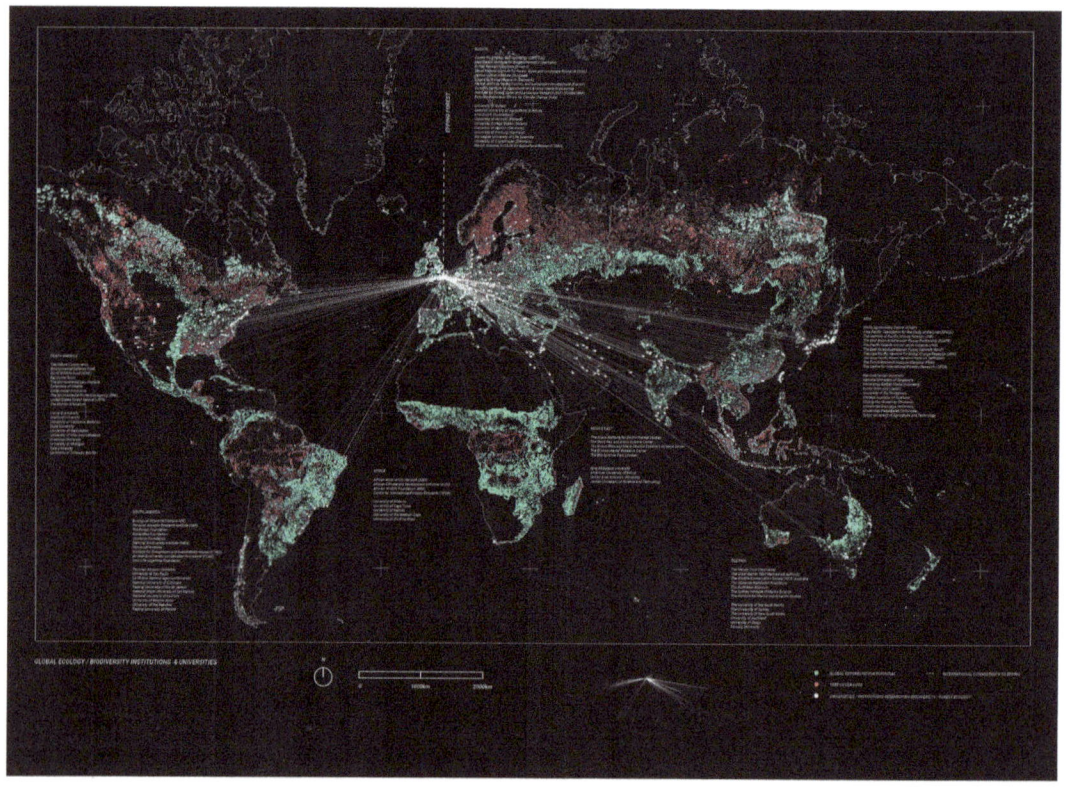

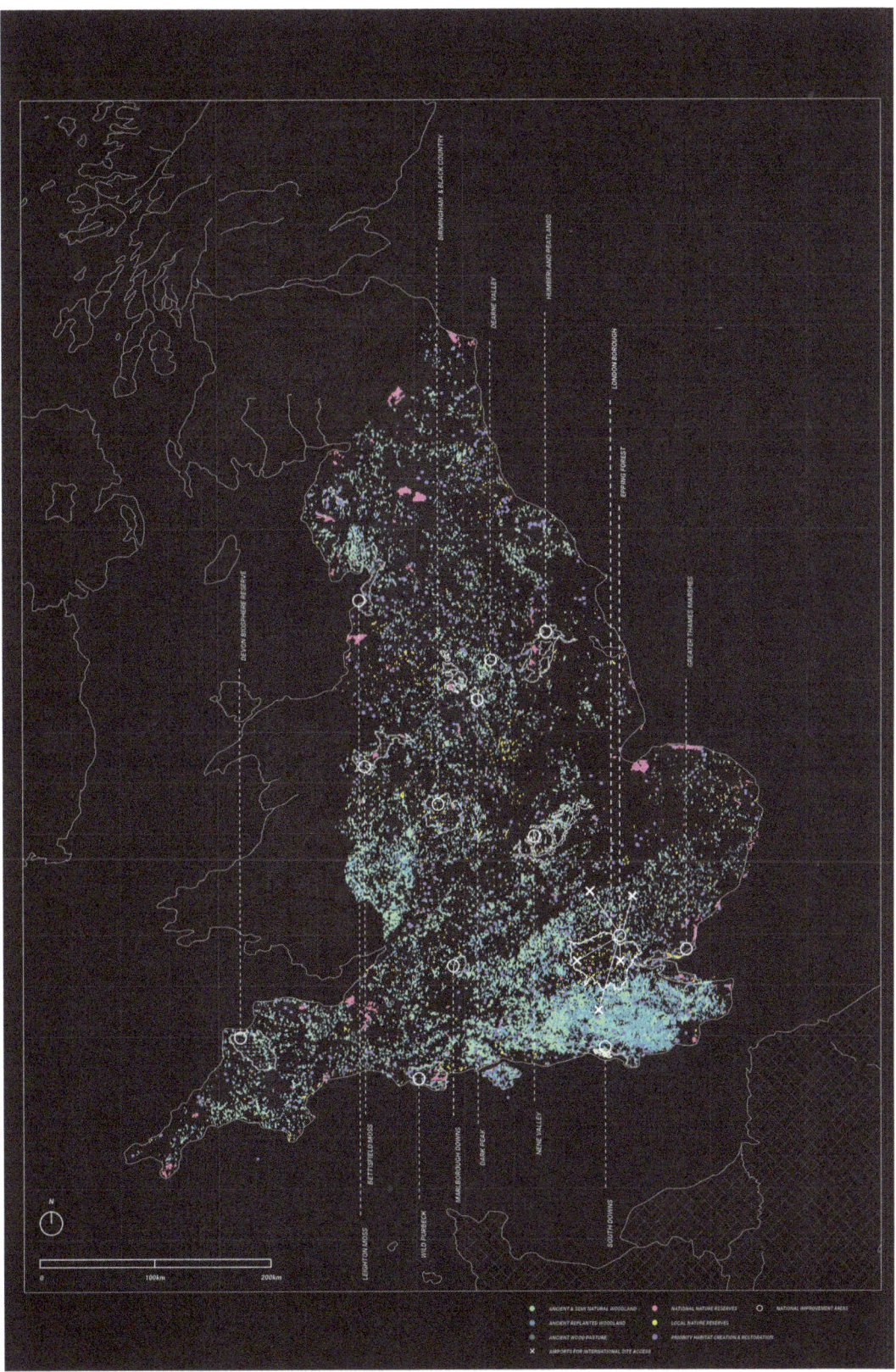

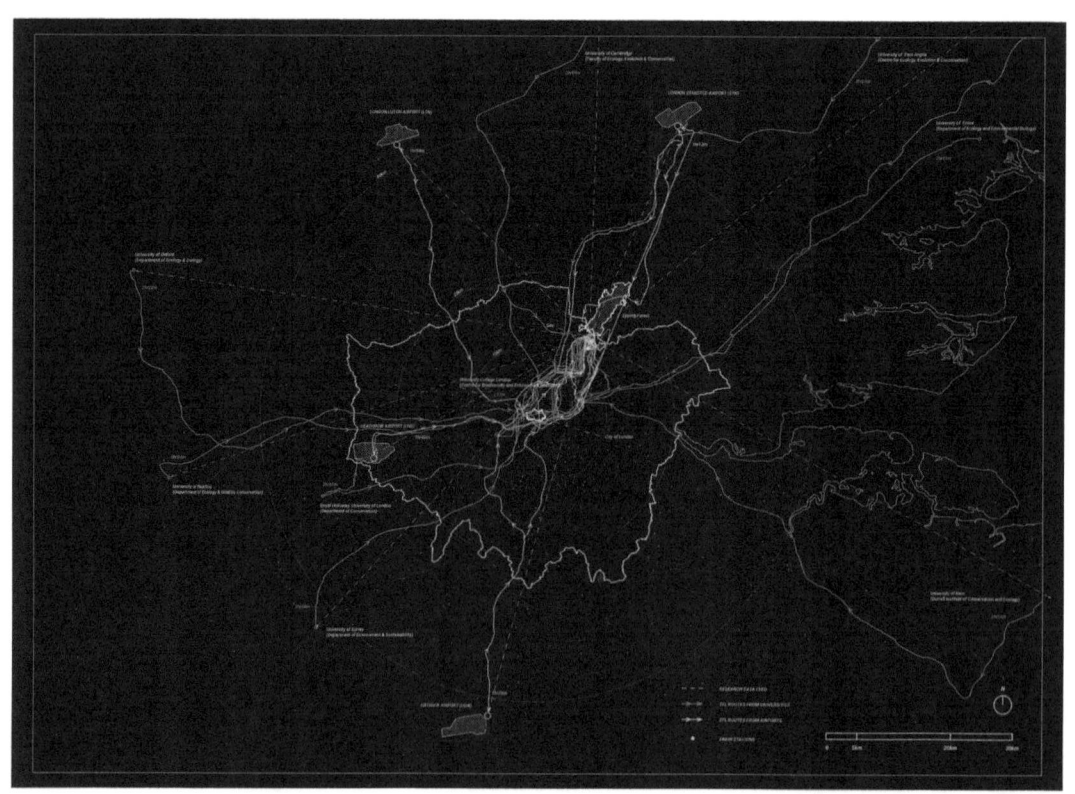

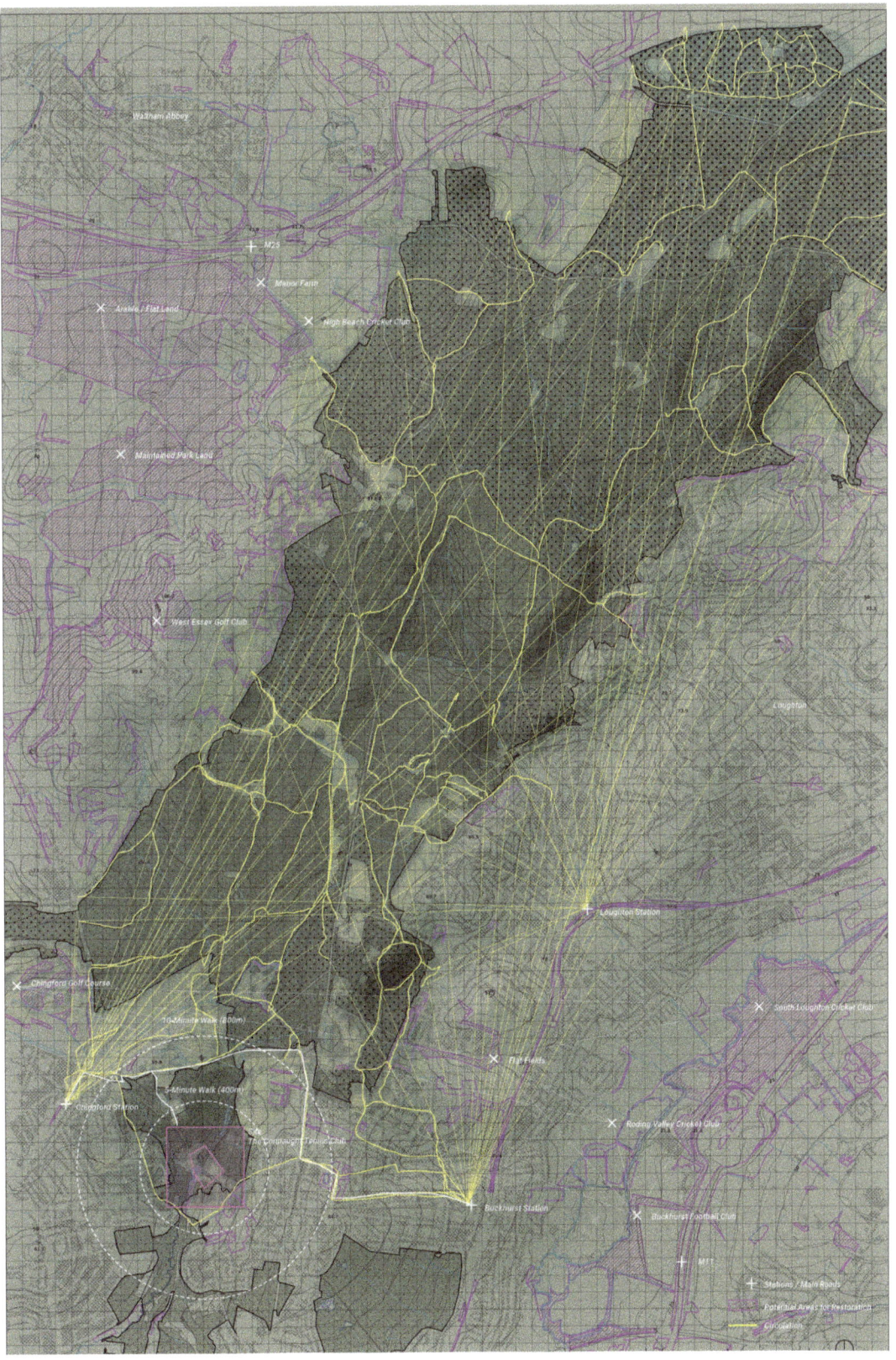

- Unlawful use of force and misuse of less-lethal weapons 
- Military force used against protesters 
- Protesters treated as a threat 
- Repressive legislature

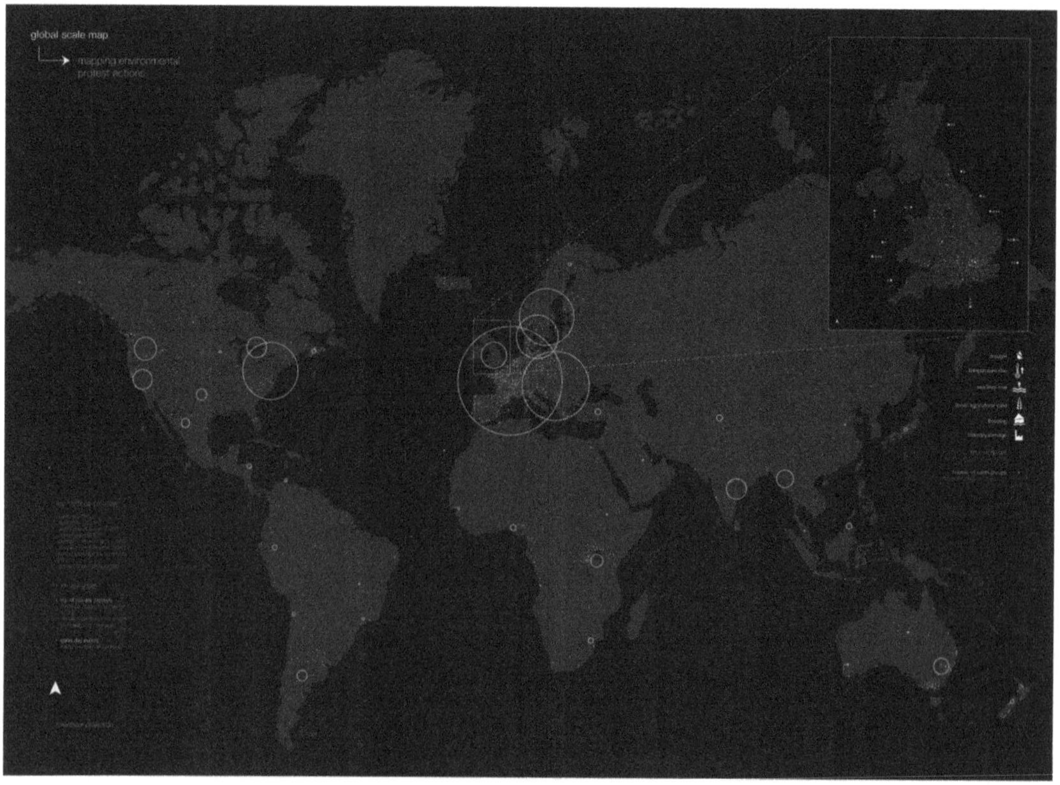

global scale map
mapping environmental protest actions

Benjamin Grafham developed over both semesters a mapping of environmental activism at multiple scales, from the global with an analysis of the legislative frameworks and enforcement in regards to activism *(opposite, top)*, and the activities of the activist group Extension Rebellion *(opposite, bottom)*, to the context of Whitehall where both of his project were located. This included a map of the then recent Extension Rebellion occupations of the area around Whitehall in 2019 and 2021 *(right)*, and an isometric of one of the protests on Whitehall *(below)*.

Semester 1: *Deployable Typologies for Environmental Uprising*
Semester 2: *The unseen labyrinth:*
"there's something in the walls"
Benjamin Grafham

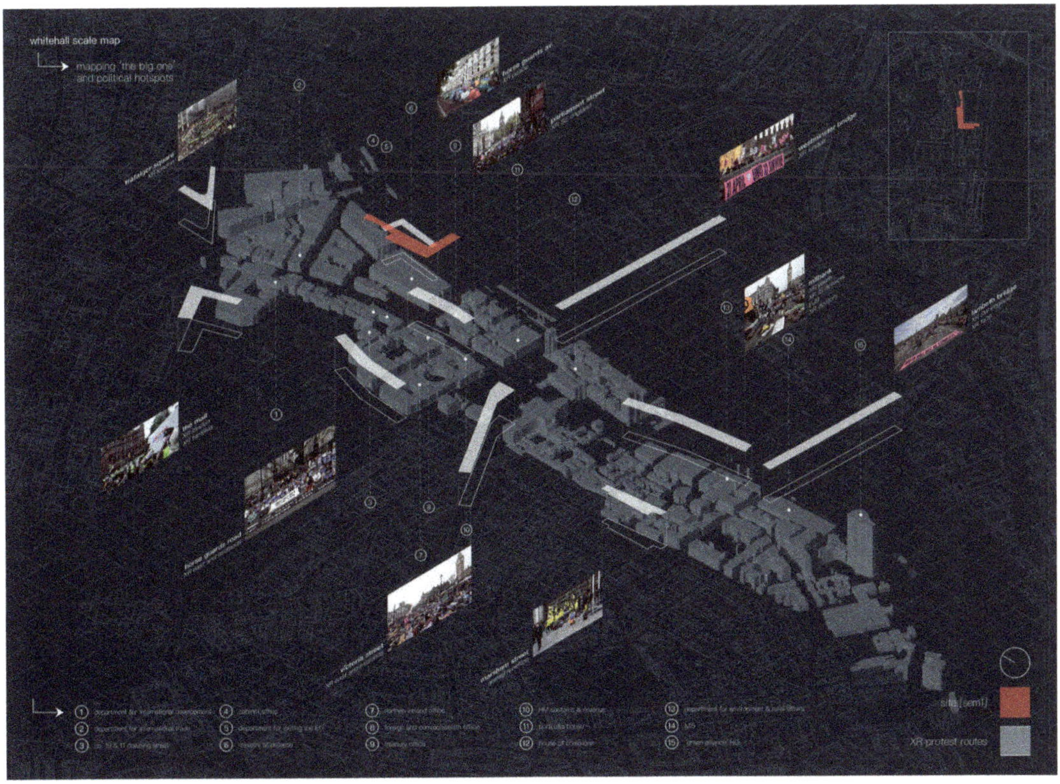

Benjamin Grafham developed over both semesters a mapping of environmental activism at multiple scales, from the global with an analysis of the legislative frameworks and enforcement in regards to activism *(opposite, top)*, and the activities of the activist group Extension Rebellion *(opposite, bottom)*, to the context of Whitehall where both of his project were located. This included a map of the then recent Extension Rebellion occupations of the area around Whitehall in 2019 and 2021 *(right)*, and an isometric of one of the protests on Whitehall *(below)*.

Semester 1: *Deployable Typologies for Environmental Uprising*
Semester 2: *The unseen labyrinth:*
"there's something in the walls"
Benjamin Grafham

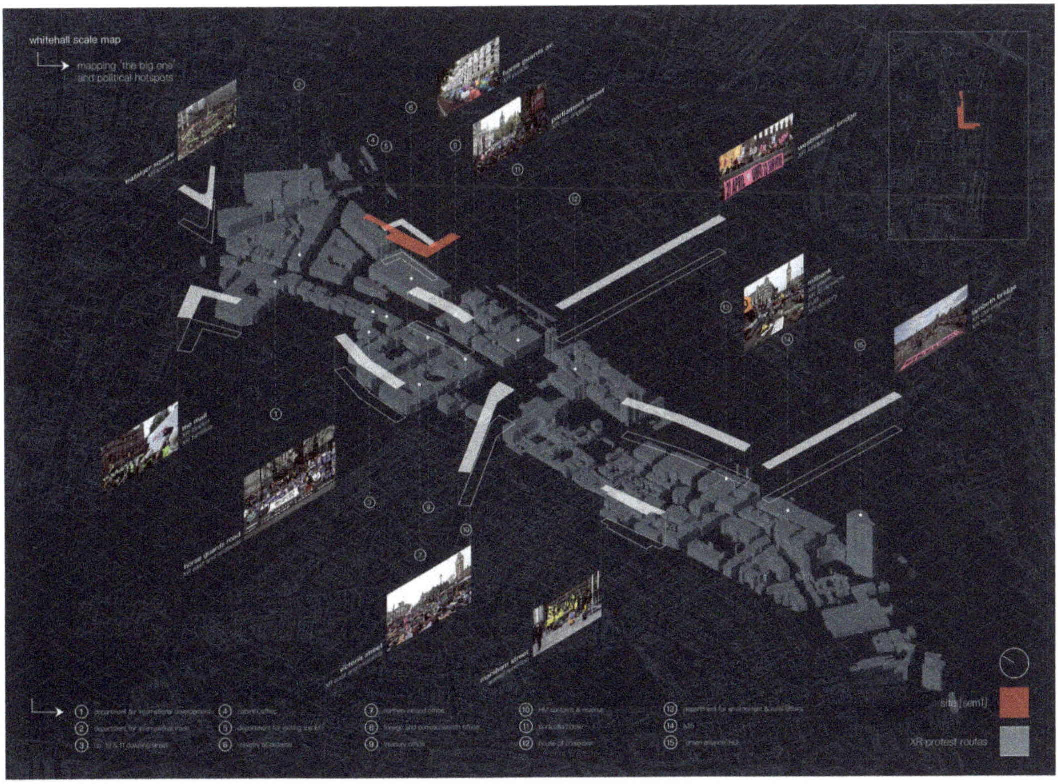

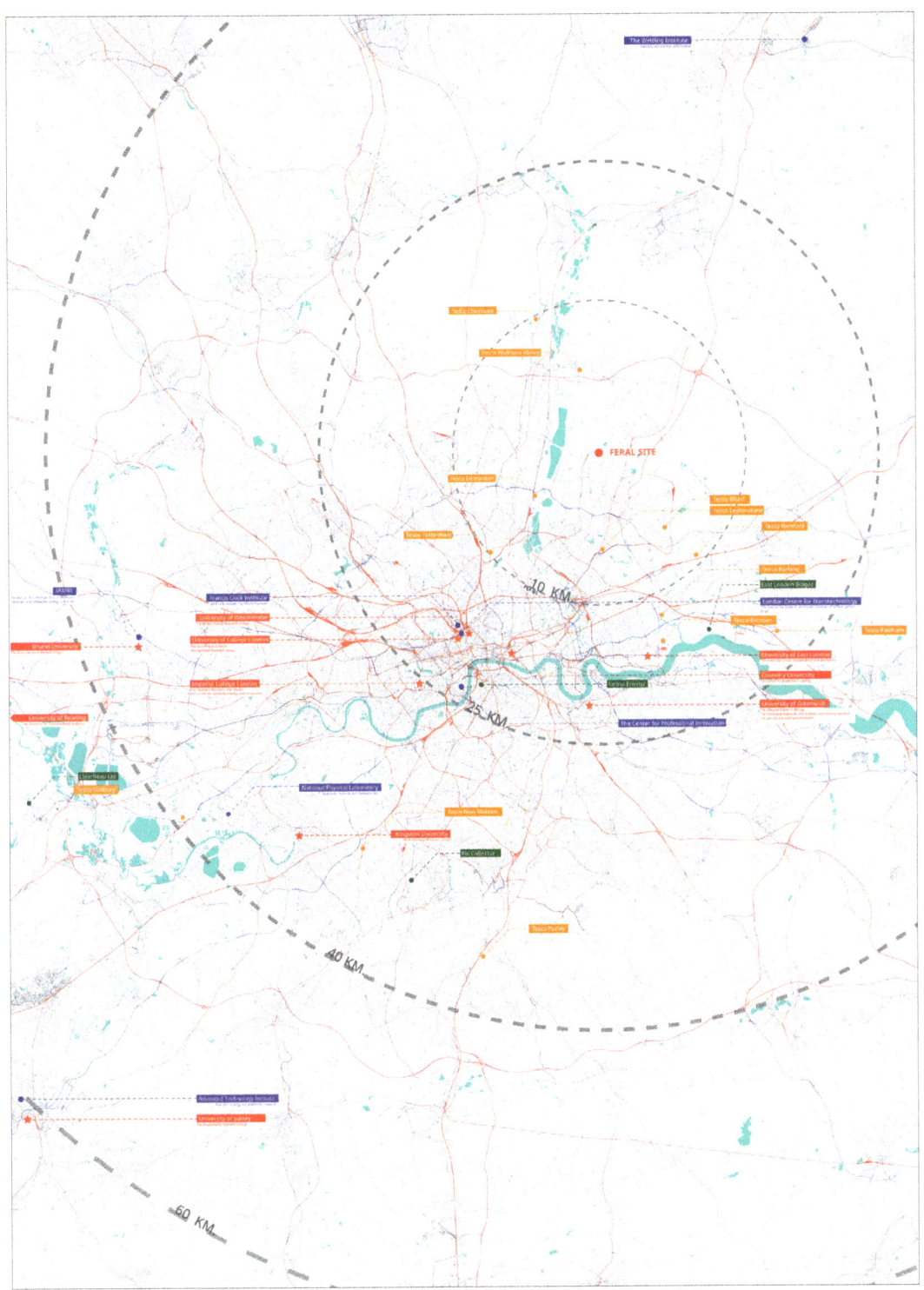

Yohei Yamane's mapping focussed on locating the potential for material to be used in this centre for locally upcycled materials and low-carbon fabrication.
Regenerative Site Plan/ Ecological Site Planning *(opposite, top)*,
Ecotonal Interface Map / Threshold Mapping of Urban-Wild Ecotone *(opposite, bottom)*, Ecological Fabrication Network Map / Territorial Network Mapping for Regenerative Infrastructure *(above)*.
NaturaeVIVA
Yohei Yamane

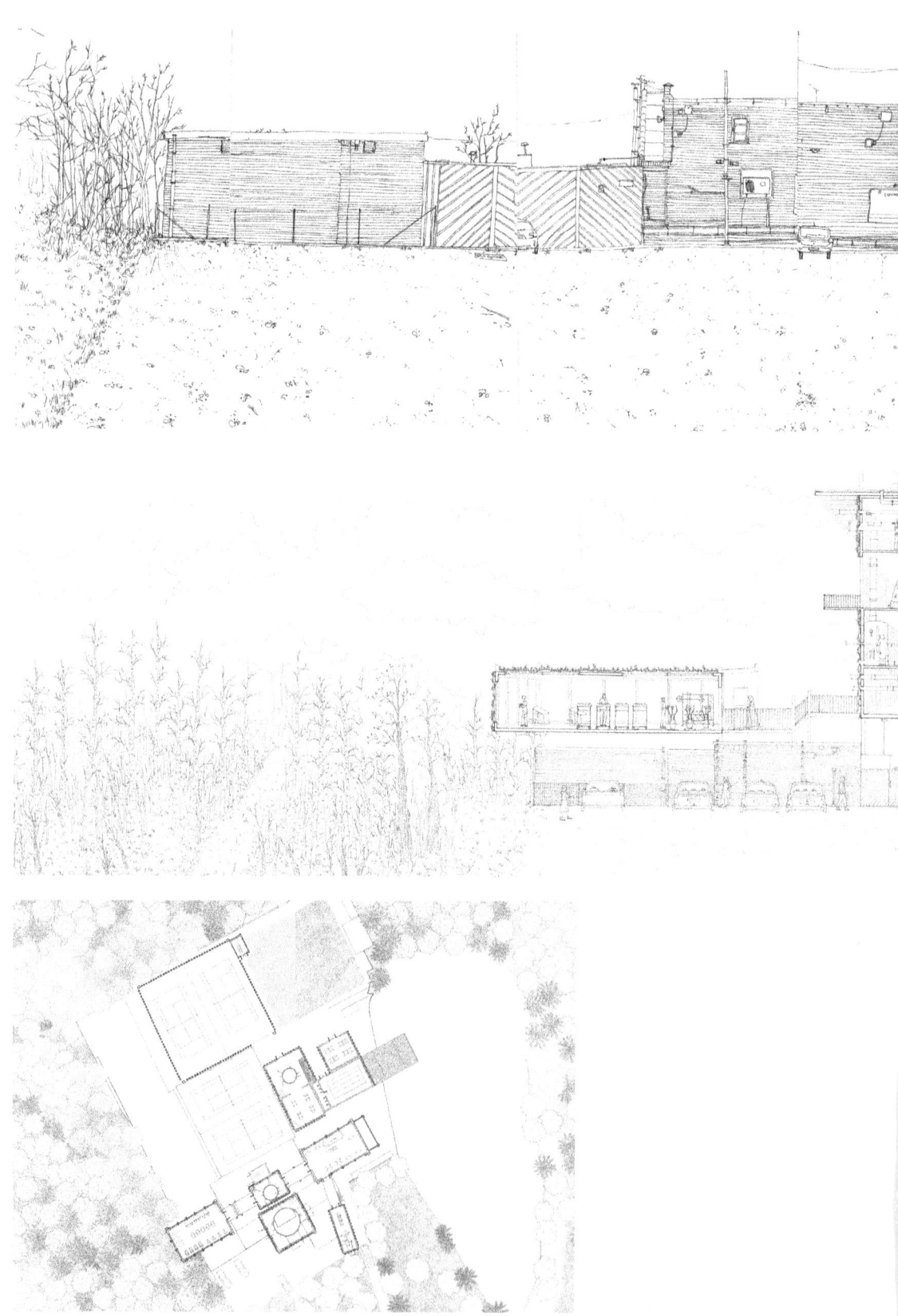

Nondita Jessica Abdul Matin mapping was based on detailed drawing of the site in situ in elevation and plan. This allowed her to develop a precise knowledge of the existing ecosystems and buildings.
This understanding led to a project that delicately re-used and framed the qualities of constructions and habitats already present on site .

Waste-to-Energy Hub
Nondita Jessica Abdul Matin

SCORE 3
ONTOPOLITICAL MODELS

Eric Guibert

Models have been a key medium for architectural design at least since the Renaissance, but models in architecture have tended to be abstracted; they are usually devoid of life, whether other-than-human or human inhabitation, and at times materiality. This may be a sign that for the modern mind, the realms of architecture as sculptural object, architecture as technical resolution, architecture as environmental design, and architecture as function (human use), are kept distinct. The other-than-human species and ecosystems are virtually entirely ignored, and even human use is abstracted (although it does appear in perspectival views). There was a tendency in the 90s architectural schools, still occurring occasionally today, for tutors to deride models that showed inhabitation as childish through terms such as "model railway" or "dollhouse" like. Abstracted sculptural form was presented as the ideal architectural model that created meaning by itself, separated from life.

As all life and most materials are not represented, the impact of architecture on biological and human communities on site and locally, as well as on the sites of extraction of the material used to build it, is out of sight and out of mind. This is a symptom of the capitalism on steroids of a neo-liberal society (I am thinking here mostly of the 1990s and 2000s) that celebrates an iconic architecture discussed primarily as a marketable language of forms, made possible by various consultants using the high operational carbon emission of air conditioning and material with high embodied carbon, such as concrete. A society that has destroyed ecosystems exponentially and led to the dangerous levels of climate change appearing today, and a drop of biodiversity of 73% since the 1970s [1].

NEW MATERIALISM

In response to these pressures, the modern and mechanical approaches (positivist) have been criticised and new philosophical models developed. We have seen a 'material turn' developing since the 1990s (new materialism, ecofeminism, cosmopolitics, ontopolitics [2]), which focuses on critically researching physical and societal phenomena, more than language, to reveal the complex situations on the ground.

Central to all their thinking is that if we are to avoid the destruction, and hopefully nurture the remaking, of our ecosystems and societies, we will have to combine different forms of knowledge and the ways of perceiving and understanding the world that are associated with them.

This means that we can no longer design with one dominant factor or problem, or even a few. Regenerative architecture works towards regenerating ecosystems of different scales simultaneously: global climate, diversity of ecosystems and associated species, human communities and individuals.

Concretely, this has meant a material and ontopolitical shift in architecture. Materially, the systemic concept of circularity – understanding where materials and energies come from and go to, from the impact on the sites of extraction, to the sites of disposal at the end of the building life. Ontopolitically, how architecture and its practice impact the different overlapping worlds of other-than-human and diverse human communities.

A recurring question for the studio has been how models should be made to allow the designers to think about both the circularity of materials and energies in relation to the coexistence of multiple species and communities. What could an ecological tectonic be?

ONTOPOLITICAL MODELS

The core of the ONTOPOLITICAL MODEL SCORE is to bring together human and other-than-human inhabitation, with building, climatic elements, structure, and materiality. It is a three-dimensional version of the ecological section. Models of course are commonly used in architectural design processes; some architectural communities of practice do integrate materiality [3], but it is rare that they are thought in relation to the inhabitation of multiple species. This leads to a different quality of models created with the inhabitation within and around the building.

This is essential to avoid a symbolic use of ecological and biological themes – eco or biomorphism – the green washing of buildings that look like biological beings but don't function like one, or that have a thin layer of plants without ecosystemic value.

The act of making ONTOPOLITICAL MODELS lead the designer towards understanding the building as a system exchanging matter and energy with its surroundings and composed of a mosaic of ecosystems for multispecies inhabitation. A building functions as a living system would, and is also a mosaic of ecosystems hosting other life. The approach can be termed 'ecomimicry' [4].

This is not only a question of how it is made and inhabited; it is also an aesthetic question. The sense of beauty, meaning, and ethics, is created not from the built elements in themselves, from the building as object, but from the relationship between the architecture and the life it hosts and nurtures, to the point, as mentioned earlier with ECOLOGICAL SECTION, that often the building somewhat disappears in the midst of the thriving inhabitation. It is an architectural aesthetic based on the assemblage of architectural and non-architectural elements, a composition of living and inert matter.

INHABITED SKETCH AND CONCEPT MODELS

As with the previous two scores, this is a gradual process, beginning with a phase of sketch and concept models. It is useful to understand this as an exercise in expanding the early ecological processes section into a three-dimensional version. As a result, the score is usually first brought in after these drawings and before the ecological sections that include the building. As is usually the case, they begin from sketch models of varying scales that can be quickly made, which have to include building and some elements of human and other-than-human inhabitation. These are then synthesised into a concept model that adds key elements of site information: topography, existing ecosystems, and other elements. These tend to be at 1/100 or 1/200 scale.

MASSING MODELS ONTOPOLITICALLY

With the more complex and larger projects in semester 2, a massing stage is necessary, a form of concept massing that locates different uses so that they establish relationships with each other and the context, these associations and positions create symbolic qualities, prominence or concealment, or gain particular views. Of particular focus is the relationship between spaces that are more for humans – interior or exterior – and those mostly or equally for other-than-human life, ecosystems, with attention to create the wildlife connectivity of nature recovery frameworks, grids of linear landscapes that give porosity for wildlife through the site.

These models have been inspired by the large programmatic foam models of OMA, such as those found in S, M, L, XL [5], that test the organisation of different functions represented by different colours as the central driver of the design process. Ours are different as OMA is primarily focused on the human programme and does not include other species or ecosystems (with the exception of their few landscape projects, of course).

In order to model the programmatic shapes to scale, students need an analysis of precedents to develop a list of areas, their size, and possible relationships. From this, they can test multiple arrangements from which to choose the most desirable option.

TRANSECT MODEL

Later on, usually after a first set of plans and sections has been produced, a more detailed model is created. At the beginning, we used entire site models at a sufficient scale to be able to model easily the structure, indicate cladding, and elements of inhabitation (at 1/100 or 1/50). This was conceived as a first stage, preparing the students for the technical module final exercise of a 1/20 model of a portion of the building, which had been developed by Scott Batty, who led the 2nd year of the BA technical module.

The aim is to add clearer materiality and environmental design, and more developed inhabitation and spatial qualities. On most projects, 1/100 is often used to keep the scale manageable (cost and storage). On a smaller project, they can be 1/50.

With the larger projects of 3rd year, the entire site model was unmanageable, and we shifted to a transect model. This is a slice of the project, including a significant portion of the landscape. It was inspired by transect sections and models used in landscape architecture that also focus on specific slices that are representative of the diversity of ecological conditions to develop the design in further detail, with the spatial, material, temporal and financial economy of only modelling part of the site.

Key to support this exercise is a lexicon of renewable or recycled materials used in the project, so that the students can work with the dimensions of the material available.

This exercise generally leads to the 1/50 or 1/20 scale models of the ECOTONE FACADE score.

THE LIVING MATERIALITY OF ONTOPOLITICAL MODELS

To the dismay of some architects, these models are resolutely aiming to convey the life and materiality envisaged, trees are generally made with organic matter, wood with balsa wood, clay for masonry and rammed earth... This is essential to develop an architectural expression that is defined by its inhabitations, and ethically sourced materials.

Our key references are the large models made by the office of the Swiss architectb Peter Zumthor for his Norway projects and others that were exhibited at the 16th Venice Biennale [6], the inhabited models of Junya Ishigami, especially Garden House [7], Bow Wow's models that include furniture [8] [9], and the furry models of Duncan Lewis & Édouard François [10] [11].

The hill of models in the studio exhibition at the OPEN Summer show in June 2023 at the School of Architecture and Cities, University of Westminster
(Photograph Eric Guibert)

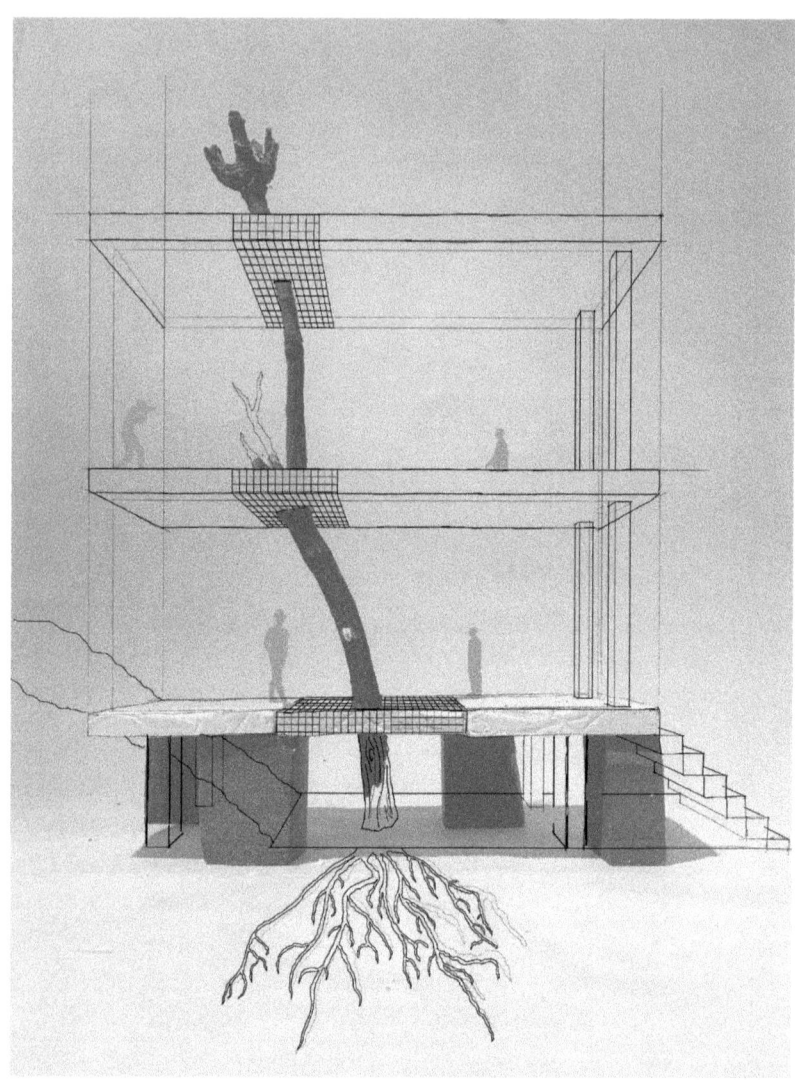

An early example of an enquiry in the potential relationships between living trees and buildings in our studio, in 2020.
Concept model by
Giovanni Musumeci

Earlier in the same academic year as the model opposite, in 2019, Nicholas Wood produced this model for a building hosting the practice of the land artist Robert Smithson. The project was conceived as a regenerative version of the artist's *Hotel Palenke* project.

The use of a diverse range of materials and tectonic clarity inspired many students in the following years.

Entropic Model
Robert Smithson Studio
Nicholas Wood

EMBRACING THE IMPERFECTION OF INHABITABLE SCALES

A traditional approach for architectural models is to make them small and perfect so that they appear fully controlled, often at 1/500 or 1/200 scale, but it is impossible for our imagination to inhabit such models, and they end up being thought of and judged purely as objects, as sculptures. The artefacts have to be large enough for the voids of their interiors, and the thickness of their facades to be unavoidable; a minimum scale is necessary to reveal the openness and porosity of architecture.

Working at larger scales in order to conceive of multispecies inhabitation and materiality is necessary for regenerative design and unavoidably leads to some imperfection, to models that are raw and slightly rough in ways reminiscent of the contemporary French artist Laure Prouvost [12]. Prouvost's work is also based on creating worlds by composing installations, assembling multiple inert and living elements around surreal and humorous narratives. As in our studio, there is a high degree of refinement, achieved through the trial and error of iteration; there is control but it is not the perfection of mathematics or craft, smoothness of form and detail. This looseness is key for the work to be approachable, familiar, and alive.

An architecture pregnant with life, as life itself, cannot be perfectly controlled, and neither should its representation be in model form.

Endnotes

(1) 'The Living Planet Report 2024 highlights the average change in observed population sizes of 5,495 vertebrate species. It shows a decline of 73% between 1970 and 2020.' in Living Planet Report: A System in Peril (World Wide Fund for Nature, 2024) https://livingplanet.panda.org/en-GB/ [accessed on 03-08-2025]

(2) These will be described in the BOOK & DRAWING score.

(3) A London based example of such a community is the Architecture Department of the Kingston School of Art who use large tectonic models as seen in their summer show in June 2025. A few examples can be found on https://www.instagram.com/ku_archland/ [accessed on 03-08-2025]

(4) Alan Marshall, 'The Theory and Practice of Ecomimicry', in Sustaining Gondwana, Issue 3, Working Paper Series (Alcoa Foundation, 2007). https://is.muni.cz/el/1423/jaro2013/HEN631/um/The_theory_and_practice_of_ecomimicy.pdf?utm_source=chatgpt.com

(5) Rem Koolhaas & Bruce Mau, Small, Medium, Large, Extra-Large: Office for Metropolitan Architecture (010 Publishers, 1995, 1st edition)

(6) Atelier Peter Zumthor, exhibition Dreams and Promises: Models of Atelier Peter Zumthor (Venice Biennale, 2018) photographs in https://worldarchitecture.org/article-links/ehghz/explore_peter_zumthors_neverbeforeseen_models_at_venice_architecture_biennale.html#:~:text=The%20exhibition%2C%20titled%20%22Dreams%20and,mining%20region%2C%20as%20well%20as or https://www.designboom.com/architecture/peter-zumthor-models-venice-architecture-biennale-05-28-2018/ [accessed on 03-08-2025]

(7) Junya Ishigami, Freeing Architecture (catalogue of the exhibition at the Fondation Cartier pour l'Art Contemporain, 2018)

(8) Atelier Bow-Wow, House Behaviorology (Venice Architecture Biennale, 2010) some images on https://www.designboom.com/architecture/atelier-bow-wow-at-venice-architecture-biennale-2010/ [accessed on 03-08-2025]

(9) Atelier Bow-Wow, Behaviorology (Rizzoli International Publications, 2010)

(10) François & Lewis, Maquette de rendu, of the Hameaux de gîtes ruraux, Jupilles, Pays de la Loire (in the Centre Pompidou Collection, 1994-96) https://www.centrepompidou.fr/en/ressources/oeuvre/crgdXRE [accessed on 03-08-2025]

(11) Édouard François, Duncan Lewis & associés, Construire avec la Nature / Building with Nature: Vingt Architectures dans le Paysage (Édisud, 1999)

(12) I have here in mind her installation at the Whitechapel Gallery for which she won the Max Mara Art Prize for Women, but much of her work, including her later exhibition at the Palais de Tokyo in 2018 shares these qualities. The London installation combined elliptical walls covered with hand drawings, collages, and screens, including the main video piece Swallow. Laure Prouvost, Farfromwords: cars mirrors eat raspberries when swimming through the sun, to swallow sweet smells (installation, Whitechapel Gallery, 2013)

In addition to her ECOLOGICAL SECTIONS represented in the previous score, Finola Simpson's first semester project *The Purple Emperor* benefited from a series of INHABITED MODELS that grew in parallel to the sections.
The models were instrumental in the definition of the geometry of the project in relation to the ecosystem. The building brings the lepidopterist close to the willow canopy where the caterpillar lives and pupates. The models were also central with the design of the structural system and materiality of the building.

Final Model at 1:50 *(above)*
Concept Model *(opposite)*

The Purple Emperor
Finola Simpson

Darya Prokopets used her models intuitively to create tactile and vibrant worlds. Whereas earlier students used similar materials in the models to those imagined (*balsa wood for timber, clay for rammed earth...*), she creatively re-used waste material of a different nature, but transformed them so that they resemble those envisaged. At times the same model medium is used for multiple purposes, such as polystyrene in this model that is marked and at times coloured to convey both the re-used concrete rubble and brickwork.

Physical concept model *(opposite)* and digital collage of the proposal in a photograph of the site *(above)*

Dwelling for a Chiropterologist
Darya Prokopets

Edmund Alcock was inspired by our visit to Knepp where Tamworth pigs roam freely. They rout the ground to feed, disturbing the soil creating patches of bare soil where rarer species of plants can germinate and grow.
He proposed a feral relationship where pigs are nurtured and yet live outdoors through the year.
Some pigs are culled to avoid overpopulation, providing wild meat for human consumption.
The models were essential at thinking the relationships between landscape and buildings, including a veranda where humans and pigs meet. The brickwork chimney is used for the smoking of the meat for preservation.

Two photographs of the final model.
Immersive view with Tamworth pigs at the crossing *(above)*
Aerial view of human and pig dwelling.

The Cycle of Pannage
Edmund Alcock

In dialogue with the ECOLOGICAL SECTIONS reproduced in the previous score, Benjamin Leathes further developed the understanding of an inhabited materiality through a series of models using multiple organic materials.
The small buildings that provide the only fixed elements create a series of habitats, the stony and dry ecosystem of gabion construction, and the climbers growing on trellis like façades.

Multiple photographs of the final model. *(above and opposite)*

Anthropic Tropism
Benjamin Leathes

One of the key concepts of Kacper Sehnke's RIBA President Bronze Medal project was to construct the buildings with waste organic materials found in Epping Forest and the rubble from the suburban area.

The harvesting of the timber nurtures biodiversity by pollarding some of the trees to creates the varied mosaic of different light levels within the woodland that is beneficial to biodiversity.

In parallel to the ECOLOGICAL SECTIONS, Kacper produced many models, especially TRANSECT MODELS slicing through different parts of the project *(above)*.

This was based on a rigorous analysis of the sizes of the available material to be used for construction, which were modelled in CAD *(opposite)*. Once the design was settled, Kacper made a digital model of the buildings which was used for the renders of his VISUAL SPECULATIVE FABULATION.

The combination of a first phase of intutive physical models, followed by a rigorous digital replica was central to the development of the language of the building in relation to multispecies inhabitation, and the refinement of a regenerative tectonic.

The Council for Ecosystem Restoration
Kacper Sehnke

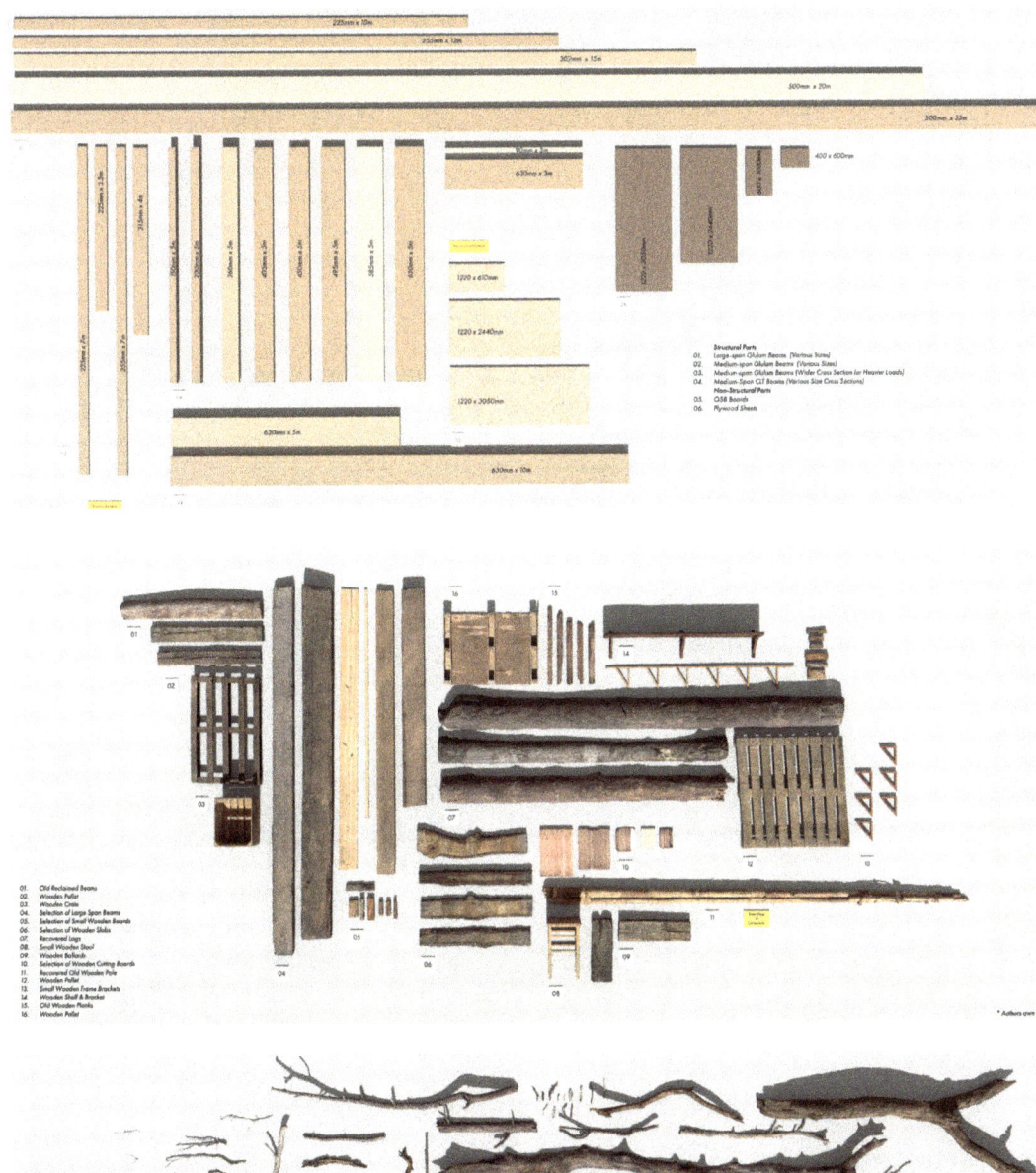

SCORE 4
VISUAL SPECULATIVE FABULATIONS

Eric Guibert

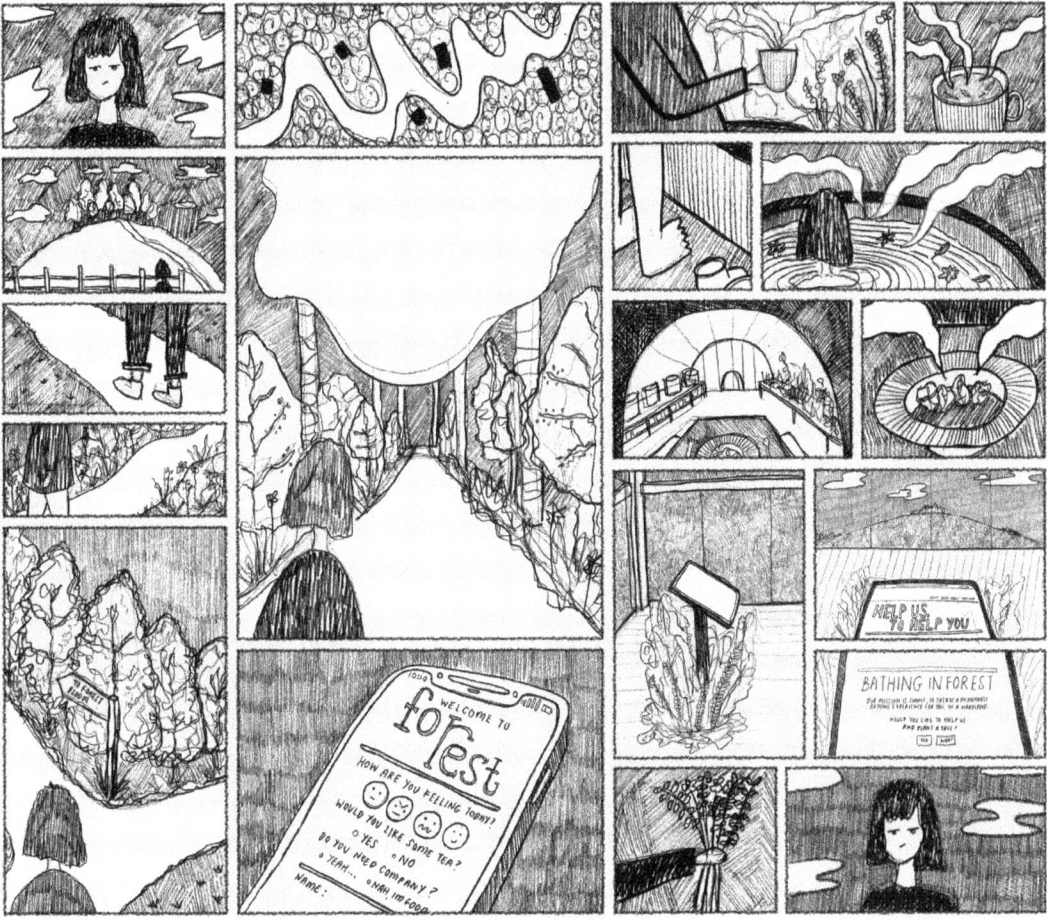

We have already seen three ways of designing architecture by shaping relations between the various actors in the projects: human and other inhabitants, climate, matter, energy, buildings... ECOLOGICAL SECTIONS do this two-dimensionally and vertically, and at the scale of buildings. PANARCHIC MAPPING connects across scales within the site and beyond. ONTOPOLITICAL MODELS do this three-dimensionally within the site. GRAPHIC SPECULATIVE FABULATIONS use narratives to show how these multiple actors relate to each other through experience, through time. It is important to point out that this type of narrative is not the story of the design process often used by students in architecture schools to describe their projects, where the narrator or persona is the student and/or the design. Our studio stories are closer to that of a film or a novel, where the voices are those of the inhabitants.

This has been one of the slowest scores to develop. There are three primary reasons for persevering in including and developing this method in order to design complex worlds where intangible qualities and change matter more than the sculptural quality of a static object.

In 2021, two students created the first convincing VISUAL SPECULATIVE FABULATIONS. Both used these as central tools to imagine both the program of their project and the architectural qualities.
Syafiqah Aziz developed a community bathing experience that unfolds both in the landscape and inside the buildings. The early sketches are reminiscent of Japanese animated films and manga with shifts between architectural scale views and details of paths, or of the smart phone app that gives form to the forest spirit.

For-Rest by **Syafiqah Aziz**

WORLDING

Most importantly, designing regenerative architecture is an act of 'worlding'; architecture is a medium for speculating on possible regenerative futures, or it might be more precise to say for reinterpreting existing realities, towards the regeneration of ecosystems, social groups, structures of meaning, and human individuals.

Donna Haraway has explained how ecological futures cannot be created for a society that functions like ours; it is necessary to imagine altered ways of living. Inspired

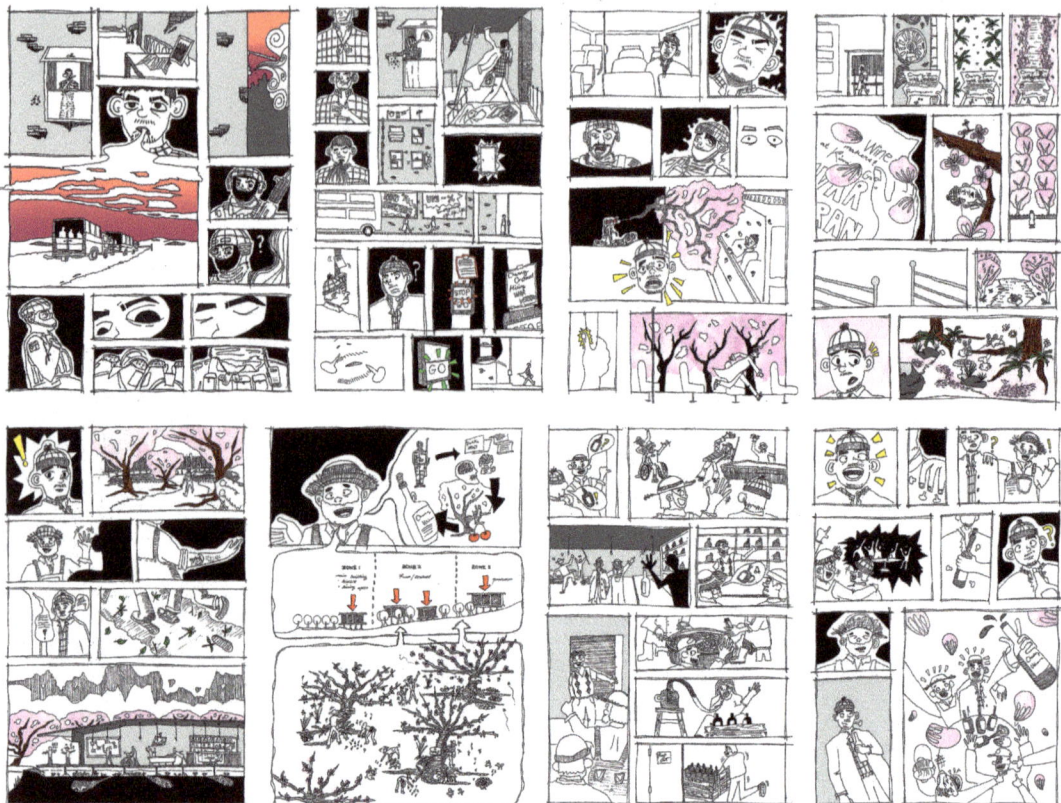

by speculative fiction, in particular the work of Ursula Le Guin, she conceives of this process of creation as Speculative Fabulations, ways of investigating possibilities that may inspire societal change through – in her case written – narratives, not because what will happen is what has been imagined exactly, but because these exercise show possible directions of travel, openings [1]. It is to some extent a utopian exercise, but one grounded in the concrete, in matter. Like good speculative fiction, it attempts to reveal existing challenges and show possibilities based on a developed understanding of the way living beings engage with the world and each other, as well as technology and science.

The most striking impact of this exercise is that it forces students to challenge their assumptions about our present condition in relation to the world they are speculating on. When it is first applied, many draw normative worlds that contradict their ambitions, at times highly consumerist and corporate. The act of drawing reveals their imagination, and implicit political position; the sketch becomes a starting point for a discussion on whether this is what they wish for our future.

These have had the broadest range of qualities and tones from childlike (but not childish) imaginations of cute worlds, to dystopian visions.

In the same year as the story board overleaf, Changsoo Yoo drew a graphic novel (above) that communicates the life in a refuge for soldiers suffering from PTSD that heal by gardening a farm producing food products by bringing in synergy pisciculture and agroforestry.

His narrative powerfully communicates the emotional and daily life of humans in connection to the ecological processes (movement of nutrients...) through the site. Some of these vignettes were redrawn at the end of the project (opposite)

Captain Charlie and the Cherry Factory
Changsoo Yoo

DESIGNING WITH THE COMPLEXITY OF SYSTEMS

Designing systemically is designing with complexity. As complex systems can never be entirely described [2], it is necessary to simplify while retaining sufficient coherence for the artefact to be understood. In plans and sections, this is done by drawing what is cut by the section line, while removing – most of – the third dimension. In stories, the coherence is given by the narrative thread, and complexity is simplified by removing what is not in the scene or the direction of view. It is time, more than space, that connects the parts.

THINKING THE FORMLESS

The third benefit of narratives is their temporal nature that represents 'formless' or intangible qualities: growth, decay, weather, inhabitation, meaning that is not created by the architectural object as symbol... It helps with understanding the concrete dimension of the brief as activities or changes taking place in space and time. Often, it reveals opportunities to harness and challenges to negotiate. It is revealing that the only year when it was not a compulsory exercise, 2021-22, is when the inhabitation of more projects was less understood, in the cases of students who didn't use the score, or only at the end.

Since my architectural studies, I have had a fascination for narratives in architecture, whether written or drawn or both. They have always seemed to me necessary to connect the broad range of architectural qualities that matter (to me), these qualities that are formless, alive, changing, partly unpredictable [3]. The inclusion of these intangible qualities was the original reason for attempting to include narratives in the design development of projects in a previous studio, with limited success at the time.

Of all the media we use, this may be the least object-centred, with the exception of TEMPORAL DRAWINGS. ECOLOGICAL SECTIONS, INHABITED PLANS, PANARCHIC MAPPING, and ONTOPOLITICAL MODELS are all systemic, and all engage with inhabitation, but they nonetheless also represent the building as a static object. The narrative tends to either bring the focus on the affordance of the architecture – what can happen within it as if it were a stage – or the non-permanent nature of architecture, as it shows the evolution of the buildings.

TOWARDS VISUAL SPECULATIVE FABULATIONS

It is in the second year of this studio that we began including written narratives of a journey through the site and building (2019-20). In the following year (2020-21), this was tested as a visual form – graphic – speculative fabulation. We referenced two multi-narratives graphic novels: *Building Stories* by the American cartoonist Chris Ware [4] and *Citizens of No Place* by the architect Rimenez Lai [5], as well as story boards from films, and the late medieval miniature serie of the months in the *Très Riches Heures du Duc de Berry* [6] where a typical scene for each month expresses the rhythms of rural production, seasons, and astrology.

We were convinced by a few excellent results from Syafiqah Aziz and Changsoo Yoo that led to the exercise being developed further in the following years, increasingly including other forms of visual narratives such as videos.

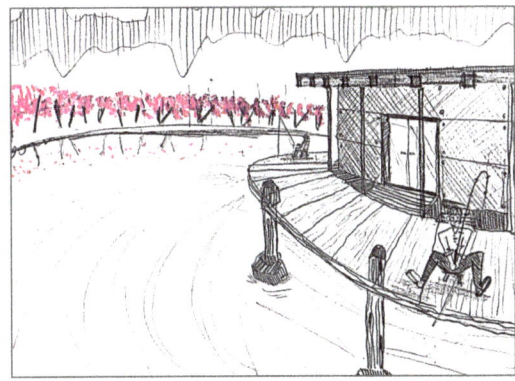

PARAMETERS – FREE AND MULTI-SCALAR

Over time, a few rules were developed to ensure the effectiveness of this score. These define a freedom of media, which we broadened over the years, while encouraging the narrative to cover multiple systemic and spatial scales (context, site, building, interior, details) as well as multiple temporal scales (human experience and evolution of years or decades). These connect to the multiple scales of Panarchic Mapping and Temporal Drawings. Here are the usual rules:

- *A visual narrative(s)*
- *It can be any type and medium: graphic novel, storyboard, video...*
- *Total freedom in terms of how the final version is produced, whether by hand, digitally collaged, using AI to generate the inhabitation, or a combination*
- *There must be multiple time frames within the story(ies)– day, year, decades... to deal with both experience and evolution over time*
- *It must be ambitious and beautiful*
- *A minimum number of outdoor spaces are represented (varies from year to year, but often 3)*
- *A minimum number of indoor spaces are represented (varies from year to year, but often 3)*
- *Inhabitations must be present throughout – human and other-than-human*
- *Context must be present in many views – topography, buildings, trees and ecosystems, water...*
- *Details of the building must be present in some views*

STAGES

The process is usually in two or more stages. A first iteration is used relatively early in the process, which is then redrawn towards the end.

The first stage is in three parts:

- *Draw quick sketches in whatever order as they come to mind*
- *Organise them as a story*
- *Draw/sketch a first complete version*

Many draw this by hand, whether on paper or on a tablet with a stylus, but some use collages from the start.

This first version often lacks architectural qualities, focusing more on the actions taking place, which are often the main focus at this stage – the frames of images are too narrow to show the spaces sufficiently, and there is a lack of detail. During the second stage, the views are broadened to show more of the spaces and add detail, further designing their architecture.

These early stages reveal the student's imagination, whether they are designing for a normative world, or understand their project's brief. This realisation leads to further development of the program with a higher degree of ecological speculation. It ensures that the architecture is designed to enable this inhabitation, instead of the latter being fitted in it at the end loosely and unconvincingly.

Usually, later in the design development, these early visual stories become the basis for the final views, which are often presented as a journey through the project that sometimes combines a walk through the spaces with an evolution of the building and landscapes through a longer, ecological or seasonal timeframe as this is most obvious with Kacper Sehnke's Bronze Medal entry (INTERLUDE 1). The final visual narrative can either be presented as a graphic novel, or as a video created from the still images an earlier story board.

REPRESENTATIONAL STRUGGLES

The understanding of the program of the project, relationships between multiple factors, and of the architectural experience substantially rises from this score but some students struggle with the medium.

For some it seems to be a misunderstanding that it can only be drawn by hand, which they are unconfident with. We do recommend the first sketches to be drawn by hand for speed and ease, but any making process can be used for the more developed artefacts.

For others, the lack of understanding of the chosen briefs blocks their capacity to imagine what may take place. This is generally due to a lack of the rigorous research; without a concrete understanding of how similar places function today, it is impossible to speculate on how they might change in the future.

The other common struggle is to think activities and architectures simultaneously, to shift away from the building as object first, within which inhabitation is massaged, to defining a way of living that the architecture is then designed to support.

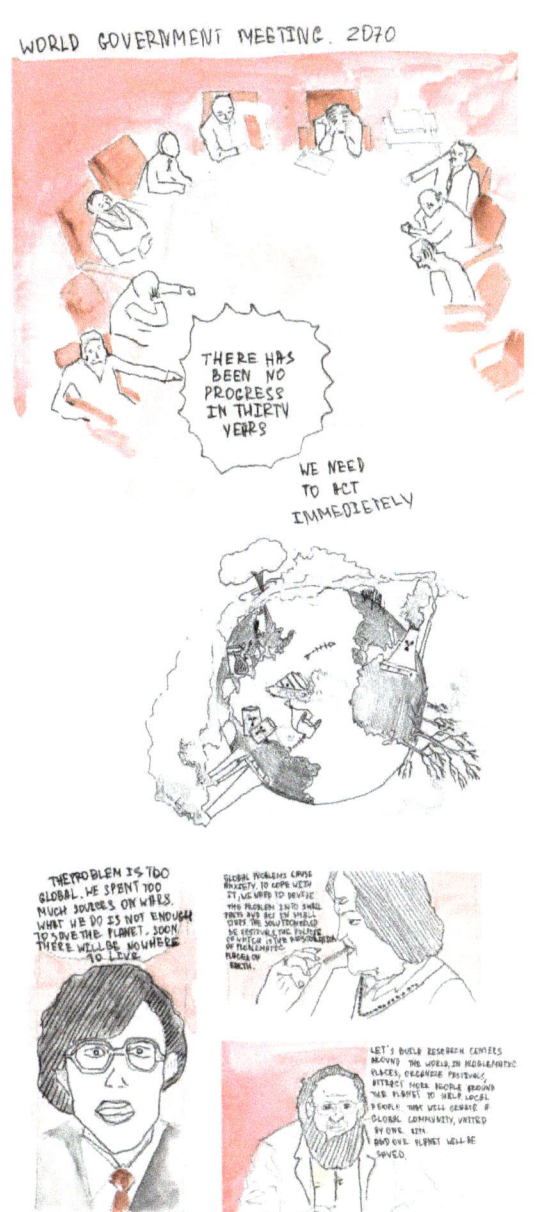

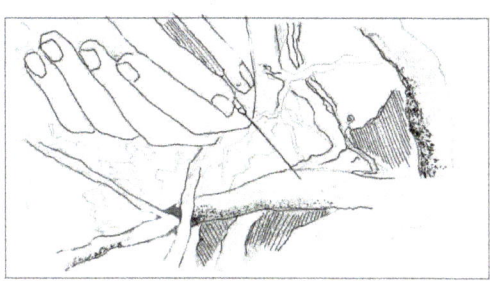

VISUAL SPECULATIVE FABULATION

Sanctuary for the dispossessed
Darya Prokopets

Endnotes

(1) Donna J. Haraway, Staying with the Trouble: Making Kin in the Chthulucene (Duke University Press, 2016) ch. 6, which also refers to Ursula Leguin 'The Carrier Bag Theory of Fiction', and ch. 8 for the example of 'The Camille Stories'.

(2) Quote on complexity...

(3) Eric Guibert, 'The Gardener Architect: designing with the emergent natures of places' (unpublished doctoral thesis, KU Leuven, 2018).

(4) Chris Ware, Building Stories (Jonathan Cape, Random House, 2012).

(5) Jimenez Lai, Citizens of No Place: An Architectural Graphic Novel (Princeton Architectural Press, 2012)

(6) Paul, Johan and Herman Limbourg, Les Très Riches Heures du Duc de Berry, 1412-1416, illuminated manuscript, Musée Condé, Chantilly, France.

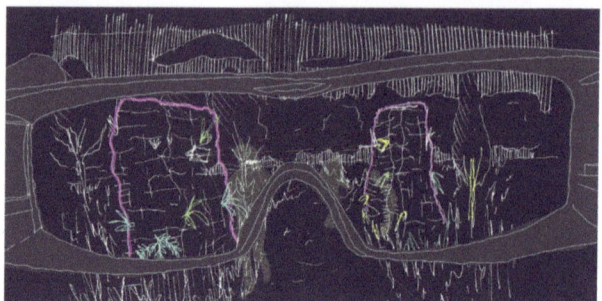

Benjamin Leathes' project is for a forest regenerated by a dynamically moving silent dance rave (the music is played on headphones).
The creation of the VISUAL SPECULATIVE FABULATION both allowed him to conceive and communicate the fluid experience of the forest. Ecological ravers are guided in different areas by augmented reality glasses to optimally spread the disturbance of humans.

Anthropic Tropism
Benjamin Leathes

149

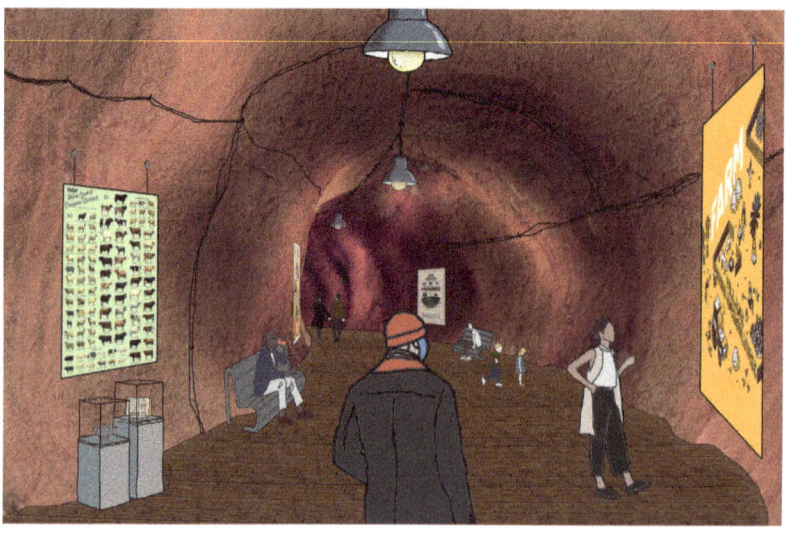

Previous spread:
Shah-Ree Tasaddiq's project for a new ecological assembly to the Houses of Parliament in London, weaves the Bengali folk-tale 'Nakshi Kanthar Math' into a new ritual based on the weaving of a quilt to record the evolution of global and national ecosystems to both give them a voice, and reveal the shifting baseline syndrome, the way society forgets how ecosystems used to be from one generation to the next. Central to the design process was a dialogue between physical and later digital models with a storyboard of views and renders that gradually brought together the ecological ritual and political palaver, with the woven architecture supported by a biomorphic structure that resonates with both Islamic and Gothic architecture.

Nakshi Kanthar Math
The Field of Embroidery Quilt
Shah-Ree Tasaddiq

This spread:
Diego Gallardo,s project for a ministry of regenerative agriculture is a humorous political statement that places a giant cow shaped building with its eyes facing the prime ministers windows at no. 10 Downing Street.
The visual narrative conveys the combination of this confrontational activism with spaces for diplomatic discussions and education on ecological food production both within and in demonstration gardens in Green Park .

Botanical Co[w]liseum
Diego Gallardo

SCORE 5
INHABITED PLANS

Eric Guibert

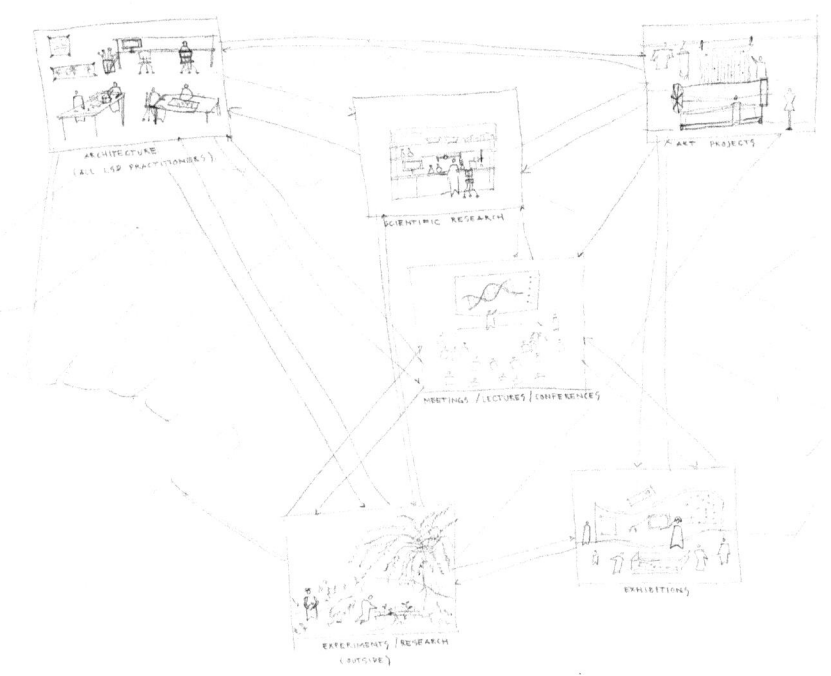

A SPATIAL DIAGRAM drawn by Thais Ribeiro Rodrigues. this example can also be read as a sketched VISUAL SPECULATIVE FABULATION organised as a spatial diagram. (left)

The Institute for Sympoiesis
Thais Ribeiro Rodrigues

Inhabited plans can be seen as zooming from the local context scale of the PANARCHIC MAPPING further into the site, while integrating the massing strategies developed in the massing modelling exercise. They define the mosaic of habitats within the site and the connectivity between them, both those for different human activities and those for other-than-humans. Central to this is how these plans form wildlife corridors, steps, and patches for the movement of wildlife to connect to broader nature recovery frameworks.

Similar to the vertical systemic thinking of ecological sections, inhabited plans focus on horizontal inhabitation by multiple species in relation to each other, defined by the building fabric and the neighbouring context. Climate is present in terms of different degrees of shelter and light, both outdoors and indoors, and is conceived as another life-like element.

SPATIAL DIAGRAMS

The process has evolved over the years, testing multiple modes.

Often, the brief has already been described as a diagram and/or models in the nested mapping stage. If the original diagram is not indicative of the areas needed for each function, it is best to begin with re-drawing the abstract diagrams spatially, with scale, either as shapes of the area needed or – better – as activities (furniture, equipment…), usually in plan so that the drawings of activities can be re-used in later drawings.

As we are speculating on alternative ways of living, assumptions on how spaces may be inhabited need to be checked and drawn rigorously in the plan medium. This process was inspired by the drawings of a number of Japanese architects also questioning normative ways of life such as the work of Ryue Nishizawa from SANAA, especially the plans of Moriyama House that redesign a single dwelling as a constellation of micro buildings spread in a small garden offering a new form of flexibility and relation between outdoors and indoors [01].

It is usually around this time that the massing models of the previous score are produced.

COLOURED AND HATCHED PLANS

After the ontopolical models have been made, a first set of plans is usually produced that is then investigated during a coloured plan workshop [02].

These are plan diagrams that represent formless or intangible spatial qualities as gradients of colour or texture, for example:

- Gradient of privacy (entirely private / shared / communal / public)
- Gradients of shelter from more static to more variable (conservative – fully heated, dynamic internal, sheltered outdoors, exposed)
- Different longevities of elements of the built fabric: permanent (structure, risers and cores), adaptable (partitions...), ephemera (furniture...)
- Degrees of control of ecosystems (wild, feral, gardened, totally controlled indoor) – this reveals the degree of wildness of habitats and wildlife corridors

These diagrams are used by students to develop strategies for a few intangible qualities of their choice, allowing them to refine the typologies of their design, construction system, and environmental strategy, to improve the movement of living beings, and the flexibility of buildings...

THE TEMPORALITIES OF "SHEARING LAYERS"

It is worth pointing out that the coloured plans representing the life spans of different materials are a way of thinking about long-term flexibility. They integrate the 'shearing layer concept' of Steward Brand described in his famous book *How Buildings Learn* [03], with those of adaptability. Our central reference in terms of conceptualisation and representation of flexibility are the plans in Jeremy Till and Tatian Schneider's book *Flexible Housing* [04] that convey the permanent structure in dark colour, and other elements in increasingly light colours depending on their ease of change.

DIVERSE INTANGIBLE QUALITIES

Applying this exercise raises the student awareness of the diversity of experiences that can be created from carefully designing the building to create a diverse range of intangible qualities, and as a result, develop a richer and broader range of habitats, a diversification of the mosaic, at a granular scale. Architecture is formed of a broad range of environments for both human experience and other-than-human. It is not a standardised private indoor sharply distinct from a uniform public outdoor.

Most of these qualities have a temporal quality and are best understood in conjunction with the narratives of the VISUAL SPECULATIVE FABULATIONS and TEMPORAL DRAWINGS scores.

Many architects' drawings have inspired us, such as the environmental plans of Philip Rahm [05], the watercolour plan sketches of Stephen Holl, 19th century plans with poche colours for cut areas expressing construction materials and thus their longevity and thermal mass, as well as hatched house plan studies of inhabitation through the day by Cedric Price.

The workshop allows for the free use of some of these qualities. They both choose two or three intangible spectra, and the colour and/or texture medium that forms the key: watercolour or other paint, pastels, pencils, but it is best to use something that is quick to use in order to freely test multiple typologies. Key is also an analysis of relevant typologies, usually the same as those used for the ontopolitical massing.

This tool helps students look at a plan, or section, to read formless qualities that are defined by the architecture but otherwise not visible. In my view, these are the real architectural qualities that matter; the sculptural quality of solid form is beneficial and important, but secondary to life and agency.

Another benefit of this method is to reveal the in-between spaces, thresholds, the thick boundaries and edges between ecosystems and buildings, and between conditions. We will discuss these liminal and interstitial spaces further in the ECOTONE ENVELOPE score.

POLYCENTRIC TYPOLOGIES

Many of the projects develop polycentric typologies; they are made of multiple units carefully placed to shape the landscape into a diversity of conditions, of external rooms. They can either be entirely separated, or more akin to finger like typologies. Brook Muller defines this as 'architecture-as-furnishings' where the "bounding entity" defining the relevant space is not the building envelope but the landscape. It communicates that the human inhabitant lives in the landscape, the "buildings-as-furnishings" are mediators, they add the comfort and other requirements to allow us to exist in this landscape [06].

THE CRITICAL DIMENSION OF INHABITED PLANS

Once the overall organisation has been settled, the final stage is a drawing of the plan of the building with all forms of inhabitation, inside and outside, human, vegetal and animal. In order to be able to draw these, the scale tends to be between 1/50 for small projects, to 1/100 (or 1/200) for larger. This requires many iterations, of course.

They were heavily influenced by a number of architects, many from the global south, often queer and/or feminist. The oldest examples are by Sri Lankan fellow gardener architect Geoffrey Bawa of plans combining houses and their garden [07] from the 1950s to 1990s, and the most recent are the vibrant plans of Wall House, in Auroville, by the Indian architect Anupama Kundoo [08]. A wave appeared in the early 2000s in Japan: Ryue Nishizawa's plans of Moriyama House mentioned above, Atelier Bow Wow's, as well as Junya Ishigami's. In all these examples, the landscape elements, internal inhabitation (furniture and floor finishes), and the building itself are all drawn with an equal level of detail.

The results are drawings within which you can easily imagine living and how humans would relate to other life forms. There is a clear sense of appropriate scale.

Drawing them takes time; they require making many decisions that are often overlooked in student projects, such as interior qualities and design, landscape, careful calibration and detailing of openings... Yet, these elements that are often considered as secondary to the more "permanent" and "masculine" aspects of architecture (structure and external form) are deeply political, as it is within these fields that a speculation on how we may live differently can be tested rigorously. INHABITED PLANS and the narratives of VISUAL SPECULATIVE FABULATIONS challenge a designer's tendency towards the political apathy of normative imagination towards the imagining potential regenerative living. Form that isn't tested by imaginaning scenarios of inhabitation is unlikely to be more than surface symbolic design that neither critically interrogates how we live now nor or we could in the future.

This is one of the earliest developed INHABITED PLANS in our studio, drawn in the first year by Daniel Berende.

Grow.Kill.Eat.Repeat- Aquaponics and the Architecture of Self-Sustaining Ecologies
Daniel Berende

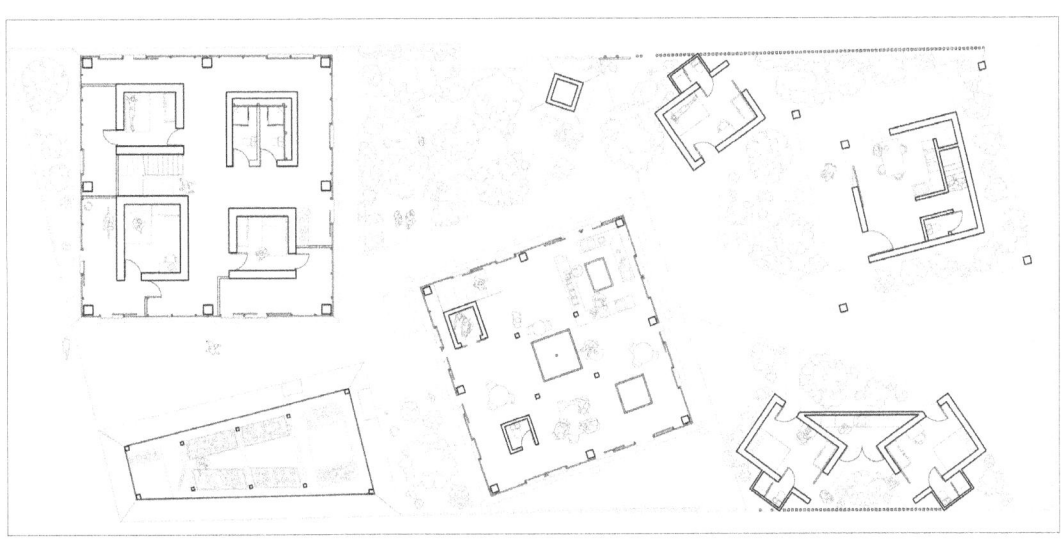

(below) Inhabited plans can lead to drawings where the landscape is more visible than the buildings. This is particularly the case here with the ground-floor plan of this environmental governance institution where most spaces are semi-external and act as a sheltered park also used in the warmer months for deliberations. The heated spaces are in a ring around the amphitheatre as well as a small rectangle that is the access level for the office building.

Department of Half-Earth Socialism
Rebecca Thompson

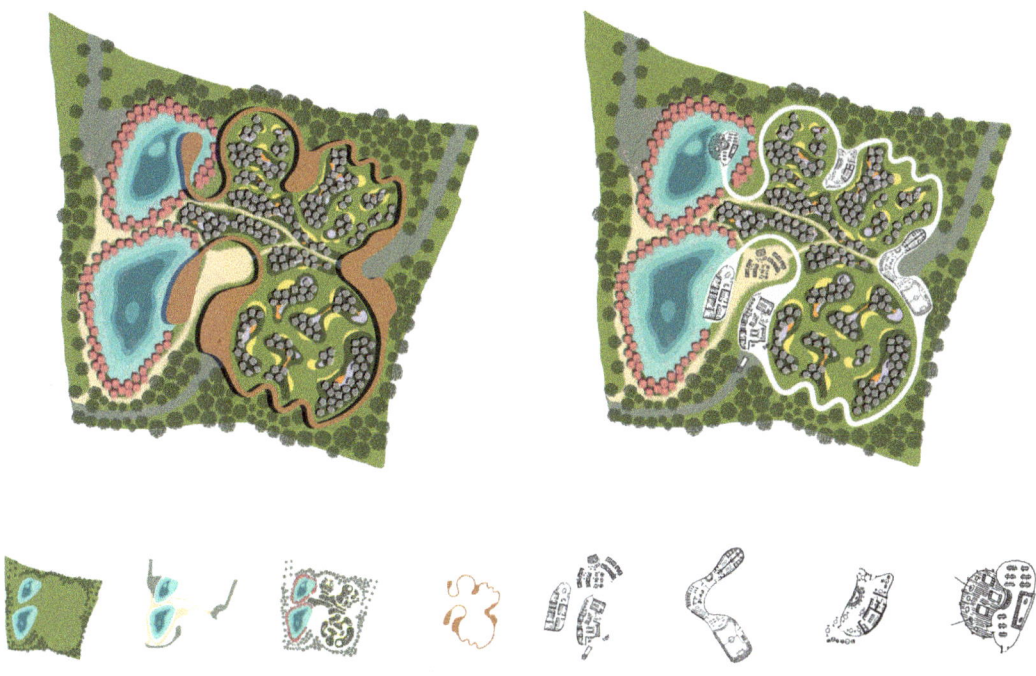

Endnotes

(01) Olivier Meystre, Pictures of the Floating Microcosm: New Representations of Japanese Architecture (Park Books, 2017)

(02) This is a further developed version of a lecture and score I originally created during the year I was teaching in the Live Project studio at the University of Westminster led by Maria Kramer.

(03) Brand Steward, How Buildings Learn: What happens after they are built (Phoenix Illustrated, Orion Books, 1997 revised paperback edition, first edition in 1994) p.13

(04) Tatian Schneider and Jeremy Till, Flexible Housing (Architectural Press, 2007)

(05) Philippe Rahm, Architectures Météorologique (Archibooks + Sautereau éditeur, 2009)

(06) Brook Muller, Ecology and the Architectural Imagination (Routledge, 2014) p.81

(07) Generously recommended by the London based architect and educator Hwei Fan Liang who has been a regular reviewer during our studio reviews. David Robson, Geoffrey Bawa: the complete Works (Thames and Hudson, 2004 reprint with revisions, from a 2002 first edition)

(08) Anupama Kundoo, Ground and first floor plans, Wall House, Auroville (MOMA collection, 2022) https://www.architectural-review.com/essays/revisit/revisit-wall-house-auroville-india (accessed on 03-08-2025)

(above) An earlier example, to the one facing, of a typology where buildings and landscape interweave to form a single organising framework based on a polycentric typology.

This type of massing strategy is often misunderstood by building architects that often perceive them as disconnected from context, whereas the design decisions establish a dialogue with the landscape context that the buildings also redefine. External and internal spaces are given equal value and attention.

Captain Charlie and the Cherry Factory
Changsoo Yoo

There are different types of typologies that establish positive porous relationships between internal and external spaces. Some shape buildings as grids of lines that define in between garden spaces that can be read as courtyards when small, or larger gardens.
Others have a feathered, hand like quality, with fingers connected to a central node. Others are constellations, like this project by Finola Simpson. She carefully placed multiple pavilion like grieving tower houses by precisely defining the in between spaces between them, and the connections created by paths, as well as ramps. The drawing of INHABITED PLANS representing multi-species inhabitation inside and out is central to developing such positive relationships.

Ground floor *(opposite)*
First floor *(above)*

Ritual Rewinding
Finola Simpson

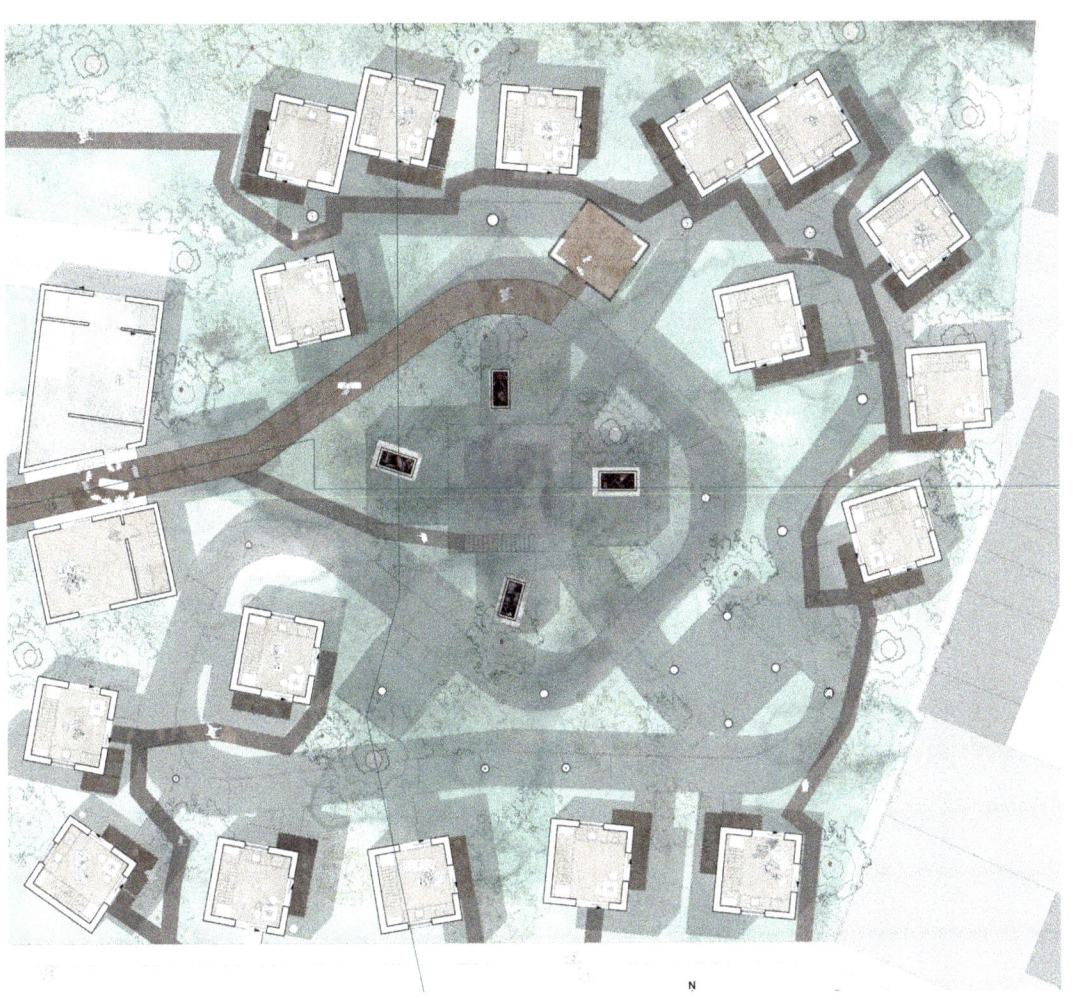

Benjamin Leathes developed this centre for nurturing diversity in Epping Forest, London, through a dialogue between models, visual narratives and plans. The design establishes a series of trellis like planes that create deep evanescent façades within and along which paths take the visitors to the forest and a tower. This tower is a launchpad for the daily ritual of the flock of monitoring drones that survey the various ecosystems and bring samples to the laboratory for testing. The design is lifted from the ground to limit the impact on existing habitats.

The Silvaesium
Benjamin Leathes

Overleaf spread:
Kacper Sehnke's project combines pavilion like elements with linear connecting wings and walkways.
These buildings shape multiple lines of movement and sight through the site, as well as define gardens with different conditions.
The range of qualities achieved can be seen in INTERLUDE 1

Ground floor plan
of *The Council for Ecosystem Restoration*
Kacper Sehnke

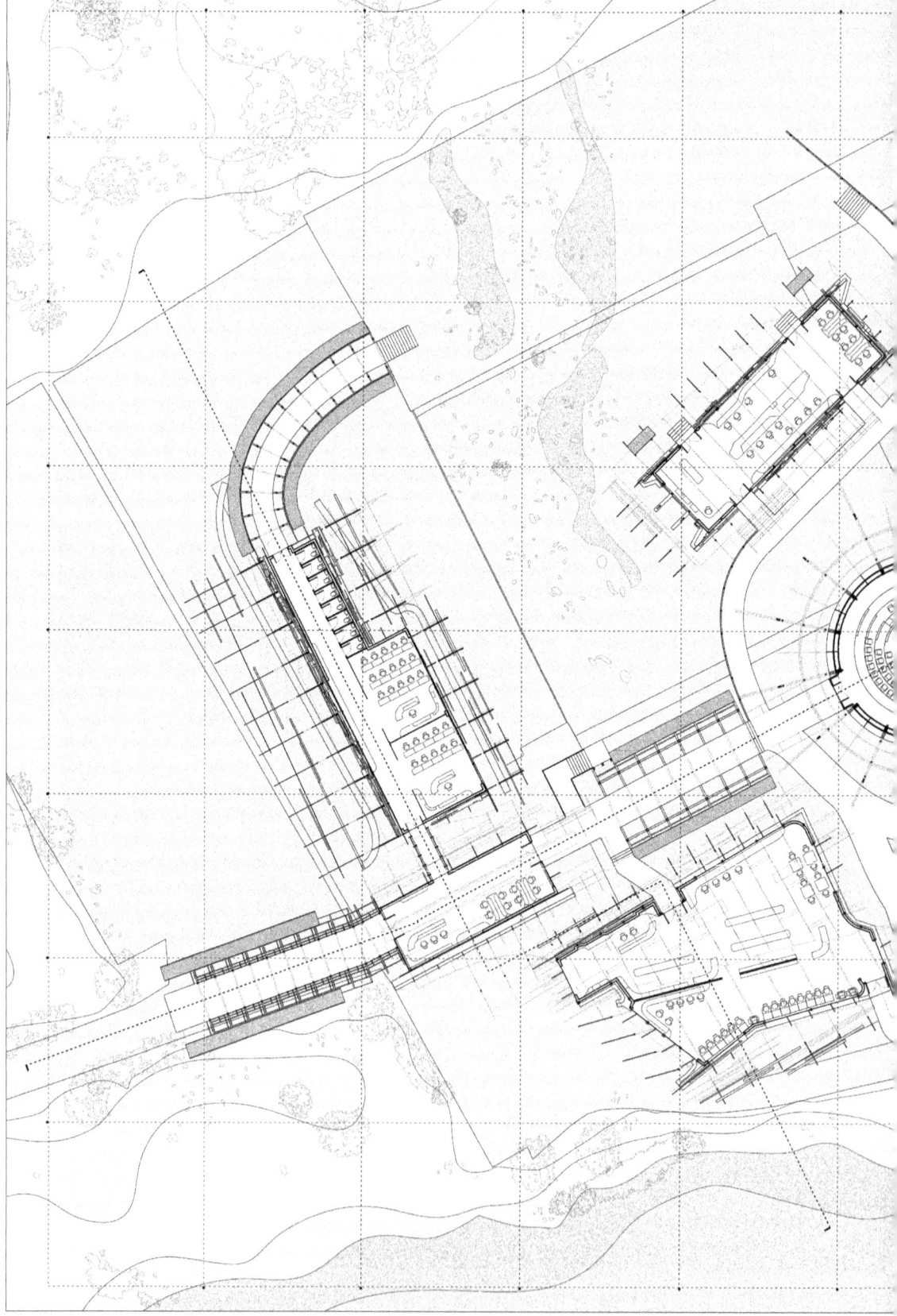

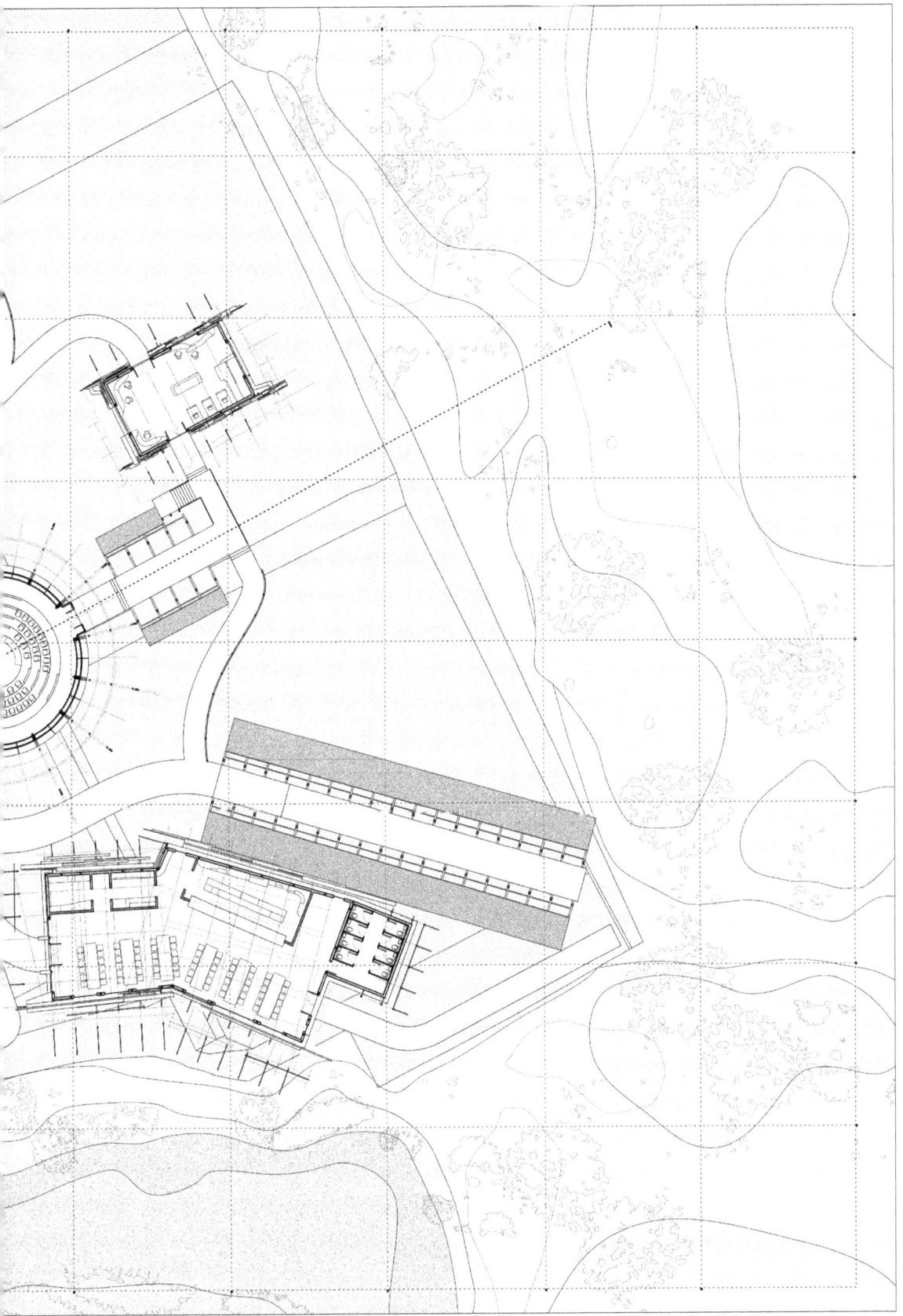

SCORE 6
TEMPORAL DRAWINGS

Eric Guibert

Socio-ecosystems are constantly changing following different rhythms at different temporal scales. Regenerative architectural design is thought through different temporalities (types of time).

There is our human experience, which is itself of varied scales: the live experience of the moment, the evolutions we experience through our life, which we engaged with in the Visual Speculative Fabulation narratives. There is the rhythmic time formed of the polyphony of living rhythms, daily, seasonal, life stages between creation and decay, that respond to each other. The rhythms of intangible qualities that were implicit in the coloured plan exercise of the previous score: inhabitation of other-than-humans, humans, climate, matter... There are also the longer temporalities of history, biological evolution through natural selection, and geology.

Thinking ecologically requires us to think and design some of these temporalities: both the rhythms and the evolutions. Accepting nonetheless that the complex systems we design with are non-linear, they are unpredictable, and as a result, designing with time is not in order to predict exactly what will happen, but to create architectures that work with the existing rhythms, and negotiate the clashes by bringing rhythms in resonance. For synergy to exist, there is a need for exchanges of matter, energy, or data, as well as synchronicity. These exchanges need to happen at the right time. For example, a large flexible workshop open for use by both the users of the institution it is in and the locals cannot deal with large numbers of both simultaneously.

Timelines have been present every year since the beginning of the studio, but not always with the same prominence, and some students engage with time more than others. They are described here in the order in which they tend to be useful.

As we have seen for the PANARCHIC MAPPING score in terms of space, it seems to be the understanding of multiple time-scales in relation that brings the most insight. This is a form of nested temporalities, as ecosystems and communities are spatially nested, their rhythms are temporally nested.

HISTORICAL TIMELINES

Timelines can be used politically or theoretically. We usually mention the circular timelines developed by the lobbyist nurse Florence Nightingale, which record war deaths during 1854 and 1855, to visually demonstrate that more soldiers died from preventable causes than wounds resulting from combat. She used this timeline to convince those in power, such as Queen Victoria, and achieve the radical change in the support given to soldiers that reduced these unnecessary deaths.

Many students have developed their understanding of their critical ambition for their project through a timeline that conveys the history of the key concept or theme and the reasons leading to this development. Kacper Sehnke, for example, traced the history of ecological thinking and institutions in response to biodiversity collapse since the 20th century to describe the role of its Council for Ecological Restoration. Ben Grafham has looked at the history of ecological demonstrations in Whitehall and globally.

THE LONG NOW

These historical timelines have so far been mostly looking from the past to the present, but we are beginning to see them as being able to speculate on long-term thinking. Many have shown how our contemporary short-term thinking is one of the key causes of our contemporary ecological challenges. Such writers encourage us to think in longer timeframes – centuries and millennia – through concepts such as Steward Brand's concept of 'The Long Now' [1].

Encouraging the development of historical timelines that look to the past as much as the future is what we intend to pursue in the coming years.

RHYTHMANALYSIS

In 1074, the French sociologist Henri Lefebvre wrote The Production of Space, a seminal book that is the foundation of many thinkers of architecture as a social practice, such as 'spatial agency' [2]. In this he describes that space is more than a physical quality, it is socially produced, and therefore political, in three ways: as everyday spatial practices ('perceived space'), as professional representations of space ('conceived space'), and as direct, subjective, and meaningful experience of space ('lived space').

Less known is the temporal evolution of his theory, which he began developing towards the end of his career as 'rhythmanalysis' and which begins to integrate biological, climatic and ecological rhythms within an otherwise human-centred research. He acknowledges that space cannot be detached from time and to understand how space is produced, it is necessary to analyse the rhythms of the three kinds of spaces: perceived, conceived, and lived [3].

In this series of essays, Lefebvre is highly critical of mechanical time, that of the clock, as a form of temporal prison. For him, time is not constant and predictable; it is rhythmic; events repeat roughly within certain timeframes, but there is no exact repetition, rhythms interact with each other not in a static way, but polyphonically, coming together each time in a specific way. These rhythms resonate.

The human rhythms coordinate with climatic and biological ones. The ecological rhythms are studied by the scientific field of phenology, the science of ecological and biological rhythms.

FROM PHENOLOGICAL TO RHYTHMANALYSIS

In the studio, we usually begin temporal design with these phenological rhythms when the first ecological processes sections are made in the first semester.

Later on, in the second semester, we encourage a rhythmanalysis of each project to help develop an understanding of the architecture through different temporal scales:

- The inhabitation of the building by different species and human communities through the day, week or year
- The evolution of the built and grown architecture as it grows, or is transformed and extended, through the years and decades
- The longer ecological evolution of the site and context, through decades and centuries.

The aim is to develop in the student a sense that their buildings, and the life they host, evolve through different scales of time: the day, seasons, and decades.

The process usually asks them, through the workshop, to draw three types that are relevant to their project and that have different timeframes, such as:

- *daily*
- *weekly*
- *seasonal / year*
- *epochal / decades*
- *centuries and beyond*

Inspired by Robert Smithson's *Hotel Palenke* project, Nicholas Wood developed a school for art and design docussing on entropy and negentropy, decay and growth. The design of the buildings, like the Hotel Palence, grows and shrinks, using a modular system on a grid of pad foundations.
This drawing was central to conceiving this process of evolution.

The Institute of Entropic and Negentropic Art and Design
Nicholas Wood

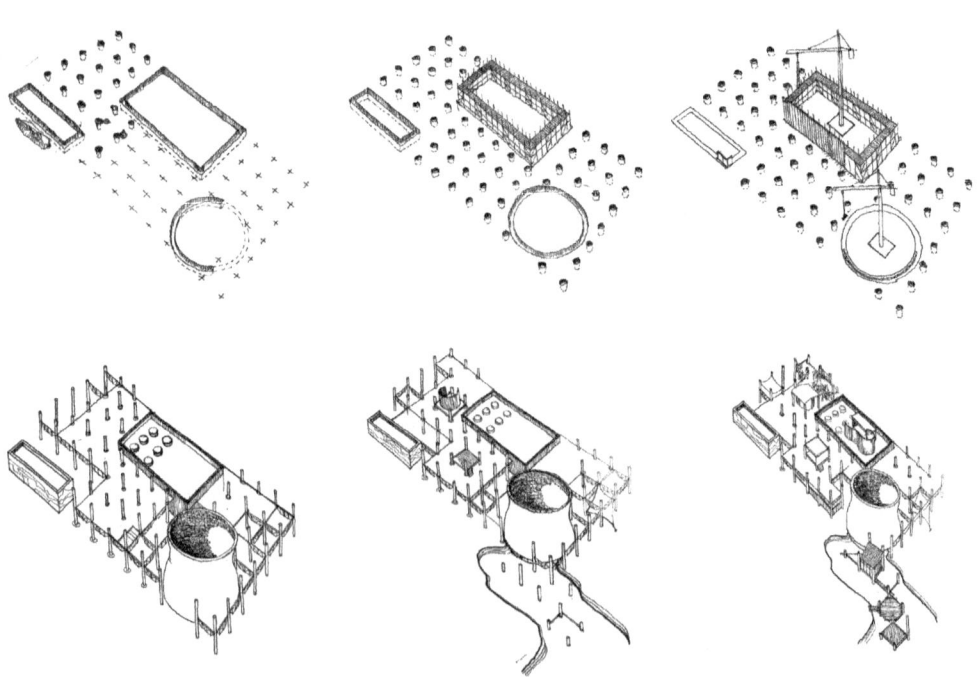

ECOSCORES

A central reference of the studio is the work of the American Landscape Architect Lawrence Halprin, in particular his work on Sea Ranch, an ecological residential community on the Sonoma County coast of California, which he designed with close attention to climatic rhythms, historical and ecological evolutions. Multiple timelines were created, but the most tantalising is his Sea Ranch Ecoscore [4], a diagram that represents the multiple temporalities of the site as spirals with different temporal scales converging to the same point. Human culture, Sea Ranch Site Culture, Animals, Vegetation, Sea-Climate, Geology. The diagram is a temporal portrait of this place.

INHABITATION TIMELINES

A usual example is timelines that represent the intensity of inhabitation rhythms over a day or a year. These were inspired by a seminal drawing by the Dutch architectural practice OMA drawn for their unbuilt Yokohama Masterplan [5]. Their central aim was not tangible. They designed the project to achieve for the site the highest possible urban intensity throughout the day. They designed towards maintaining the existing intense use in the

This drawing investigated the yearly rhythms of occupation for this foraging centre. As the production has high seasonal peaks, the project is conceived as a combination of permanent buildings and tent like structures erected during the months to house the increased workforce.

Esther Calinawan drew this in parallel to a timeline of foraged plant productivity. The architectural design responds to the ecological rhythms of the area.

This is one of the very first TEMPORAL DRAWINGS produced in our studio in its first year in 2019.

morning of a fish market, and added other functions taking place later, such as concerts, shops... To design this, they drew multiple timelines to show how the variations in intensity of the varied uses added to a constant high level of use.

ARCHITECTURAL EVOLUTION

When describing the evolution of architectures over years and decades, students tend to use a series of more standard architectural drawings such as elevations, plans, or isometrics...

Change is usually represented in two ways: either a succession of the same view redrawn for each stage, or the evolution is drawn within the same drawing, for example, from left to right.

Different evolving aspects are represented:

- *The evolution of the building, which was inspired by similar drawings by the German architecture research practice Baubotanik, who investigate buildings in part constructed of living trees.*
- *The landscape and modes of care applied – discussed in the ecological section score*
- *The building extensions and/or contractions, often done through multiple plans or isometric drawings*

GRAPHIC LANGUAGE

Most of the timelines produced tend to be digitally made with precise lines, but some are done expressively, with hand-drawn or made techniques that are more expressive, that communicate more subjectively. These are reminiscent of and inspired by the multiple examples of alternative musical scores in Theresa Sauer's book Notations 21 [6].

Controlling the language of these timelines is a balance between a sufficient degree of accuracy so that they are useful, yet they are approximate, as the rhythms do not repeat with identical beats.

The temporal tolerance, the appropriate level of accuracy required for nurturing desired synchronicity without constraining life's development.

As with PANARCHIC MAPPING, TEMPORAL DRAWINGS are useful in two ways. In terms of defining the position and program brief, through developing a spatial or temporal understanding of the relevant contexts and communities. It is with this understanding of context, of the relevant sociological and ecological systems they belong to, and their place in their evolution today, that the designers gain clarity and confidence in their aims and, as a result, in their design decisions. If mapping describes these contexts and communities at present and locates them, temporal drawings describe how they became what they are today and how they might change, in part in response to the project.

Both scores are also useful in designing the buildings themselves. With PANARCHIC MAPPING, it is primarily massing; with TEMPORAL DRAWINGS, it is their flexibility and evolution, the way ecosystems and biological beings, including humans, inhabit and transform the buildings over time.

Endnotes

(1) Stewart Brand, The Clock of the Long Now: Time and Responsibility (Basic Books, 1999)

(2) Nishwat Awan, Tatjana Schneider, Jeremy Till, Spatial Agency: Other Ways of doing Architecture (Routledge, 2011)

(3) Henri Lefebvre, Rhythmanalysis: Space, Time and Everyday Life (Bloomsbury, 2013)

(4) Lawrence Halprin, RSVP Cycles: Processes in the Human Environments (George Brazilier, 1969) p.122.

(5) OMA, 'Yokohama Masterplan Assemblage of Programs' timeline (Urban Design Forum, Yokohama, Japan, 1992), in Rem Koolhaas & Bruce Mau, Small, Medium, Large, Extra-Large: Office for Metropolitan Architecture (010 Publishers, 1995, 1st edition) An example can be seen here: https://www.oma.com/projects/yokohama-masterplan [accessed on 03-08-2025]

(6) Theresa Sauer, Notations 21 (Mark Batty Publisher, 2009)

Through the representation of the
process of construction and decay of the buildings, the project is conceived as
growing from and returning to the peri-urban soil.

of *The Council for Ecosystem Restoration*
Kacper Sehnke

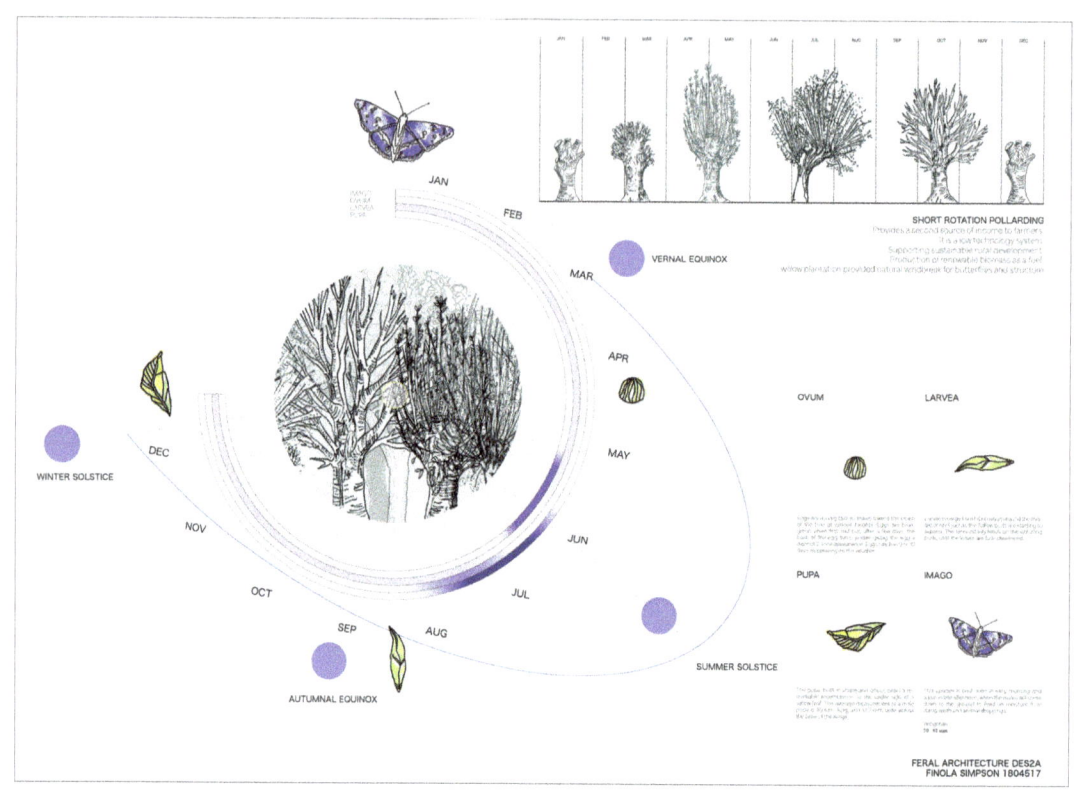

Two phenological timelines synchronising other-than-human species and/or systems, technical, and human rhythms. This temporal understanding is essential to the architecture of the project and equal to spatial dimensions, typology, and form.

(above) The interraction between the decade long rhythm of willow pollarding and the annual cycle of the purple emperor catterpillar that feeds on its foliage.

The Purple Emperor
Finola Simpson

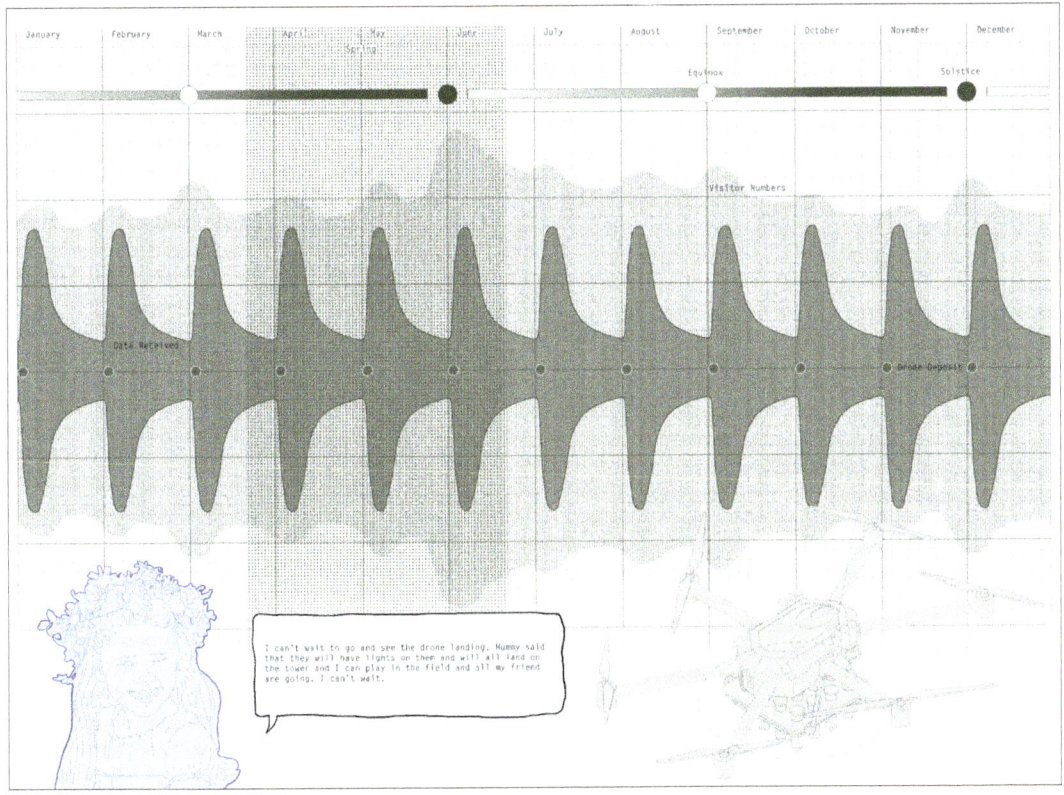

(above) Synchronised rhythms of human visitors over the week and years, and ecological drone monitoring in the

The Silvaesium
Benjamin Leathes

Three examples of architectural evolution temporal drawings. These show how the building evolves over seasons or years as vegetation and ecosystems change.

(above) seasonal changes of the trellis facade covered with climbers through the seasons (elevations and sections).

The Silvaesium
Benjamin Leathes

(opposite, top) Facade timeline of the evolution of a bioreceptive concrete facade, showing years 0, 10, and 20
Earthly Hills

Epping Forest Centre of Ecologies and Climate Change
Farah Mazloum

(opposite, bottom) Progression of the growth of a living tree facade over decades. This was inspired by the Atelier Baubotanik system.
The evolution is drawn on the same elevation from left to right.

Progression of living facade growth of
Department of Plants
Eunseo Lee

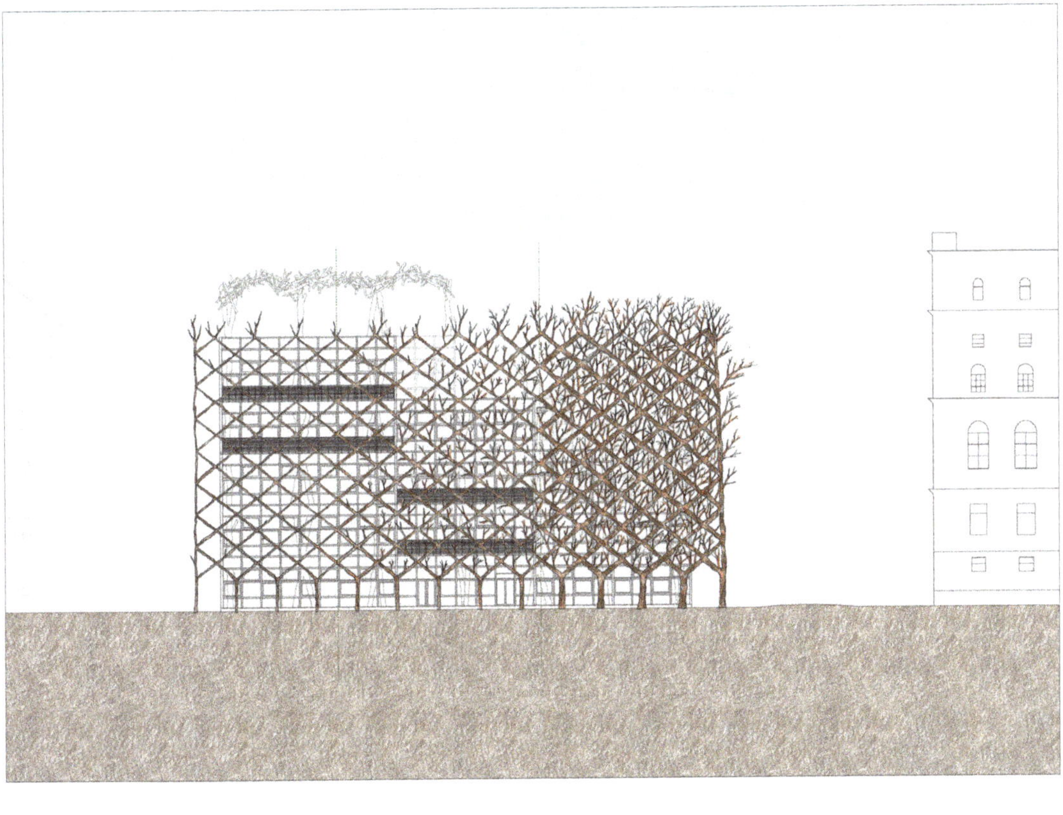

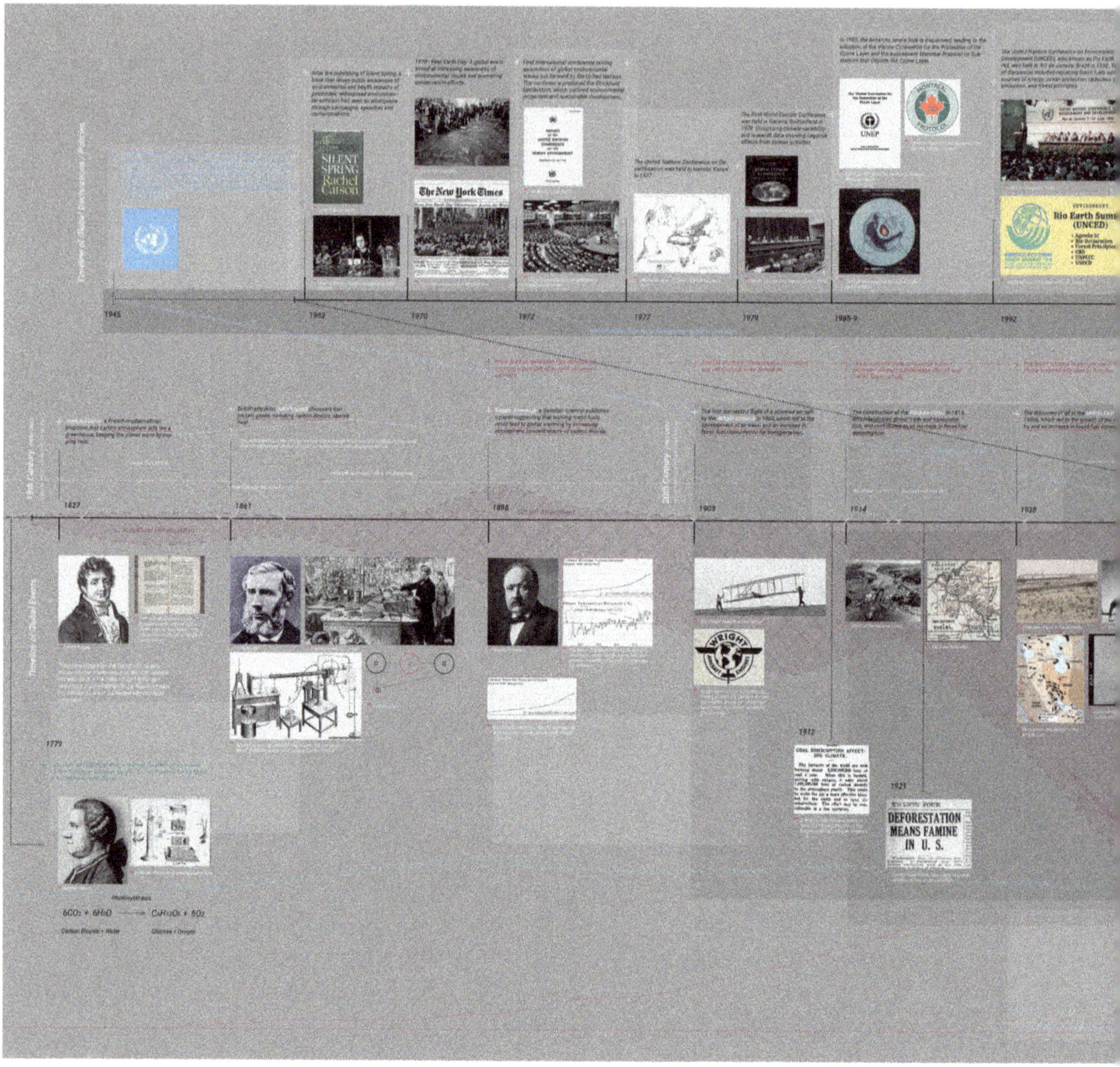

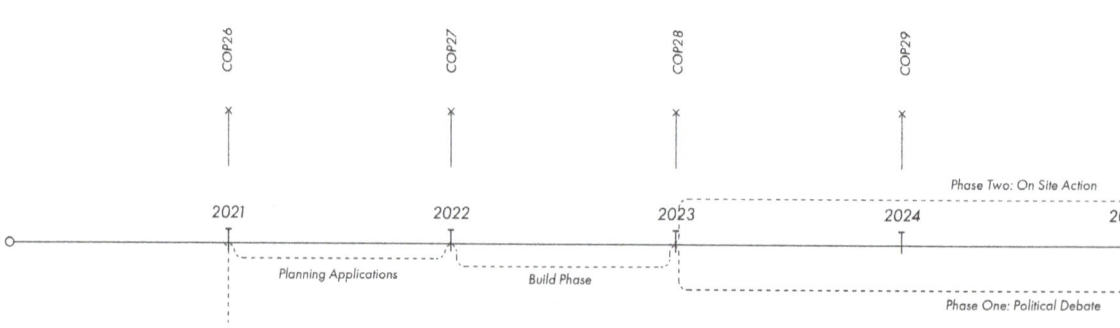

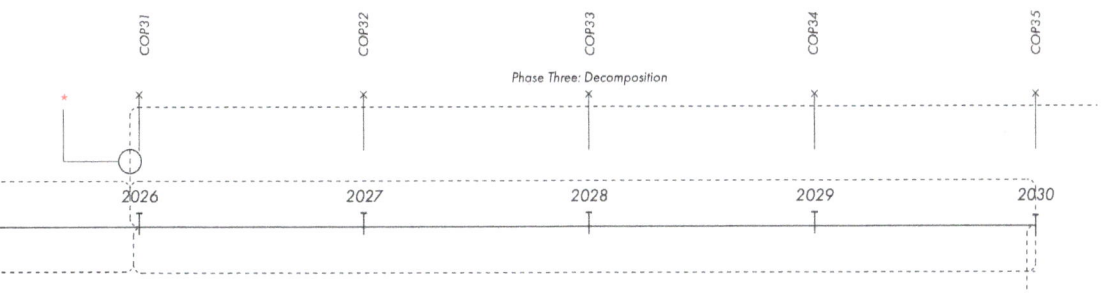

Kacper Sehnke's use of timelines was central to the definition of the critical ambition of the project and the role of the building understood in time.

The geopolitical timeline of global events related to resource exploitation, environmental activism, and regenerative policy development allowed the visualisation of the environmental movement in relation to global politics. (above)

This led to a temporal strategy for a temporary building that will be built in phases, and predicting its obsolescence, would be in part dismantled and in part left to decay to form a new ecosystem. (below)

The Council for Ecosystem Restoration
Kacper Sehnke

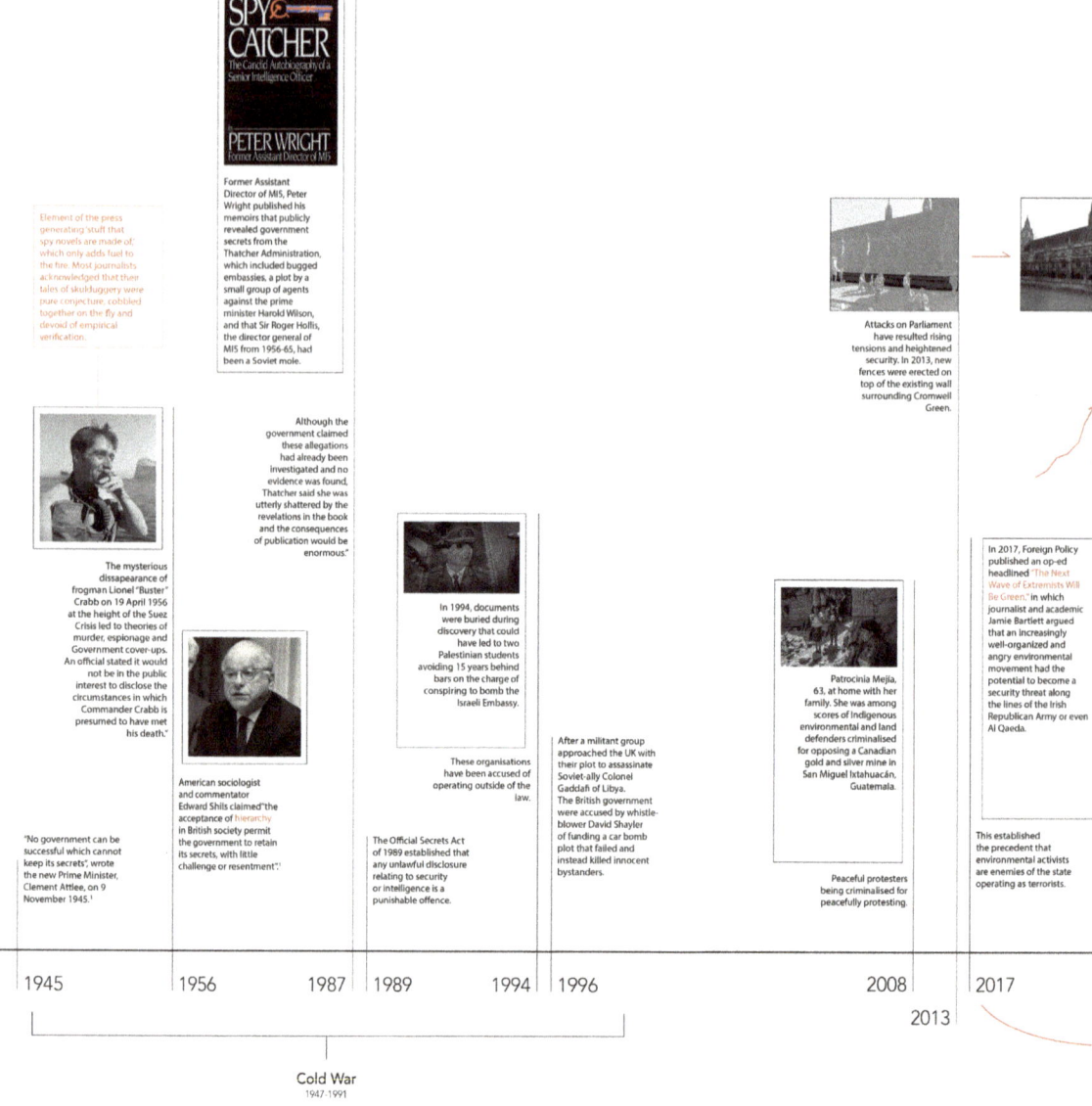

"We will not allow them to criminalise the noble tradition of non-violent civil disobedience."

- Sarah Lunnon, a spokesperson for Extinction Rebellion

are criminalised

2020 was the deadliest year on record ate activists,

- The War on Climate Activism Is Reaching Dangerous New Height

"
So called eco-crusaders turned criminals,.. a shameful attack on our way of life, our economy and the livelihoods of the hard-working majority. The very criminals who disrupt our free society must be stopped. And together we must all stand firm against the guerilla tactics of Extinction Rebellion."

"
What we are seeing looks very much like political decisions to charge people and to take them to court for very minor offences, and that is extraordinary. I can not think of a precedent (in the UK) where that has happened before on anything like this scale."

- Graeme Hayes, Sociologist from Aston University, who is part of a team of researchers following the XR court cases.

Manuel Esteban Paez Terán, a brave environmentalist known as Tortuguita, was shot and killed by the police on January 18th 2023.

He was peacefully trying to defend from being razed and turned into an enormous $90m "urban warfare" style police academy.

Climate defenders gather at Parliament to resist UK Government's 'deadly' new oil and gas bill.

If passed, the bill will allow fossil fuel corporations to bid for new North Sea licences every year. The bill comes after the Government and North Sea Transition Authorities already announced their plan to give out more than 100 production licences for new oil and gas in the North Sea.

2020 was worst year on record for UK government secrecy

- 'Access Denied' OpenDemocracy Report, 2021

Just 41% of Freedom of Information (FOI) requests sent to government departments and agencies were granted in full in 2020, down from 43% the previous year.

- Priti Patel, UK Home Secretary

Following on from the idea of violent environmental groups that emerged in 2017, the largest climate activist group in the UK are labelled as criminals by the government.

"
Over time, we may see citizen frustration and activism evolve into violence against both government and fossil fuel companies— perhaps a new and more violent wave of eco-terrorism as Earth becomes even less inhabitable.

- Maha Aziz, Political risk specialist and professor at New York University speaking at COP 27, 2022.

The concept of a eco-terrorism is widely acknowledged as a possibility.

Handcuffed activists from the group Just Stop Oil lie on the road as they are arrested after they blocked a road in London in October 2022.

More than 1,000 people who took part in environmental direct action organised by Extinction Rebellion were taken to court in one of the biggest crackdowns on protest in British legal history.

This tragedy is an obscene escalation in the decades long war the United States has been waging on climate activists.

Between 2012 and 2022, at least 1,733 people around the world were killed while trying to protect their land.

Although the UK aims to be net-zero by 2050, they're still funding new fossil fuel projects in the North Sea. They have stated that all oil and gas extracted would be sold on the international market.

| 2020 | 2020 | 2020 | 2022 | 2023 | 2023 | 2024 | Now |

2022

Benjamin Grafham similarly develops a historical understanding of the relationship between environmental activism and politics through a timeline of the last century (above), revealing the increased reduction in activist freedom of expression in the recent years (below). This led to conceiving the role of the Ministry of the Future, inspired by the eponymous speculative fiction by Kim Stanley Robinson, as a part public facing, part underground pressure and lobbying group.

The unseen labyrinth:
"there's something in the walls"
Benjamin Grafham

SCORE 7
BOOK AS DRAWING

Eric Guibert

In the introduction, we mentioned that the development of regenerative design happened in parallel to that of ecology and of new grounded vitalist philosophies. I discovered these various new materialist, ecofeminist, cosmopolitical and ontopolitical thinkers during my PhD and the early years of the studio, and they have been gradually integrated within our pedagogy through the BOOK AS DRAWING score, starting as a yearly monoculture, soon after moving towards increased theoretical diversification.

In our first year, a single theoretical reference was given: Retrosuburbia [1]. This was the latest book from one of the fathers of permaculture, David Holmgren, that applies these ecological principles to regenerate existing suburbia. Although there was diversity in the projects, the students designs ended up being overly similar. The students had a broad range of briefs that followed their own interests, and there was a degree of formal diversity arising from different architectural and artistic precedents, but the positions, architectural and graphic languages, were fairly aligned.

They had created an ecological poster early in semester 2 that aimed to convey their position and critical ambition. This could be an advert, a political poster, or any large drawing that also includes a limited amount of text. As I do not have records of these, I can only base this reflection on my memory. The posters engaged with ecological positions, but tended to be overly earnest and idealistic, possibly in echo of Holmgren's book. This felt unproductive for multiple reasons. The lack of diversity in outputs came from a uniformity of position, a position that was little critiqued by the group.

We sensed that for a diversity of approaches to appear, which was our central aim, the studio needed more than a specific student brief and one shared theoretical reading. In order for each student to develop and convey a personal critical ambition, they needed a project-specific philosophical or theoretical frame.

Our first attempt at diversification, in the following second year, was to introduce a range of "living system design" practices. At the start of semester 1, each student chose from a list of artists, landscape architects, makers, and composers who work with the unpredictability of living systems. These became their client. There was an immediate improvement as each practice is a specific aesthetic vision. We also realised that the students were also gaining from the different worldviews and political or ethical positions embodied in these practices.

This highlighted to us that for a diversity of speculative approaches to arise around ecological themes, designers need a speficic philosophy, a way of understanding the world, an ontology, which forms the substrate for a specific brief. As we were teaching in the second year of the Bachelor's in Architecture at the time, I had originally

BOOK AS DRAWING from
Ian L McHarg, *Design with Nature*
Changsoo Yoo

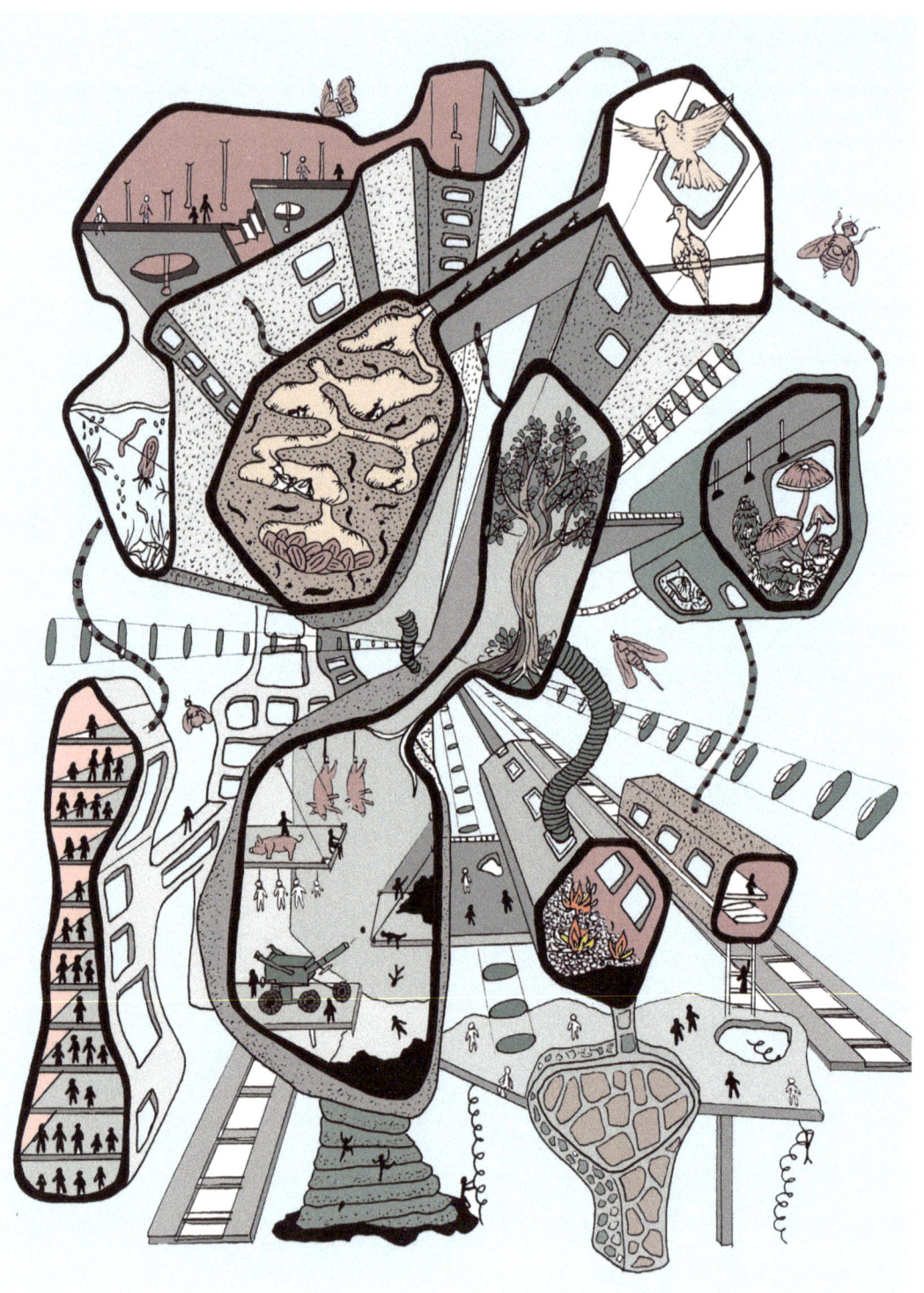

BOOK AS DRAWING from
Donna Harraway, *Staying with the trouble*
Betina Menescal

avoided a diversity of complex theories. My concern was that most students would not be able to productively use theoretical ecological writing. I was wrong.

NURTURING A DIVERSITY OF ONTOLOGIES IN A COMMUNITY OF PRACTICE

In the second year of the studio, this theoretical diversification was integrated fully into the pedagogy with the BOOK AS DRAWING score. Each student draws an architectural drawing that communicates key concepts of their chosen book in the form of an ambitious architectural drawing.

Each book is specific to each student – a rule is that there no two students read the same book in one year – and chosen at the end of the first semester through a discussion with them based on the interests that have appeared in the previous months. They are taken from a broad range of ecologically connected references from ecology, speculative fiction, ecofeminism, new materialism, and ecological forms of politics… The list can be found at the end of this chapter.

There is a double aim. First, the intrinsic motivation of each student is nurtured to enhance their existing knowledge, interests, and specificities. Simultaneously, it is a community of practice exercise, as each student researches a different book and explains it to the entire studio during a short presentation of their drawing; the studio as a whole develops a common bibliography and a shared lexicon of concepts, which they are encouraged to discuss with each other.

This presentation also reveals how varied the field is, how different philosophies (ontologies), types of knowledge (epistemologies), engage with a similar range of questions, helping students realise that they have to position themselves, that there isn't a single universal truth that the educators impart to the students. This allows them to situate themselves in relation to both the studio community and the broader theoretical context. Many find this positioning difficult, but it is a key dimension of university education, beneficial to society as it leads to more critical citizens, and architects…

The bibliography shifts and expands each year; it tends to have some books around the yearly theme, such as systemic design thinking, fermentation, and wilding. Other, more philosophical books, reappear from year to year, such as Jane Bennett's *Vibrant Matter* and Donna Haraway's *Staying with the Trouble*, books about vegetal and other forms of cognition.

BOOK AS DRAWING from
Ursula Leguin, The Dispossessed
George Darlington

This is one of the scores that is most mentioned by students as key to their development during the end-of-year debrief and feedback session. This does not mean that they fully understand these books; I didn't understand theoretical text as comprehensively as I do now at their age either. More than a set of concepts that can be rigorously applied, the books open their minds to new ways of seeing, leading to creative inspiration, as well as a passion for a position that may align with, or occasionally react against, their reading. However imperfectly understood, these texts create the cognitive disturbance that is needed to imagine alternative ways of being. This is a transformative experience that hopefully nurtures the paradigmatic change needed in our society towards systemic understandings.

ARCHITECTURAL DRAWINGS

In order to connect theoretical and philosophical dimensions to architecture, the students are asked to draw an architectural drawing of their choice as an ambitious and beautiful A2, or larger, drawing, combining hand-drawn and digital means. There are many sections, perspectives, plans, masterplans, iso and axonometric drawings… These are expected to be entirely speculative and should avoid being the first drawings of the project per se.

Originally, the exercise was less abstract; it aimed towards a poster, manifesto, advert, or similar arrangement of primarily an image and some limited amount of text or logotype. This shifted towards architectural drawings to act as a transition between concept and building design, and allow for a more intuitive creativity. Whereas the first year posters communicated a position through a brief, the latter are more abstract investigations of the potential architectures embodying a concept.

The process recommended each year is to begin sketching while reading, small drawings of ideas as they come. Once the book is finished, these pieces are merged together into the ambitious drawing, first sketched at a smaller scale and then redrawn to its full large size (A2 minimum).

These are often impressive both because they tend to be beautiful and, more importantly, as they convey multiple layers that will be seeds for the main project development.

The drawing is a catalyst for a process of translation

BOOK AS DRAWING from
Colleen Myles, *Fermented Landscapes*
Giorgia Bresciani

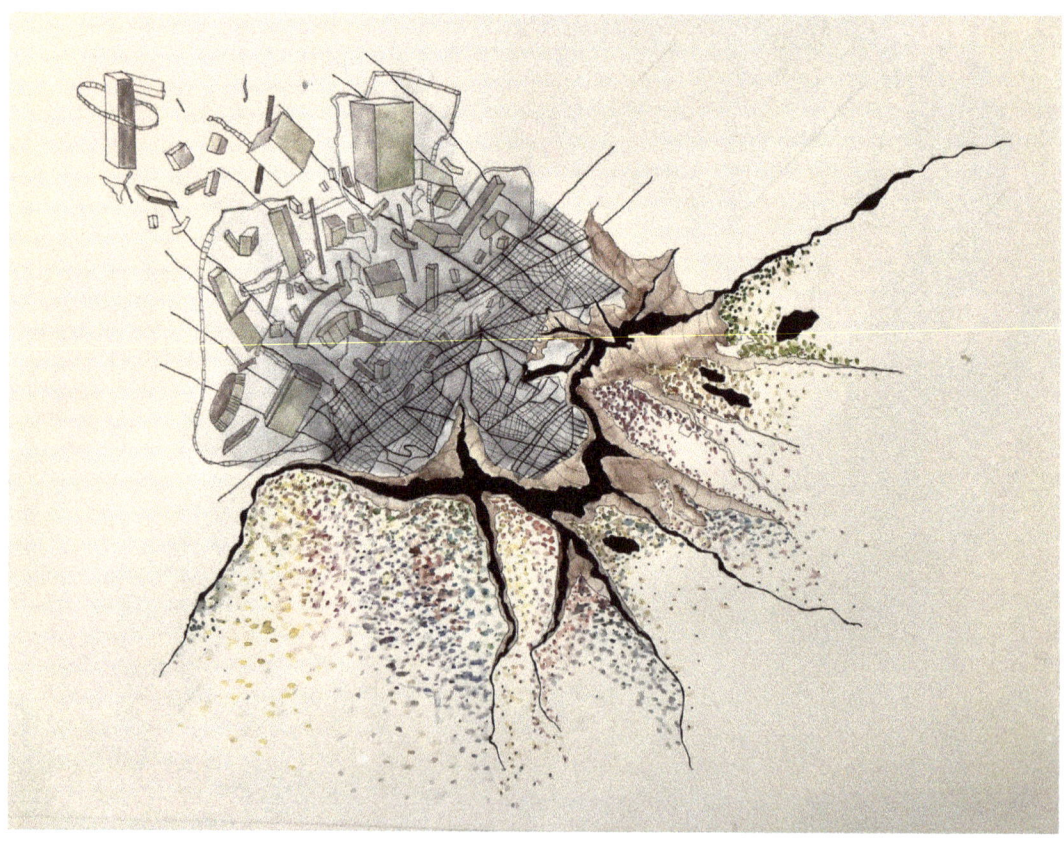

of a philosophy into multiple architectural dimensions, inspiring spatial qualities, typologies, formal language, inhabitations… It is also the clarification of a relevant and personal drawing style and graphic language, using specific media, process, viewpoints, and colours that convey these concepts.

The least successful drawings tend to be those that attempt to symbolise a single concept in a building form.

TIMING

The choice of book is usually made at the end of the first semester so that it can be read through the Christmas break. During our yearly debriefs, some students have asked if this could be introduced earlier. We originally avoided this as it is difficult to guide students towards an 'intrinsic motivation' earlier, as we need to see enough work developing.

In response, in recent years, we included shared shorter theoretical texts early in semester 1, such as Freya Mathews' definitions of nature [2] and Ecology and Architectural Imagination. We have also begun introducing books to students as soon as we sense what their position or direction might be. This can be very early, usually with the more committed students, or sometimes takes the entire first semester.

TWO BOOKS AND ONE DRAWING

We intend to experiment this coming year, by reversing the order and starting the year with a student-specific theoretical reading, and later analysing a specific ecosystem in response. We envisage either randomly giving texts in the very first week or making students choose on the first day from a list. With this earlier theoretical introduction, we are considering that each student will read or watch a narrative during the Christmas period. In reaction to the theoretical book, they will choose their own speculative fiction novel or film that will further disturb the creative process.

The reason for not doing so until now is that we sense that the ecological concepts we introduce in the first semester are already complex, and they already lead to diversity for the first project. Waiting a little longer for them to have found some degree of ease, clarity, and confidence and then disturbing this again with another layer of complexity seemed the best approach. In other words, the students first deal with ecosystems and ecology, including human communities and the processes involved, before the more philosophical or political dimensions are introduced. But this limits the extent of influence of these philosophies, and we need to test an earlier introduction.

REVEALING AN ECOSYSTEM OF EVOLVING ONTOLOGIES

The key benefit of this exercise is that it is a catalyst for each student's ontological shift towards regenerative thinking, without being a dogma. There is a diversity of ecological ontologies present in the range of books, and transformed by each student. Our role is to curate a landscape of positions.

The drawing exercise allows students to think through the medium of architecture, and/or its representation, a way of thinking that they have some experience with. The resulting drawing makes the position and this shift visible, and thus allows a discussion.

Over the years, we have seen patterns of reactions emerging that convey different ecological understandings. These ontologies often reflect those found in society. The most striking is the categories of porous versus hermetic architectures.

About a quarter to a third of the students originally draw architectures that protect ecosystems internally, forming impermeable envelopes, bubbles, against polluted and human-made environments. These echo the 1960s and 1970s early ecological architectures that recreate entire ecosystems within more or less sealed environments. A striking example is the Biosphere 2 experiment in the 90s [3]. The spatial configuration that this expresses is anthropocentric; nature is a passive patient protected by humans from humans in glass bubbles. It is also dualistic. This is often in opposition to the texts they have been reading that tend to describe humans as being part of nature, although not all.

Others imagine a more porous relationship with polycentric typologies. Fragmented and feathered buildings that mingle with the landscape. These focus on meshworks and connectedness.

This leads to productive discussions on the question of the relation between humans and nature, architectural porosity, and how, instead of imagining a thin and impermeable envelope, and buildings as single blocks, an architecture forming fingers, or separate blocks, with thick ecotone envelopes provides a higher diversity of ecosystems, and negotiates flows of elements and beings.

As I am writing this, I realise that we rarely recommend anthropocentric philosophies, positivist ontology. We do occasionally, but this is rare. This might be a response to the students' interests, but we should be careful to equally nurture students who desire to remain within such positions.

DIALECTICAL DRAWINGS

A fascinating dimension of many drawings is their ambiguous nature, some temporal, some about the relationship between biology and technology. Many students combine references from the past with futuristic visions, which expresses a combination of ancient and modern knowledge. The architectures are often in ruins, part building, part ecosystem. In many projects, ecosystems, species and technical building elements integrate in bionic or cyborg-like systems, which we will discuss further in the ECOTONE ENVELOPE score. These are tropes often found in speculative fiction narratives. They communicate the dialectical nature of ecological thinking, in reaction to the usual dualistic separations of humans from nature, past from future, technology from biology/ecology, they create architectures that combine seemingly opposed conditions.

SHIFT TO COLLAGE THINKING?

There has recently been an increasing tendency for some students not to draw the architectural elements; many students collage images found (usually online), or created by AI. This is a strange phenomenon as the images chosen bring with them worldviews that are not those of the students, leading at times to miscommunications of the book concepts. There is a different form of creativity in these works; the pieces brought together are usually banal and generic, and the creativity comes from the juxtaposition. This may be due to a cohort that lacks confidence in their drawing skills, but it could also be a cognitive shift created by the dominance of the digital in contemporary life. The intuitive skills of many students seem to have reduced due to the lack of practice of a hand-drawing skill.

So far, this has been a minority, but we are concerned with this shift, as we are with the use of AI to produce most of the writing of essays. The thinking takes place in the use of a medium, in the dialogue that the designer has with her/himself through it. This needs evolution, time. Technology can and should be used – for example, drawing with a stylus on a tablet probably is similar in terms of design development to marking on a sheet of paper – but a designer should be careful to replace iterative thinking with technical shortcuts to produce fast artefacts that may be attractive but have limited creativity. Maybe a more refined prompting of large language models may form an iterative process, but we believe this will be more associated with hand drawing than a replacement.

Endnotes

(1) David Holmgren, Retrosuburbia: The Downshifter's Guide to a Resilient Future (Melliodora Publishing, 2018)

(2) Freya Mathews, Letting the World do the doing (Ecological Humanities, Issue 33, December 2004). http://australianhumanitiesreview.org/2004/08/01/letting-the-world-do-the-doing/ [accessed on 23-09-2021]

(3) A fascinating account of this project is the feature film: Matt Wolf, Spaceship Earth (2020)

BOOK AS DRAWING from
Stefano Mancuso, *The Revolutionary Genius of Plants*
Eunseo Lee

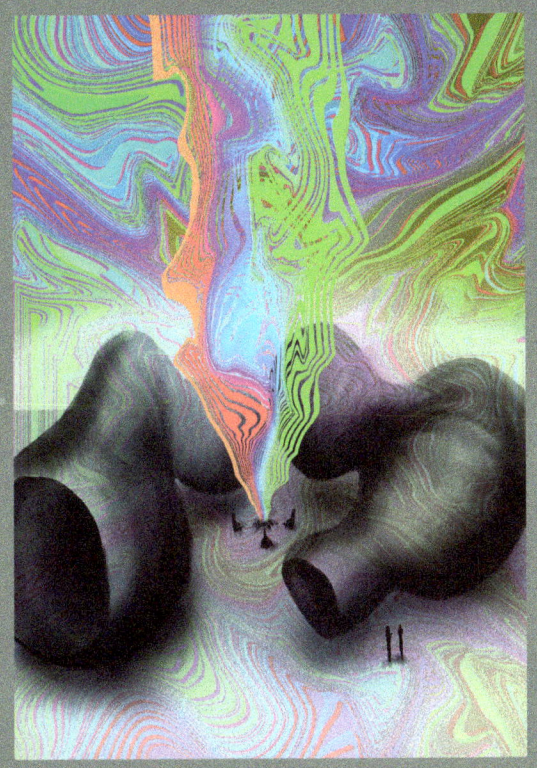

BOOK AS DRAWINGS in 2021-2022 by:

Finola Simpson (opposite, top)
Sue Burke, *Semiosis*

Darya Prokopets (opposite, middle)
Ian L. McHargh, *Design with Nature*

Isabella Tostevin (opposite, bottom)
Natania Meeker & Antónia Szabari,
Radical Botany: plants and speculative fiction

Benjamin Leathes (above, left)
Merlin Sheldrake, *Entangled Life*

Harry Mellor (above, right)
Isabella Tree, *Wilding*

Julia Lassota (below, left)
Anna Tsing, *The Mushroom at the end of the World*

BOOK AS DRAWINGS in 2022-2023 by:

Benjamin Leathes *(top, left)*
Anna Tsing, *Arts of Living on a Damaged Planet*
Farah Mazloum *(top, right)*
Janine Benyus, *Biomimicry*
Kacper Shenke *(bottom)*
Drew Pendergrass & Troy Vettese, *Half-Earth Socialism*
Saleh Sesha *(opposite, top)*
Benedict Mcdonald, *Cornerstones*
Florentine Rockenbauer *(opposite, bottom)*
Jane Bennett, *Vibrant Matter*

BOOK AS DRAWINGS in 2023-2024 by:

Benjamin Grafham *(top, left)*
Kim Stanley Robinson,
The Ministry of the Future

Danielle Elefante *(top, right)*
Jane Bennett, *Vibrant Matter*

Melody Akanji *(bottom, left)*
Graham Harvey,
Animism: Respecting the Living World

Diego Gallardo *(bottom, right)*
James Rebanks, *The Shepherd's Life*

Merla Elakkad *(opposite, top)*
Murray Bookchin,
The Ecology of Freedom

Eunseo Lee *(opposite, bottom, left)*
Stefano Mancuso,
The Revolutionary Genius of Plants

Shah-Ree Tasaddiq *(opposite, bottom, right)* Christina Cogdell, *Toward a Living Architecture?*

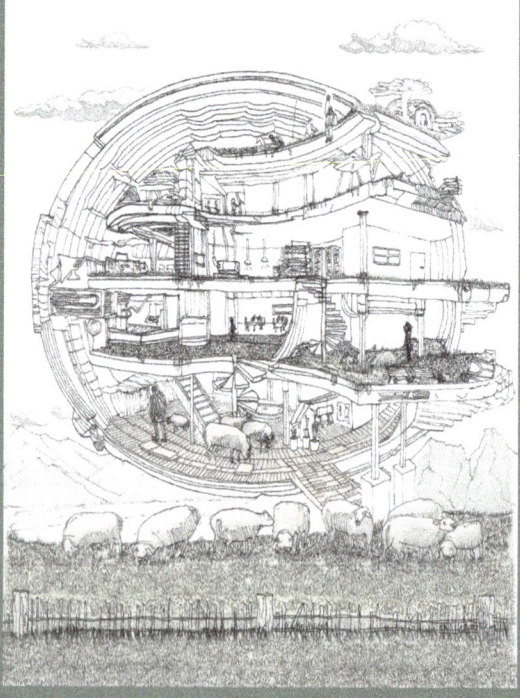

BIBLIOGRAPHY OF THEORETICAL AND SCIENCE FICTION REFERENCES

Books that were read in:	2018 2019	2019 2020	2020 2021	2021 2022	2022 2023	2023 2024
New materialist and vitalist philosophies						
Jane Bennett – Vibrant Matter		■	■		■	■
Donna Haraway – Staying with the Trouble		■	■		■	
Donna Haraway – The Companion Species Manifesto			■			
Anna Tsing – The Mushroom at the end of the World		■		■		
Anna Tsing – Arts of Living on a Damaged Planet: Ghosts and Monsters of the Anthropocene					■	
Freya Mathews – Letting the World do the Doing			■			
Traditional Ecological Knowledge / Ancestral						
Kat Anderson – Tending the Wild					■	
Robin Wall Kimmerer – Braiding Sweetgrass		■				
Graham Harvey – Animism: Respecting the Living World						■
Fermentation						
Sandor Katz – Fermentation as Metaphor			■			
Colleen, C., Myles – Fermented Landscapes			■			
Formless architecture (climatic, weathering)						
Jonathan Hill – Weather Architecture			■			
Dean Hawkes – The Environmental Imagination			■			
Mohsen Mostafavi & David Leatherbarrow – On weathering			■			
Philippe Rahm – Constructed Atmospheres			■			
Other philosophies						
Georges Perec – Species of Spaces and Other Pieces		■				
Drew Pendergrass and Troy Vettese – Half Earth Socialism					■	■
Murray Bookchin – The Ecology of Freedom						■
Systemic thinking						
Fritjof Capra & Pier Luigi Luisi – Systems View of Life		■				
Donella Meadows – Thinking in Systems		■				
Jeremy Lent and Fritjof Capra – The Patterning Instinct: A Cultural History of Humanity's Search for Meaning		■				
Regenerative design and architectural agency						
Jeremy Till – Spatial Agency: Other Ways of doing Architecture		■				
Herman Hertzberger – Lessons for Students in Architecture		■				
Janine Benyus – Biomimicry: Innovation Inspired by Nature		■				
Peter Harper, Godfrey Boyle – Radical Technology		■				
Brook Muller – Ecology and the Architectural Imagination				■	■	■
Janine Benyus – Biomimicry: Innovation Inspired by Nature					■	
Stewart Brand – How Buildings Learn					■	
Stewart Brand – The Clock Of The Long Now: Time and Responsibility						■
Roman Krznaric – The Good Ancestor					■	
Sarah Ichioka, Michael Pawlyn – Flourish: Design Paradigms for Our Planetary Emergency					■	■
Toward an Urban Ecology: SCAPE / Landscape Architecture – Kate Orff					■	
Christina Cogdell – Toward a Living Architecture? Complexism and Biology in Generative Design						■
Julia Watson – Lo-TEK: Design by Radical Indigenism						■

Books that were read in:	2018/2019	2019/2020	2020/2021	2021/2022	2022/2023	2023/2024
Science fiction and other Novels						
Richard Powers – The Overstory		✓	✓			
Ursula Leguin – The Dispossessed			✓			
Ursula Leguin – The Word for World is Forest				✓		
Karl Shroeder – Stealing Worlds			✓			
Sue Burke – Semiosis			✓			
Kim Stanley Robinson – The Ministry of the Future				✓		
Horticulture / permaculture						
David Holmgren – Retrofitting Suburbia	✓					
Dan Palmer – Making Permaculture Stronger		✓				
Carolyn Steel – Sitopia			✓			
Nigel Dunnett and Andy Clayden – Rain Gardens: Managing Water Sustainably in the Garden and Designed Landscape				✓		
Process based Art						
Robert Smithson – Entropy and the New Monuments		✓				
Gary Peters – Philosophy of Improvisation		✓				
Amelia Barikin – Parallel Presents: The Art of Pierre Huygues		✓				
Okakura Kakuzō – The Book of Tea		✓				
Charles Jencks and Nathan Silver – Adhocism		✓				
Lucia Pietroiusti & Filipa Ramos – The shape of the circle in the mind of the fish				✓		
Natania Meeker and Antónia Szabari – Radical Botany: plants and speculative fiction					✓	
Ecology or biology						
Eduardo Kohn – How forest think		✓				
Merlin Sheldrake – Entangled Life			✓			
William Bryant Logan – Dirt: The Ecstatic Skin of the Earth			✓			
Isabella Tree: Wilding				✓	✓	
George Monbiot: Feral				✓		
Jepson, P. and Blythe, C. (2020) Rewilding: the radical new science of ecological recovery				✓		
Edward O Wilson: Half Earth				✓		
Ian L. McHargh: Design with Nature				✓		
Stefano Mancuso – The Revolutionary Genius of Plants: A new Understanding of Plant Intelligence and Behaviour				✓	✓	✓
Peter Wohlleben – The Hidden Life of Trees				✓	✓	
Alan Weisman – The World Without Us				✓		
Benedict Macdonald – Cornerstones: Wild Forces That Can Change Our World					✓	
Paul Jepson – Rewilding					✓	
James Ribanks – The Shepherd's Life: A Tale of the Lake District						✓
Cognition						
James Bridle – Ways of Being: Animals, Plants, Machines: The Search for a Planetary Intelligence					✓	
Jakob von Uexküll – A Foray Into the Worlds of Animals and Humans: With a Theory of Meaning					✓	
Katherine Hayles – Unthought: The Power of the Cognitive Nonconscious						✓

SCORE 8
COLLECTIVE MASTERPLANS

Eric Guibert

Studio review of the COLLECTIVE MASTERPLAN for Southwater with Keb Garavito and Jeremy Rye in 2022

Whereas the earlier scores have been used every year, some years more than others, the score COLLECTIVE MASTERPLAN for nature recovery has been used every two years on average. This is a masterplan developed across the studio that is composed of a mosaic of all students' projects and shared communal spaces such as linear parks, squares, roads... The masterplan defines all the students' sites.

We used this in the first year in semester 2 to regenerate an entire residential suburban block. It was used again in our third year in semester 1, in part as a way of dealing with the isolation created by the COVID lockdowns. In this case, it was a simple row of buildings along a quay on the Lea Valley in London. And then the following year, to create a masterplan on the edge of a rural village.

THE SYNERGETIC BENEFITS OF THE PROCESS CREATING A SHARED VISION

The aims of this score are multiple. Firstly, it is an opportunity to lead the students to think of the impact of their collective work at a broader scale, which defines one of the contexts, as in PANARCHIC MAPPING, but in this case, a studio-designed one. It introduces the concept of the nature recovery framework as the studio develops a shared masterplan that provides for habitats, ecosystem services, and wildlife connectivity. It is often easier to integrate nature-based solutions at the masterplan scale. It also engages with surrounding human communities, of course, and their economies.

Secondly, students learn to create synergies, a process that is always an imperfect yet necessary dialogue between different beings and communities. As the neighbours of each scheme are other students' projects, the students have to engage in negotiations to form relationships and symbiosis between their projects, leading to solutions that are beneficial to all. This is true both during the charette itself and, once the masterplan strategy is drawn, during the design development of each project.

On the actual day of the charrette, the students usually arrive with a limited understanding of the point of the exercise and its benefit for their individual projects, which is the main focus of their thinking at this stage. There is usually a body language of arms closed, with students remaining on the edge of the room. As we facilitate the process, they begin to understand the value of synergy – the system is more than the addition of all individual parts. If each gives a little, for example, a little land for a shared garden, each project gains more than they give up. Very quickly, they begin to engage and contribute a flow of ideas.

Thirdly, studio cohesion is enhanced as it intensifies the exchanges and connections between students. They have to build relationships, demonstrate care towards others, and explain their projects. We had started this before the COVID period, but brought it back during one of the lockdown periods so that students would be meeting virtually more regularly without tutors and, hopefully, feel less isolated as a result.

The fourth benefit is about learning to deal with change and accept the limited control inherent to architecture. The attention to others is also towards the dynamic nature of the evolution of the built and grown environment. All students' projects co-evolve in negotiation with each other, in what Karen Barad calls "intra-action" [1], or Donna Haraway calls "sympoesis" [2], the students' learning, and their project design, become with others. In this sense, the masterplan is an analogue to practising as an architect outside of academia. The timeframe is shorter, what takes years in the real world is condensed in a few months, but there is a similarity of adapting to a world that you cannot control, accepting this, and understanding that as much as some challenges may arise, opportunities also do, as long as you position yourself with openness and generosity, but also clear in your aims.

The fifth is enhanced cross-fertilisation of ideas and skills between students through this process. This is difficult to measure, but it was clearly taking place, especially within some of the sub-groups.

The last benefit is that it leads to a diverse large-scale model, a mosaic of ecosystems and visions, that represents both the collective ambitions as well as all the individual works, something particularly useful to communicate the regenerative work of the studio in the summer show.

PROCESS

The process is essentially in three phases. The first requires developing an understanding of scale and typologies, and the development of some units. It is either an early design of their individual schemes or an in-depth study of precedents in small groups of 3 or so students. These are all modelled at the same scale so that they can be used in stage 2.

Stage 2 is the charrette, per se. It begins with a discussion on the collective ambitions of the group and the key parameters in the context. This leads to a diagram of a strategy that includes the nature recovery framework, road infrastructure, and key habitats. The models are then used, usually placed on a plan at the same scale, on which the infrastructure is drawn, and the projects are moved around to find the best agencies between them, and with

the surrounding context. By the end of the day, there is a sketched framework and each student has a location; this is drawn accurately afterwards for clarity.

The third phase is the design development of all projects in relation to their neighbours, which can include some tweaks to the framework. During this stage, at multiple points, including the reviews, the models are brought together to check the relationships and the overall masterplan.

LIMITATIONS

We do not use this every year, as there are limitations with this score. It is most striking with the most ambitious students whose creativity can be constrained by sites limited by the other projects, especially if their visions are complex and engage more directly with the broader context. These students might benefit from larger sites that are more connected to the surroundings. Since the studio has shifted to the 3rd year of the BA, we have not used this model to give freedom to students with their main project.

The less confident benefit from more restriction surrounding their site. Compared to the constrained sites in an existing context often chosen by or for such students, there is more flexibility, the boundaries can be negotiated, and the relationships of neighbouring schemes to each other.

COLLECTIVE AND INDIVIDUAL REGENERATION

Of all the scores, with the BOOK & DRAWING score and the ecological layers exercise, it is the most regenerative for the majority of students, as individuals who are part of a group. The masterplan framework has an effect similar to the entire pedagogical scaffolding of events and scores of the year, it gives the students a shared frame, further opportunities for collective learning, within which each student and project can emerge – paradoxically – more freely as there is more support, as long as the framework of the masterplan is open enough to different designs.

Compared to PANARCHIC MAPPING & TEMPORAL DRAWINGS that also help students understanding of the multiple contexts of tehir projects at different scales, with COLLECTIVE MASTERPLAN, a larger part of this thinking is collective and projective.

We have discussed earlier how we nurture our design studio to act as a community within which to learn and experience regenerative practice in action, as it is impossible to do so fully within a BA. This score is probably the moment when it is closest to what would be experienced outside of academia. Students have exposure to the tensions between individual freedom and the group, personal and collective learning, and effectiveness that can often arise from limits, if these limits are not overly throttling creativity.

Masterplanning workshop organised by Eric Guibert and Michael Spooner in January 2022 *(left & opposite)*

COLLECTIVE MASTERPLAN MODELS
at the design studio exhibition in the
OPEN Summer shows in June 2019 *(left)*, and 2022 *(opposite)*,
School of Architecture and Cities
University of Westminster

The masterplan drawing above is for the 2022 project and was drawn by Finola Simpson.

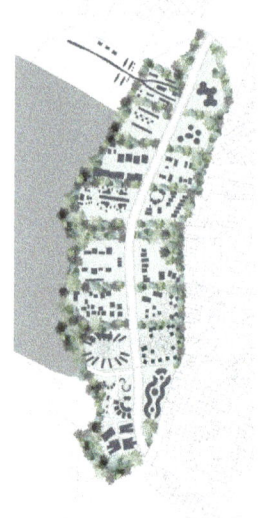

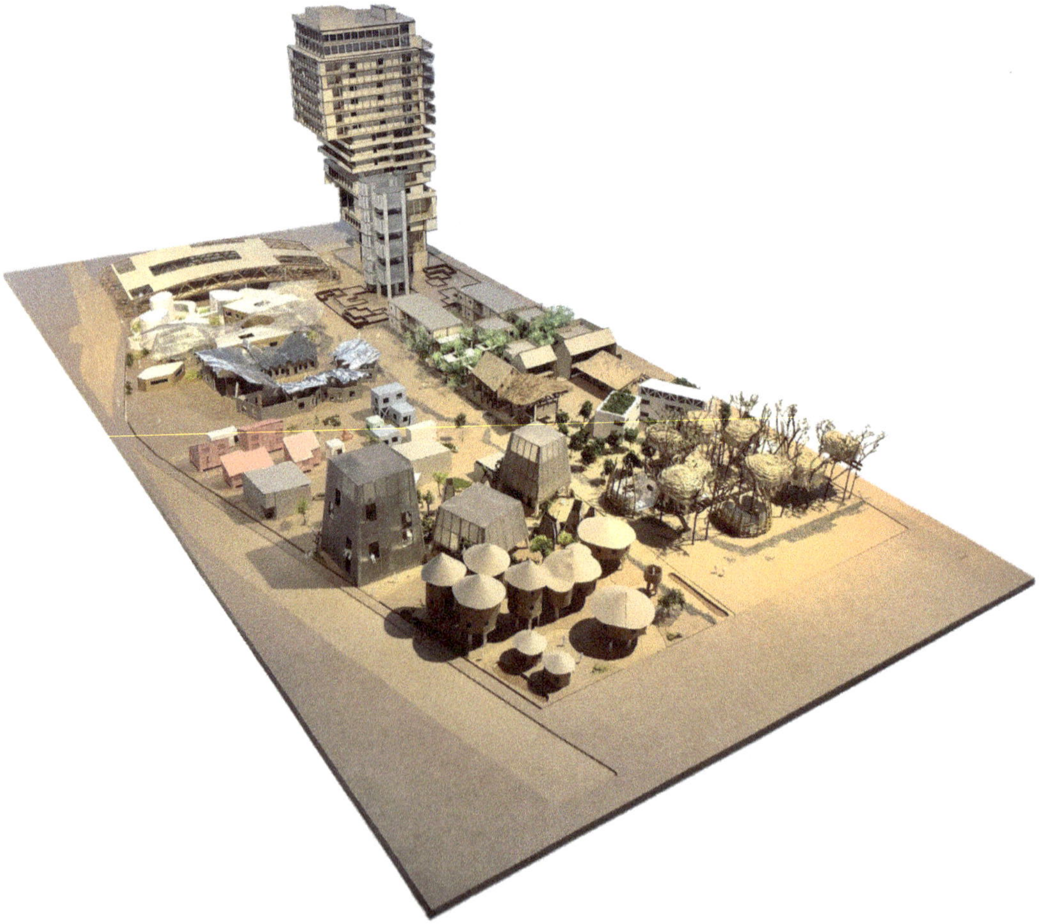

Endnotes

(1) Karen Barad, Meeting the Universe Halfway: Quantum Physics and the Entanglement of Matter and Meaning (Duke University Press, 2007)

(2) Donna J. Haraway, Staying with the Trouble: Making Kin in the Chthulucene (Duke University Press, 2016)

SCORE 9
ECOTONE BUILDING ENVELOPES

Eric Guibert

Whereas INHABITED PLANS aim to create mosaics of habitats and nature connectivity within the site, and MASTERPLAN CHARETTE through the larger site shared by the studio, ECOTONE BUILDING ENVELOPES create habitats in the very materiality of the buildings, within the walls and roofs. They are also conceived as a thick skin that controls and shapes the flows of light, air, heat and water.

The buildings using such façades resemble mountains with walls similar to inhabitable cliffs, or artificial trees, as built habitat scaffoldings [1]. Far from the students' usual understanding of walls as thin lines separating inside and outside, these envelopes are conceived as deep, porous and inhabitable boundaries.

An ecotone is a transition between two ecosystems, for example, the woodland edge between a meadow and a wood. Such edge conditions are usually particularly biodiverse as they combine species and activities that exist in one ecosystem, or the other, or both, or only in this threshold. Similarly, the porosity and cellular quality of ecotone facades provide shelter for plants, animals, humans, and other species.

This depth is used for hosting multiple living beings and negotiating their relationships: animals and plants, soil, humans, and climate. They are, of course, also part of more traditional architectural discourse in concepts such as thresholds between outdoors and indoors, or liminal space, but focusing on multispecies inhabitation instead of human-only. Ecotone facades are spaces where 'species meet' [2].

To limit energy consumption and operational carbon emission, we push projects more towards systems that do not need mechanised watering and fertilising, only the climate cares for them on a regular basis, apart from yearly maintenance. There are, nonetheless, exceptions to this when it seems desirable, most obviously in high-density urban areas.

This shift in understanding of the façade or roof from a thin impermeable line to a deep porous space is so substantial for students that we usually approach this exercise in two stages, starting with a redrawing of built precedents, and later designing this in their project. Some years, the two stages are merged into one week in the second semester.

A LEXICON OF ECOTONE ENVELOPES

First, at the very beginning of the year, each student chooses a different case study from a list. They research this and redraw either a section or an isometric, showing construction (scales around 1/50), and other-than-human and human inhabitation. This process was inspired by the research of the Japanese *Window Research Institute* led by the Japanese architect Yoshiharu Tsukamoto. Especially the combination of drawings, photographs and text in their book *Windowscape: Window Behaviourology* [3]. The students present these drawings and other images found to each other during short presentations to develop a shared lexicon of types that each student can freely choose from and adapt later. These precedents tend to be deep examples (the list can be found below).

Virtual board of the ECOTONE ENVELOPE LEXICON score, detail of the lexicon

ECOTONE ENVELOPE MODELS

The second stage, in the second semester, is a model exercise at 1/50 (or 1/20) scale of a section of the building envelope showing the same technical and living layers, which is then drawn at 1/50 or 1/20.

The exercise succeeds at bringing to the fore inhabited building envelopes. The danger with the more passive students is a tendency to only apply the precedent they drew to the building uncritically, achieving detailed designs that are not appropriate to their project. There is always a danger with scores that less committed students use them as a tick box exercise.

The benefit of the separation of the stages between the first and second semester is that it helps with the integration of this concept in their technical study. The semester 1 technical assignment in our BA is for a research project into the technical elements that are typically later integrated in the second semester main project.

LIVING TECTONICS LEADING TO FRAMEWORK TYPOLOGIES

A number of types have appeared over the years. These are all 'bioreceptive' in a way; they all are able to host biological life, but the first category is of a larger scale, more like a scaffolding covered with plants, than the second, which is more like 'architectural bark' [4]. These different scales of ecosystems lead to different architectural expressions.

These ecotone materialities and inhabitations are associated with the organising framework of the buildings and landscapes. Sometimes as frameworks shared with the landscape, sometimes as topographies, sometimes as objects, they each time define a relationship between the other-than-human and human, between buildings and landscape.

One of the earliest
ECOTONE FACADE MODEL
Nina Busz

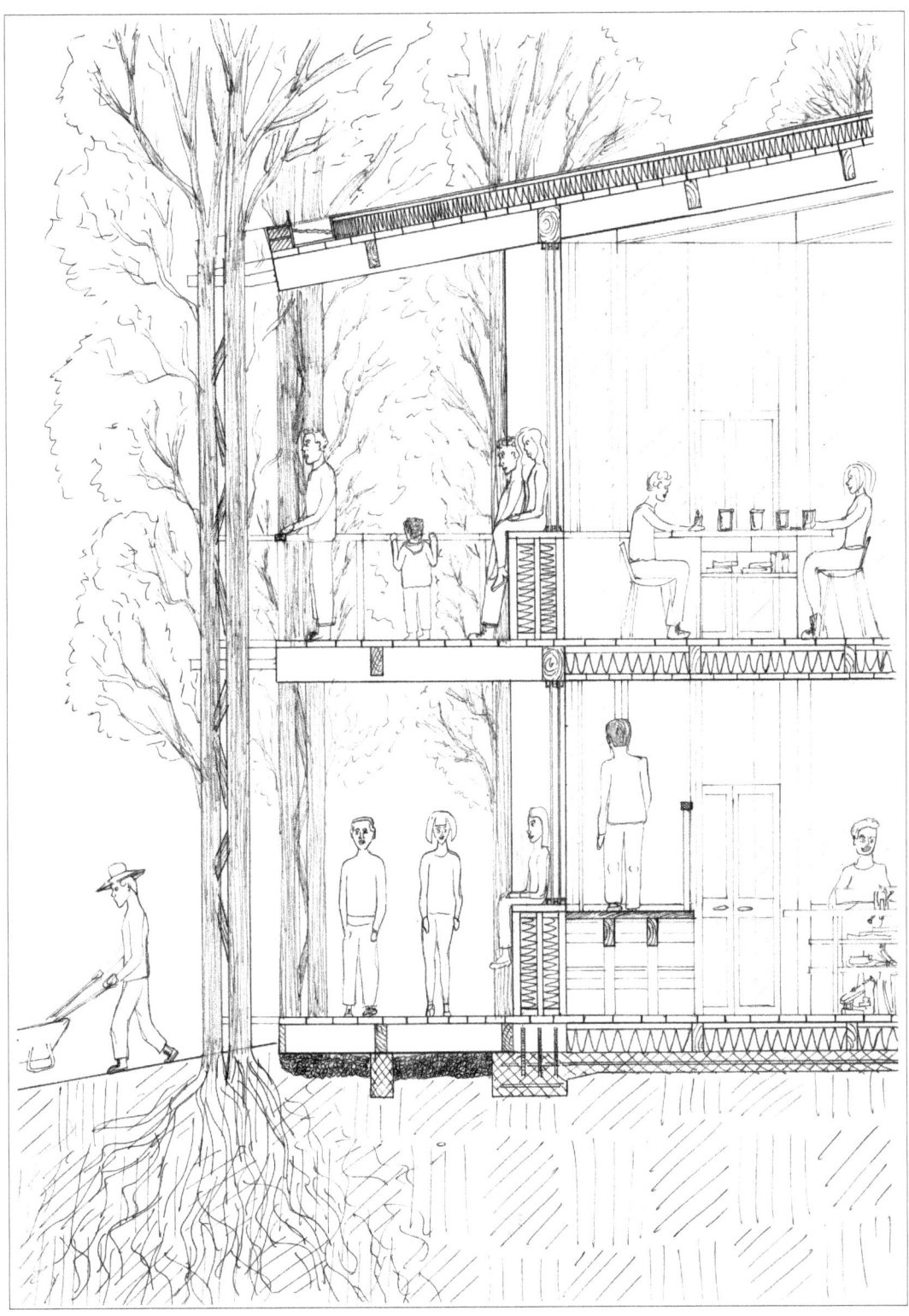

Ecotone Facade Section of
Communal Meadery,
George Darlington

FEATHERED AND DECONSTRUCTED ECOTONE ENVELOPES

Many are very deep; these are either formed of a separate lightweight structure that is lightly braced by the main building, or defined by a deep external structural system that supports the building, an exoskeleton, in a similar way to the Centre Pompidou in Paris, designed by Richard Rogers and Renzo Piano. This is efficient for flexible plans for large spans, but can be an issue with the continuity of the insulated layer. In both cases, the deep structural threshold space hosts human balconies and terraces, circulation, animals such as birds, plants such as climbers and trees.

These projects often seem to feather, or disintegrate within the surrounding landscape, as usually the ecotone envelope is extended beyond the heated enclosure in the landscape. They share the qualities of the follies in the Park de la Villette by Bernard Tschumi, a project we often visit during our study trips. In this type, it often seems that either a larger building is in ruins, has decayed irregularly, with only some pieces left, or that it is growing, with the ecotone envelope extending first, followed by insulated spaces. Either way, the typology expresses change, life, growth and decay, buildings as process, unfinished, that are both landscape and buildings, in a way similar to a pergola or colonnade in a garden. Sometimes the deep façade remains close, against the building, but if there is sufficient space on the site, it threads into the landscape to form walkways and screens, becoming a shared organising framework for both landscape and building structures. In this latter case, not only is the façade both landscape and building, the building itself is also fully integrated in the landscape structure. If structure in buildings means the supporting elements (columns, walls...), in landscapes, it means the framework, or organisation, of conditions and ecosystems created by topography, climate and hydrology. When the building structure integrates with the landscape structure, both fields coexist in coherence within the other.

SPONGE ECOTONE CLADDING

Another family of ecotone facades is thinner, skin-like, formed of cellular cladding systems, usually porous, shaped to create niches, nooks and crannies for smaller living beings, animals and vegetal, from the micro (lichen, moss, insects) to the medio (birds, plants...). They can be thin rainscreen cladding or thicker and structural. They are usually made of ceramic, fired clay, rammed earth, or biomimetic concrete, or thatch and hay.

These projects have a sponge-like quality. The buildings have solidity but without the heaviness of smoother materials; their materiality is alive as plants, animals, sometimes water and/or soil inhabit within the material itself. Human inhabitation is created by shaping the building's form to create roofs and deep window and door reveals, or fixing lightweight elements to the mass.

They tend to look like mountains and cliffs. This can aim to form objects contrasting with the landscape, or they can be shaped to discretely form topographies together with those of the landscape, seemingly disappearing within it, becoming the ground.

BROWN ROOFS

There are roofs, of course, and this is an opportunity for ecosystems. We favour the deeper systems, avoiding the thin soil layers that lack resilience, favouring microtopographies and brown roofs (low-tech solutions left primarily alone without regular gardening) to more controlled systems.

BUILDINGS AS BEINGS AND BUILDINGS AS LANDSCAPE MOSAICS

Regenerative design thinking requires constant cognitive shifts between an understanding of buildings as living entity that ingests and excretes matter and energy, which are defined by an envelope with a controllable degree of porosity to air, light and heat, and buildings as mosaic of multiple habitats that host diverse living beings, both other-than-human and human, inside, in between, outside, but equally within the thickness of the envelope itself.

This is equally a shift between systemic scales and between worldviews; between an understanding of architecture as things, as objects that have either more mechanical or more biological functions, at times cyborg or bionic, and an architecture of habitats, of voids pregnant with potential inhabitation.

This shift in understanding is similar to that of the human body, which can equally be seen as a biological being and as a series of ecosystems, such as the intestine hosting the digestive microbiome.

Both understandings are necessary, the building as being in order to conceive of harvesting heat, air, light, and water, the building as landscape for multispecies inhabitation.

LIST OF PROJECTS RESEARCHED BY STUDENTS OVER THE YEARS

- *Dry stone wall ecosystems: Francois Édouard, The Building that Grows* – https://divisare.com/projects/224057-maison-edouard-francois-nicolas-borel-the-building-that-grows
- *Pots: Luciano Pia, 25 Verde* – https://www.designboom.com/architecture/luciano-pia-25-verde-treehouse-torino-italy-03-13-2015/ – http://www.lucianopia.it/opere-e-progetti/2007-2012-25-green-25-verde/
- *Pots: Maison Edouard Francois, Tower Flower* – https://architizer.com/projects/tower-flower/
- *Climbers: Maison Édouard Francois, Eden Bio* –¬ https://www.edouardfrancois.com/projects/eden-bio-2
- *Platforms: Ot Hoffmann, Tree House in Darmstadt.* https://biotope-city.net/english-the-pioneers-tree-house-darmstadt-1970-ott-hoffmann/ , https://biotope-city.net/ein-pionier-interview-mit-ot-hofmann/
- *Climbers: WOHA, OASIA Singapore hotel project*
- *Patrick Blanc & Jean Nouvel – green wall of the Musée du Quai Branly*– https://www.verticalgardenpatrickblanc.com/realisations/paris/quai-branly-jacques-chirac-museum
- *Epythites: Lina Bo Bardi, Valéria Cirell House.*
- *Living trees: Baubotanik, Plane Tree Cube and Housing of Future Berlin* http://www.ferdinandludwig.com/plane-tree-cube-nagold/articles/plane-tree-cube-nagold.html – http://www.ferdinandludwig.com/house-of-future/articles/house-of-future.html
- *Living Trees: Maison Édouard Francois, Gites Ruraux* – https://www.edouardfrancois.com/projects/gItes-ruraux
- *Troughs: Vo Trong Nghia + Daisuke Sanuki + Shunri Nishizawa, Stacking green*
- *Under roof: Ryue Nishizawa, Terasaki House, Kanagawa* – https://arquitecturaviva.com/works/casa-terasaki-kanagawa-8 – https://www.designboom.com/architecture/ryue-nishizama-terasaki-house-japan-08-15-2019/
- *Pots: Ryue Nishizawa, Garden and House* – https://www.thisispaper.com/mag/garden-and-house-ryue-nishizawa
- *Internal garden – Ishigami, Garden House* – https://www.designboom.com/architecture/junya-ishigami-designed-house-for-a-young-couple-in-tokyo-12-15-2013/
- *Lacaton Vassal – social housing estate extension* – https://www.bettsproject.com/events#/the-imaginaries-of-transformation-lacatonvassal-druot
- *Lacaton Vassal – house in dunes*
- *Large planters: Stefano Boeri – Bosco Verticale* – https://www.stefanoboeriarchitetti.net/en/project/vertical-forest/
- *Façade as interface – Bow Wow, Pony Garden* – https://www.japan-architects.com/en/atelier-bow-wow-tokyo/project/pony-garden
- *Turf roofs: Terunobu Fujimori, La Collina* – https://www.pmq.org.hk/leisureculture/the-story-of-an-anthill/ + Iceland
- *Marco Casagrande: Ultra-Ruin, Ruin Academy,* www.casagrandelaboratory.com
- *James Wines, SITE, BEST Products' Forest Building Showroom in Richmond, Virginia, 1980* – https://storyboard.cmoa.org/2015/07/james-wines-the-architect-who-turned-buildings-into-art/
- *Geoffrey Bawa (Kandalama hotel*
- *Kengo Kuma - Nest We Grow*

Endnotes

(1) Brook Muller, Ecology and the Architectural Imagination (Routledge, 2014) p.109

(2) This is inspired by the work of Donna Haraway of course. Donna Haraway, When Species Meet (University Of Minnesota Press, 2007). Also Staying with the Trouble mentioned in VISUAL SPECULATIVE FABULATIONS.

(3) Yoshiharu Tsukamoto, Windowscape: Window Behaviorology (Page One Publishing, 2012)

(4) Marcos Cruz and Richard Beckett, 'Bioreceptive Design: A Novel Approach to Biodigital Materiality', Arq: Architectural Research Quarterly, 20, no. 1 (2016), 51–64, https://doi.org/10.1017/S1359135516000130.

Alexandra Berculean developed an ECOTONE FACADE for multi-species inhabitation through a series of physical and digital models at a broad range of scale from a 1to20 model of the entire facade to 1to1 mock ups of the cladding tiles. The facade is designed to host a broad range of species, moss and lichen on the bioreceptive textured terracotta, birds and insects in cavities, climbing plants on the trellis, and humans in the shelter of the roof overhang.
Ecotone facade model *(above)*, digital model of tile for multi-species inhabitation *(below, left)*, 1to1 tile mock-up *(below, centre)*, and ecotone facade model in the exhibition *(bottom, right)*.

Epping Forest Institute on Animal Behaviour
Alexandra Berculean

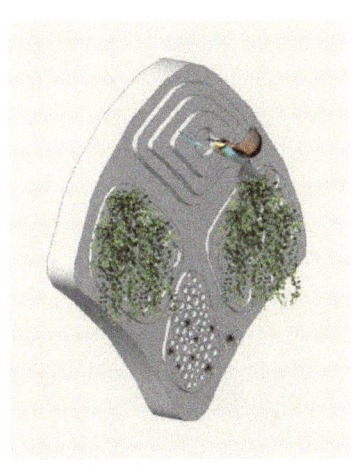
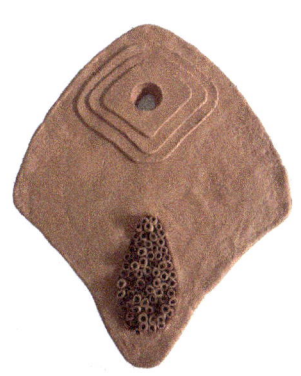

The design of this ecotone facade combines trellis like frameworks for climbing plants, paths open to both visitors and the broader public walking through Epping Forest, and fires escape routes.

The building appears from the outside as a series of diaphanous floating planes covered with vegetation.

The technical design lightly lifts the building from the ground with a thin timber structure resting on pile foundations, to limit the impact on existing habitats.

The Silvaesium
Benjamin Leathes

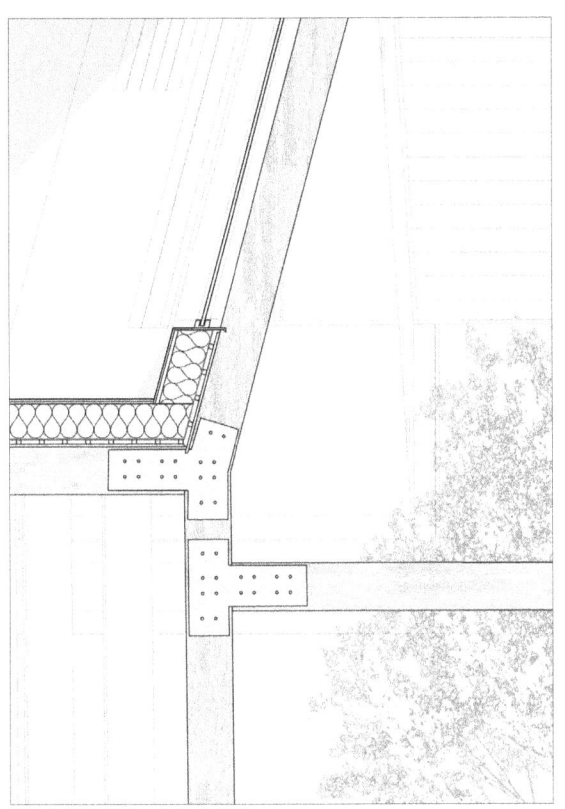
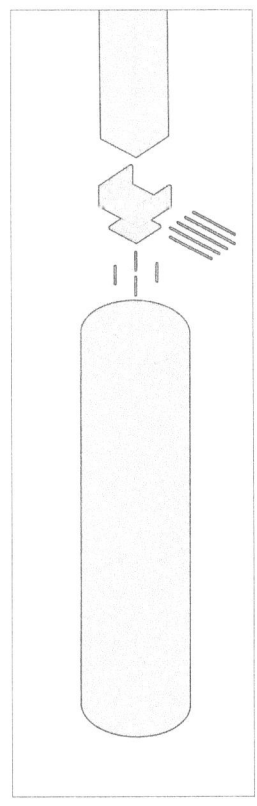

Finola Simpson's project, the ECOTONE ENVELOPE of the grieving houses includes the narrow spaces between the facades of the buildings and the processional walkways. The ecotone facade models she used to develop them conceived this space as inhabited by humans, trees and wildlife. They also guided the technical design and material choices.

Ritual Rewinding
Finola Simpson

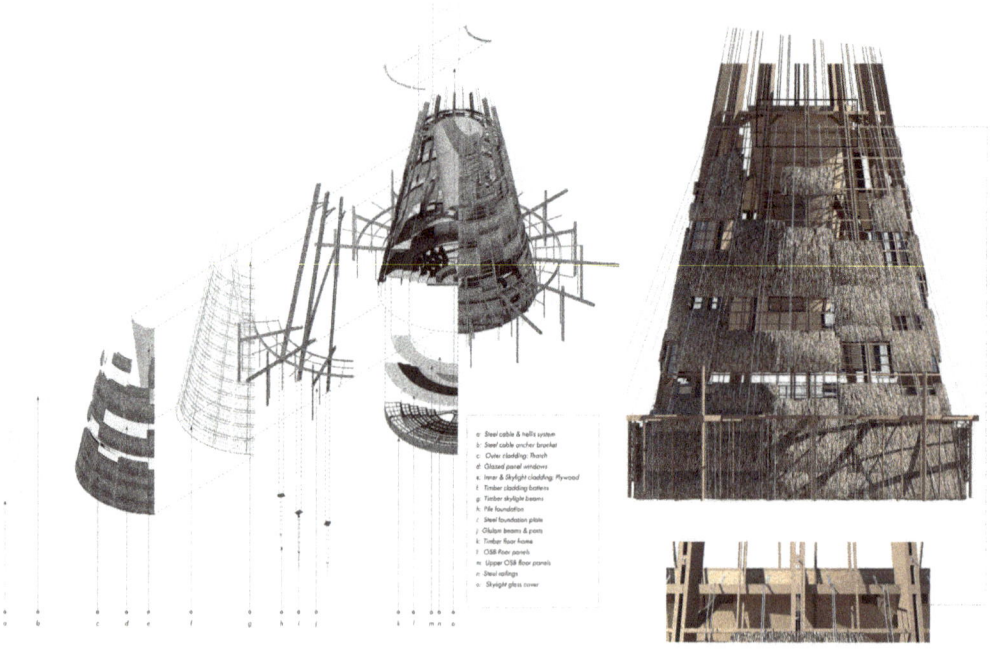

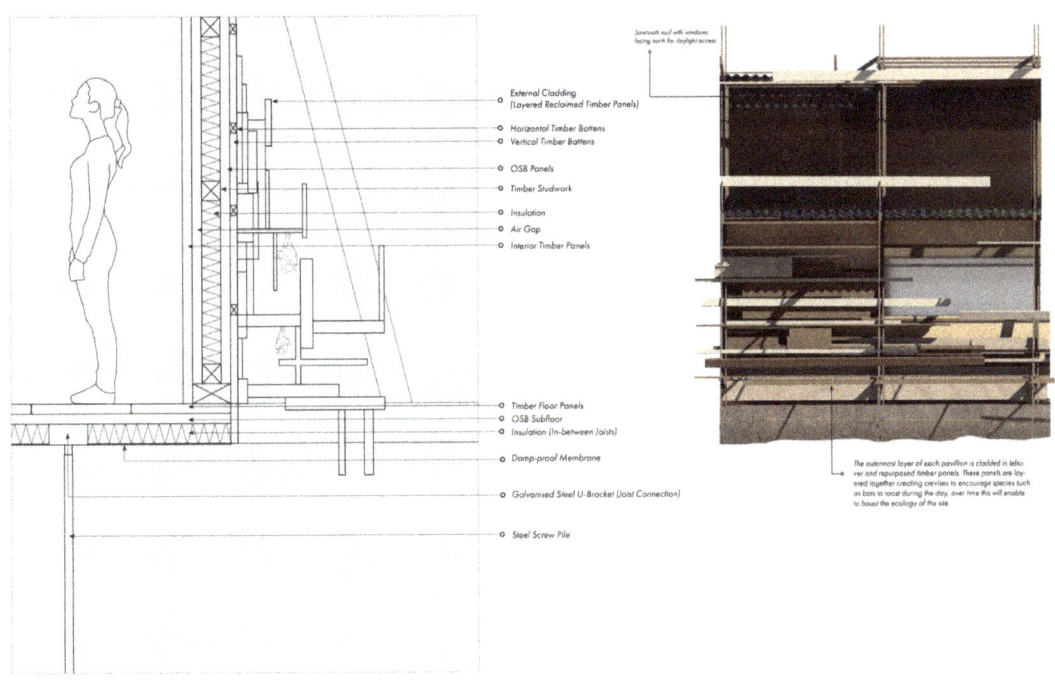

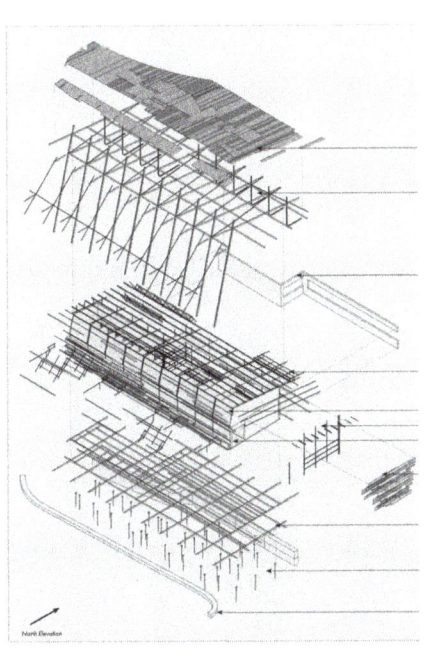

Wall Detail Model 1:20

Kacper Sehnke's facade system deconstructs the facade in layers to develop an upcycled technical system and an aesthetic merging biological and technical circularity.
It is composed of multiple layers of shading and climbing plant support, rainscreen cladding, the actual thermal envelope and an internal cladding. Each layer is expressed and the depth is inhabited by other-than-human life.

Ground floor plan
of *The Council for Ecosystem Restoration*
Kacper Sehnke

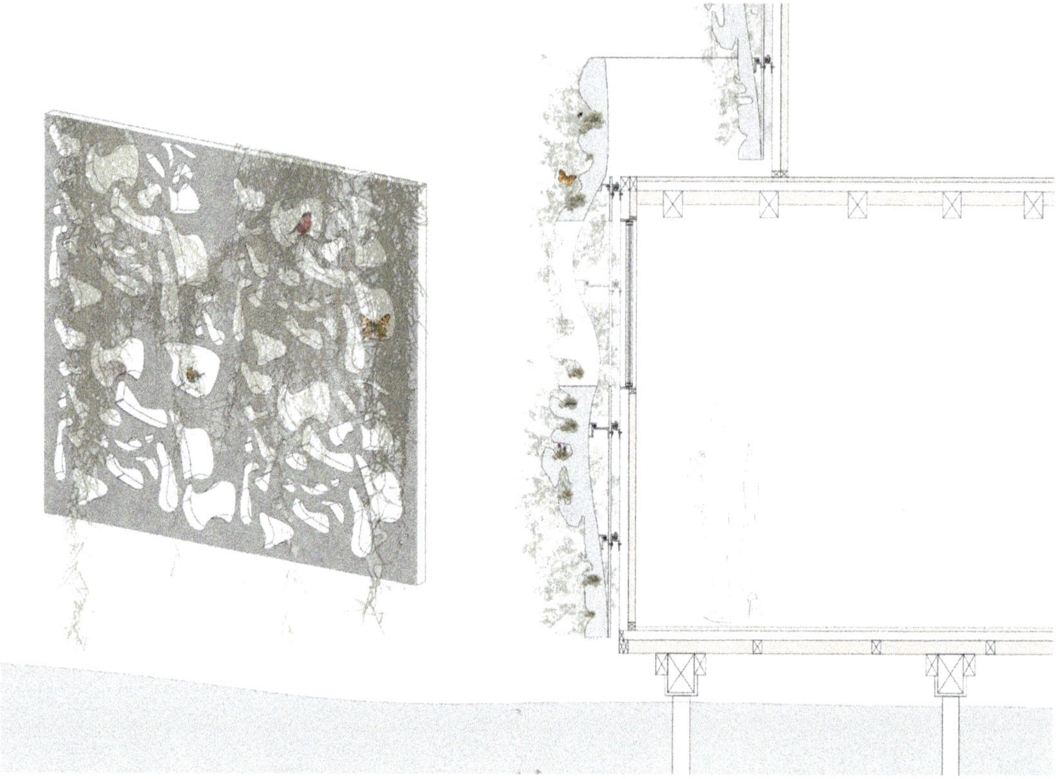

214

Ecotone facade of a rock like bioreceptive concrete facade. This type of facade tends towards hosting minute living beings such as lichen, moss, algae, but in this case it has been deeply shaped to include niches for small animals such as birds, and balconies for humans.

The cladding geometry and texture was conceived through a series of clay and plaster cast models.

Sectional detail *(opposite, top)*
Facade collage *(opposite bottom)*
Panel tests (left, top and bottom)
Clay models testing the geometry of the nooks and crannies *(right)*

Earthly Hills
Epping Forest Centre of Ecologies and Climate Change
Farah Mazloum

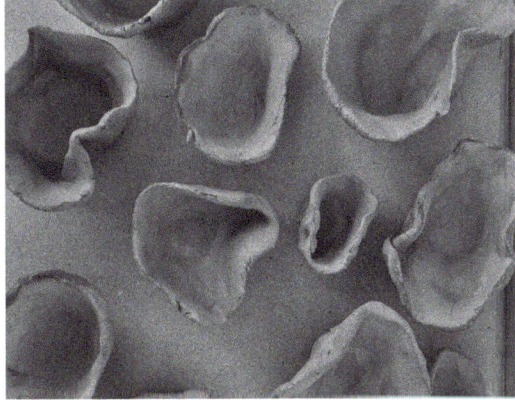

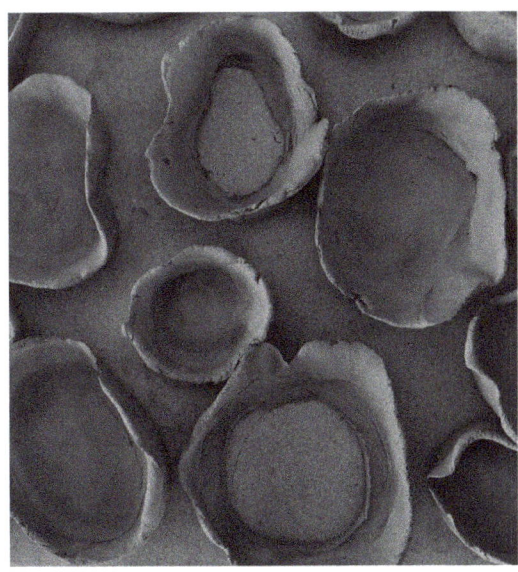

SCORE 10
NARRATIVES, CONTAINERS & CONFECTIONS

Eric Guibert

Regenerative design requires a broader range of media than most other architectural practices, and with this comes the difficulty of composing and laying out this diversity of graphic and sculptural languages into a coherent output. Over the years, we have tested how these various scores and the other media each student adds come together in both their portfolio and the presentations they perform to communicate them during our cross reviews.

Of all the scores, this has been the slowest at developing, maybe unsurprisingly, as it comes last. The designer needs the developed scores to be able to finalise the best approach to assembling them. This, as a result, is a reflection on early findings and potential next steps. Despite remaining in the early stage of development, it seems essential to include a description of how this disparate range of media comes together coherently.

We believe, as many do, that students need to reflect on what matters in their design, and move away from describing their design process chronologically ("I did this, and then I did that…") to develop a clarifying structure with project-specific titles. As a minimum, we recommend structuring portfolios along key themes [1] and organising all their work to demonstrate how each has evolved. But this minimum can be shaped more effectively to convey regenerative architectural speculations.

The key questions we have been struggling with are:

- *What are the best metaphors for the process of synthesis that leads to a regenerative portfolio that allow for a broad range of viable possibilities?*
- *What should the portfolio of a regenerative architectural project physically be? What should be its layout, materiality…?*
- *How should the various parts be connected or related? How should it be structured?*
- *How should this be exhibited and performed during presentations?*

CONTAINERS OR CONSTELLATIONS

Intuitively from the start, we conceived of portfolios as 'containers' [2] within which different elements, each with its own format, can co-exist. The metaphor of containers of disparate elements loosely held together is an expression of an assemblic mode of thinking, the multiple pieces are layers of different experiences and understandings that cannot entirely merge but can be held in resonance and dialogue. Assemblic is coined here as the adjective of assemblage, in the Deleuze and Guattari sense of constellations of elements that relate but that are not forced into a single fixed unifying structure. In this sense, Containers share the qualities of the 'carrier bag' metaphor of this book, coined by Ursula Leguin [3] and embraced by Donna Haraway [4], a narrative that does not have a single heroic narrative arch, with one uniform ontology, but is formed of pieces and moments.

The portfolio as a constellation of artefacts is analogous to an ecological understanding of architecture as a dynamic system, as an assemblage.

The portfolio as a container, as an actual or metaphorical box/bag/envelope/book, can contain the diversity of media needed to avoid the usual communication of architecture primarily as an object towards architecture as an ecosystem. Each score benefits from a specific size and/or materiality that doesn't always fit the standard A2 sheet format.

We have been inspired by multiple types of precedents. For example, the *Boxes in Suitcases* of Marcel Duchamp [5], or the box of the graphic novel *Building Stories* by Chris Ware [6], which contains different printed elements, each with its own narrative, following different characters, including animals: books, booklets, fanzines, and maps.

This has had moments of success, but most BA students find this level of reflection difficult. They already struggle with being able to separate and describe the various architectural layers (typology, mapping, architectural language…), to be able to also be conscious of the media they use and how they can be combined.

In order to help them, for a few years, we gave a prescribed list of 'containers', often combining an Atlas for the research with a box or book for the design process, larger key artefacts and scheme drawings. This was helpful as a starting point, but was also limiting because each project needs a specific type(s) of container(s), and the level of reflexivity needed for this choice to be made early enough so that it can be produced is challenging for BA students. We have, over the years, replaced this with asking students to think of a container and narratives early, at the interim review stage, to give more time for them to develop. Despite this, many students follow the more standard single large A2 portfolio form, which is also a container.

The benefit of the container concept is that it is a smooth transition to the exhibition within which the performance of the final presentation takes place.

CONFECTIONS

Another way of combining different scores is to combine some in a single drawing (or model), for example, an ecological section and a timeline, or a section and a graphic speculative fabulation. 'Visual confection' [7] is a word coined by the theorist of graphic design Edward Tufte to describe an image that is composed of multiple types of graphic systems and languages. For example, a timeline, a perspective and a section. Confections are drawings that are particularly dense in information and usually engaging. A single, large, and detailed drawing can summarise a broad understanding of the project, tell the entire story. The benefit of confections is that by bringing together different media, they also combine different types of knowledge and worldview into a layered combination, joining the experiential dimension of VISUAL SPECULATIVE FABULATIONS, with the systemic nature of the ECOLOGICAL SECTIONS, and the temporal rhythms of a timeline. In particular, the combination of time and narratives, combined with ecological sections or other more standard architectural representations, allows for a combined understanding of spatial form and speculation on how we may live in it.

Students love working on these large and ambitious drawings.

NARRATIVES AS 'LINES OF FLIGHT'

Collating multiple scores in containers or confections is not sufficient to effectively communicate the layering of the projects in the short time frame available for the assessment of the work. To be understood, the project needs a journey through the artefacts, a narrative. These connecting threads can be of multiple types, but it is not the narrative of the design development chronologically described, as they neither clarify intent nor key features of the work.

Over the years, we have increasingly encouraged students to connect their artefacts by using narratives that are relevant to their project: such as the experience of the project by humans and other-than-humans, a historical story of a landscape or person, a personal family story... Sometimes the narrator is a character in the story, imagined or real, sometimes the designer. The styles of narratives used vary wildly from literary or poetic (speculative fiction, fairy tale, myth, Studio Ghibli animations, poems) to scientific or governance reports, political manifestos, or more standard architectural descriptions.

The narratives are primarily visually constructed, bringing together all the work that is produced, located where it best conveys meaning. The great value of the narrative form is that it can string a diverse range of media seamlessly through either a story (a chronological line) or an argument (a theoretical line).

These narratives show the possibilities for regeneration created by the design, openings for change, possibilities for emergence, for what Gilles Deleuze and Felix Guattari called 'lines of flight' [8]. They are not describing what would happen, but what could happen, which creates a capacity to later imagine other ways of being, they create cognitive affordances which may call other things into being.

Most weave together different narrative lines of different styles; they might begin with an analytical description of the context, theoretical ambition and brief, and finish with an experiential piece of speculative fiction, often the developed version of the VISUAL SPECULATIVE FABULATION. This can be seen in the projects of Kacper Sehnke (in INTERLUDE 1 & PANARCHIC MAPPING) and Ben Grafham (in INTERLUDE 3 & PANARCHIC MAPPING). Other, more standard narratives may be used in between to describe different aspects of the project.

An interesting example is Melody Akanji, who combined a piece of auto-ethnographic research with an experiential dream-like storyboard (INTERLUDE 4). A few have combined all in a single narrative, which tends to be a developed version of the VISUAL SPECULATIVE FABULATION; the best example is the graphic novel portfoliocreated by Syafiqah Aziz's that follows at the end of this chapter.

The division, if there is one, often comes from the necessity for a shift in either narrator – from designer to future inhabitant – or types of knowledge, such as from a technical and rational description to an experience.

PERFORMANCE

The containers and narratives of the portfolio usually inspire, or lead to, the performance during presentation. The containers often become the exhibition, reformatted around the actual artefacts, especially the models and physically made drawings. Students often read part of their earlier narratives or integrate them into short films.

The performance brings the narrative(s) to life in a similar act of threading through the various scores. In addition, at times, they can communicate key concepts that may be difficult to communicate in the image and text form of the portfolio. The role of the performance to convey concepts difficult to communicate in print was originally inspired by Mark Leckey's performance *In the Long Tail* where he communicates the evolving qualities of images once they are available online [9]. It is his combination of moving images, the act of drawing 'the long tail' on a chalkboard, with his school teacher/scientist-like description, that brings his discourse to life; we can feel this experience of the digital image.

The most impressive example in our studio has been Melody Akanji's performance to describe her extension to the Houses of Parliament with an animistic house for ecological deliberations; she gave presence to the ecosystem's spirit during the presentation by creating a costume worn by a friend who would only move halfway through the performance, unsettling the audience perception of what is animated or inert, as a parallel to our societal blindness to the life of ecosystems (upcoming INTERLUDE 4).

COMMUNICATING COMPLEX AND LAYERED SPECULATIVE WORLDS

Communicating the layering and complexity of regenerative design, the multiple scales and temporalities, requires both the creation of assemblages of the diverse range of artefacts, of scores, in containers, whether in book, video, or exhibition form, and the connecting tissue of narratives that bring these constellations of scores and the world they describe to life.

Together, these assemblages in containers and narratives convey the building as an object – a core course requirement – as well as, fundamentally for our studio, communicate the architectural experiences and understandings of vibrant and connected other ways of living and being, somewhat altered version of the present condition and our personal histories, and yet also new.

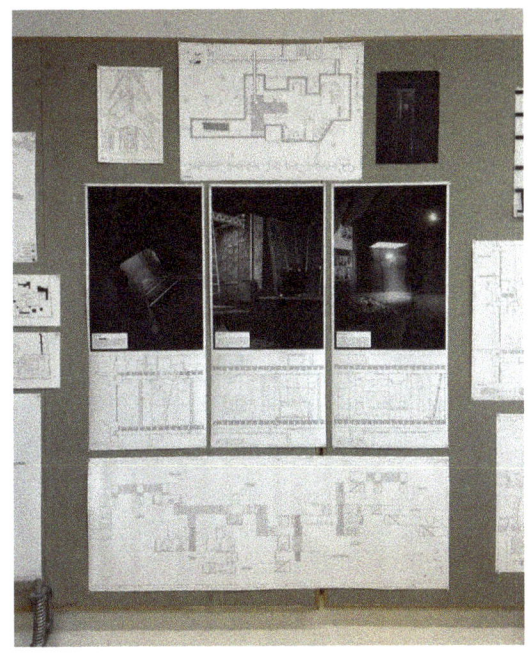

Benjamin Grafham exhibition wall for his final presentation of
The unseen labyrinth:
"there's something in the walls"
Benjamin Grafham

Endnotes

(1) We tend to use similar categories to many: critical ambition & contexts, brief & inhabitation by other-than-human and humans and how they meet, structure & materiality, typology & massing, environmental strategy, form and architectural language, any other…

(2) Hans-Ulrich Obrist et al., Ian Cheng, Emissaries Guide to Worlding (Serpentine Gallery catalogue, Verlag der Buchhandlung Walther König, 2018)

(3) Ursula K. Leguin, The Carrier Bag Theory of Fiction (cosmogenesis, 2024)

(4) Donna J. Haraway, Staying with the Trouble: Making Kin in the Chthulucene (Duke University Press, 2016) pp.117-125

(5) Marcel Duchamp, Box in a Valise (From or by Marcel Duchamp or Rrose Sélavy)(MOMA Collection, 1935-41) https://www.moma.org/collection/works/80890 [accessed on 04-08-2025]

(6) Chris Ware, Building Stories (Jonathan Cape, Random House, 2012).

(7) Edward Tufte, Visual Explanations: Images and Quantities, Evidence & Narrative (Graphics Press, 1997) pp.121-151

(8) Gilles Deleuze & Felix Guattari, A Thousand Plateaus: Capitalism and Schizophrenia (Bloomsbury Revelations, 2013, was originally published in French in 1980)

(9) Mark Leckey, In the Long Tail (2008-09) https://youtu.be/Oi4NLXHWtHI?feature=shared [accessed on 05-08-2025]

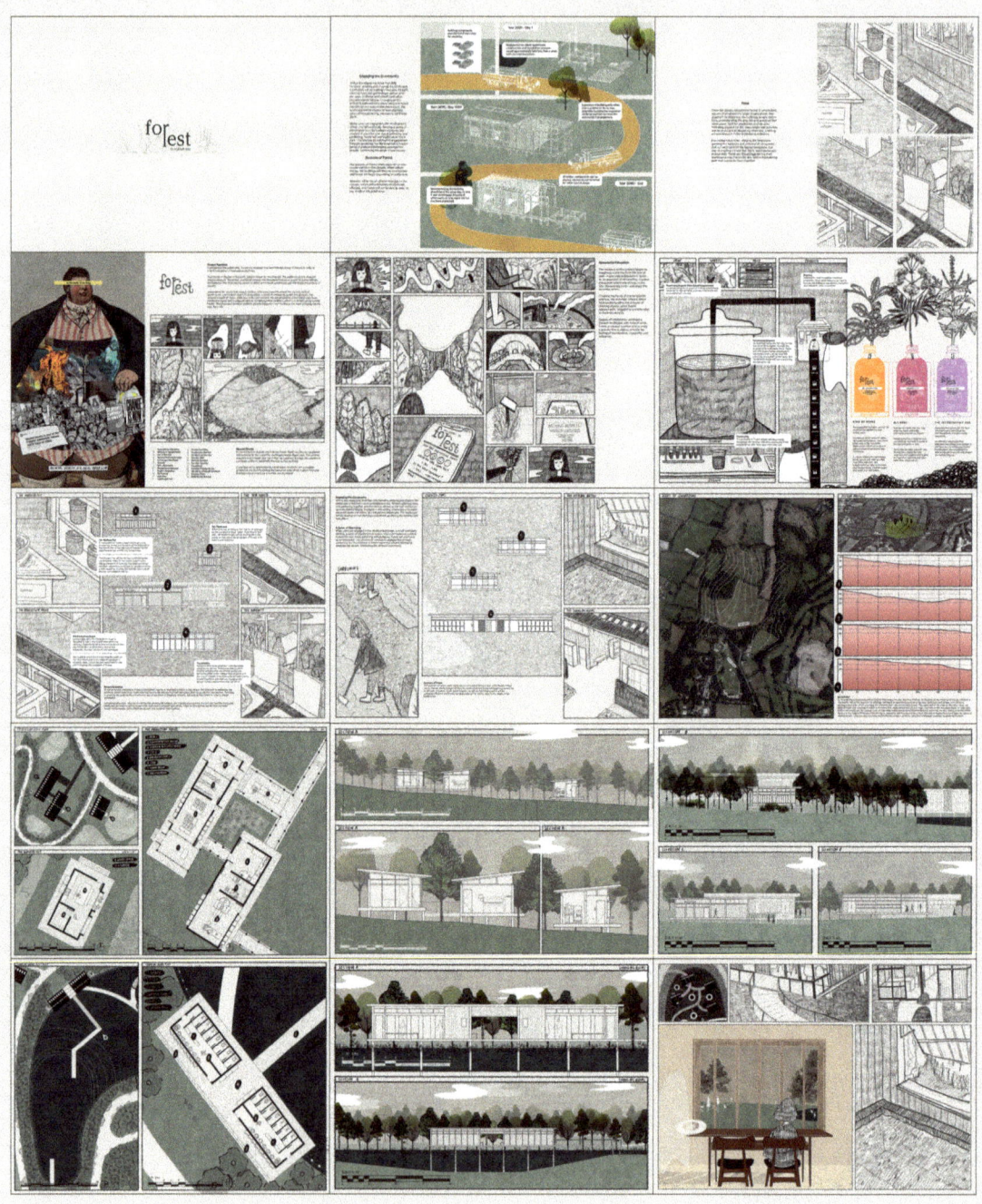

Entire portfolio as graphic novel by Syafiqah Aziz

For-Rest

Syafiqah Aziz

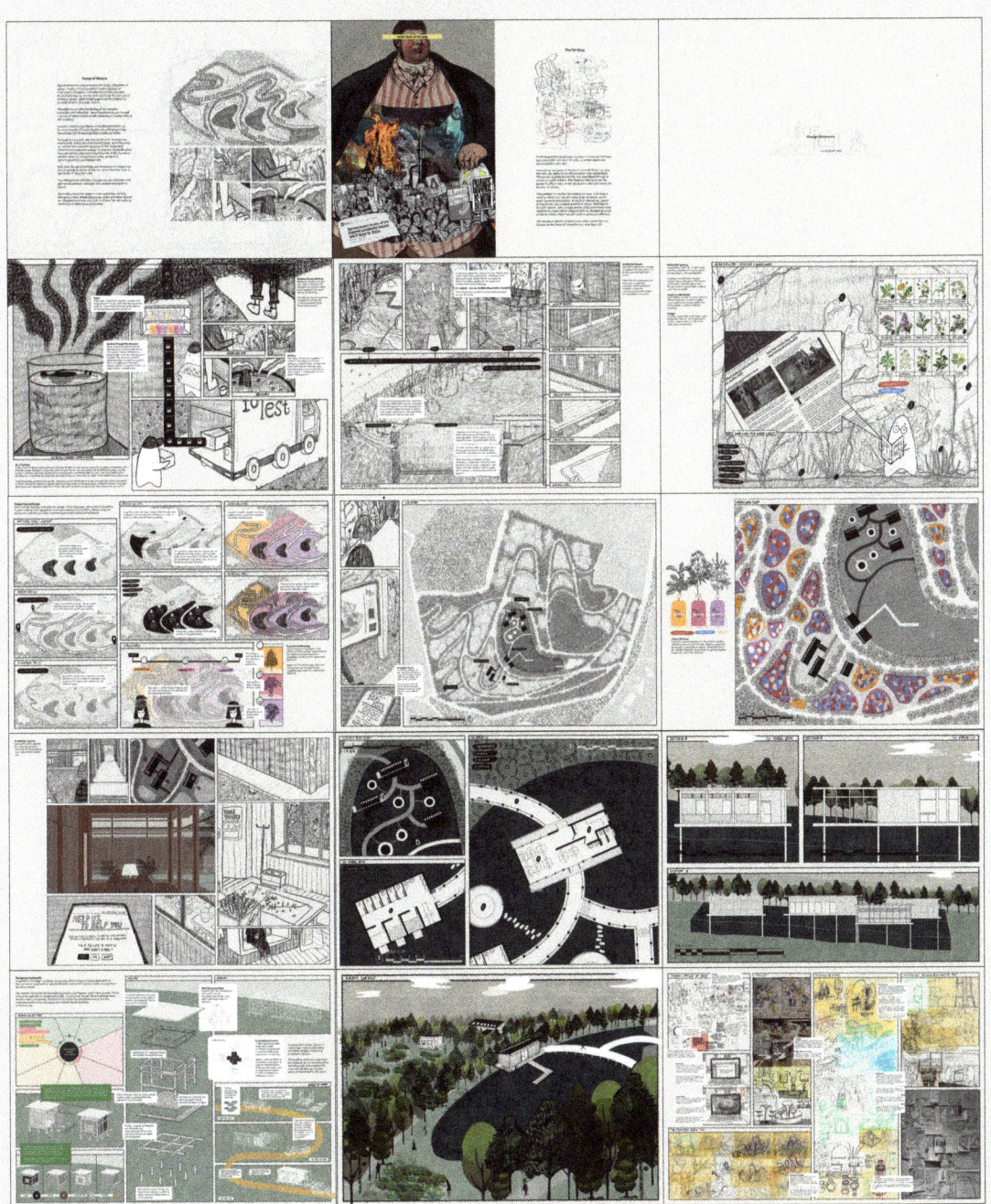

EMI'S (COSMIC) ARCHIPELAGO

INTERLUDE 4

MELODY AKANJI

ife rere
ife rere beeni ife rere
ife t'o wosan ati gbala
ife ti o mu papo
beeni ife rere
nigbati o ba gba wa ni iwọ yoo ri
nigbati o ba mu gbogbo wa jọ iwọ yoo ri
pe bẹẹni eyi jẹ ifẹ ti o dara
ife rere
rogbodiyan ife

good love
good love yes good love
love that heals and saves
love that brings together
yes good love
when it saves us you will see
when it brings us all together you will see
that yes this is good love
good love
revolutionary love

arrival/walkways

OBJECTIVE; public/circulation/procession
TOURNAMENT; archive/information/participation
VENUE; pontoon/library/between land and water

the arrival centre and the floating walkway represents public intervention dedicated to circulation and knowledge. the arrival centre is the public's first point of contact on the cosmic archipelago and houses a small public library, archive and the ecologists office and data tower. visitors at the arrival centre can find a wealth of information related to animisim, ecology and the practices of the indeginous yoruba tribe

Dividing the old and new- the animistic and the individual

CONCLUSION
TEN REGENERATIVE DESIGN PRINCIPLES

Eric Guibert

In a carrier bag, objects are constantly moving around, and more things are added or taken out. You have to rummage around to find what you need; at times, this is right at the bottom for those that haven't been used for a while, and in seeking this rarely used item, you rediscover forgotten articles along the way. Tools come to the surface and sink; the order of their use and their exact function change according to circumstances and purpose.

The same applies with this CARRIER BAG OF REGENERATIVE SCORES, with the use of the scores, or the order you read them in; you may start with a score or another, depending on need or attracted by an image or word. You might read about the regenerative design context and history of the studio, or the pedagogical framework, or not. This is not a definite version of regenerative architectural design methods, an elusive field that is very much in a process of becoming. There is no real end, but some sort of a condensation of repeating themes seems useful as a conclusion; these can be seen as principles that regenerative designers, especially students, may benefit from looking out for, or it may be best to say lenses to use, or prompts, that may help when one is stuck.

A few precedents have inspired this approach. The *Immaculate Heart College Art Department Ten Rules by* Sister Corita Kent, which have been disseminated by the composer John Cage, define an active learner's way of being [1]. Brian Eno's *Oblique Strategies* to enhance creativity or get out of a creative block [2]. Lastly, the 9 recommendations to Landscape Architecture students written by the French landscape architect Michel Corajoud as *A Letter to Students* [3]. The first two are very short, each point coming across as an order, which can be ignored, while the third is more explanatory.

The principles that follow do not specifically include a summary of the above descriptions of scores or the pouches, although they often echo many.

1. THINK AND DESIGN RELATIONALLY

The world is an entangled web of relations. Nothing exists in separation, and all elements and beings evolve in relation to everything else. The most important aim for our society and a regenerative designer is that the systems we belong to thrive and are resilient. This is what our modern society constantly forgets as it tends to focus on limited problems and deliverables instead of the health of the systems.

Learn from the various fields that engage with complex systems: ecology, systemic design, complexity theory... Develop a systemic understanding of your project, of the place and the programme. How is it connected to the world? What are the flows going through it, flows of living beings, human and otherwise, flows of climatic elements (sun, air, water, heat), and data? Where do the materials of your project come from? Where will they go at the end of the building's life?

This means that a regenerative design project is not valued as an object separated from the world, but as a habitat for living beings, and as a node through which multiple flows pass. Its aesthetic is relational; it is enjoyed as a lived architecture more than an object beautiful in itself.

2. DESIGN WITH EMPATHY AND CARE, BUT NOT TOO MUCH

Care for all life, other-than-human and human, systems, communities and beings, care for the climate; allow other lives to create. Care for those around you; help and share your knowledge with them. And do not forget to care for yourself and look at your own work with the kindness and generosity you would show to others. But don't aim for all to be equal beneficiaries; it is impossible and will only lead to exhaustion and despair.

Make everything with care. This does not mean perfection or using expensive materials. It means deciding to do something achievable, and taking a little extra time to do it mindfully, thoughtfully, and with intent.

3. RESEARCH AND NURTURE THE VARIOUS SCALES OF COMMUNITIES AND CONTEXTS

Nurturing synergies necessitates defining the relevant communities. In each situation, there will always be multiple collectives that exist at different scales. This is true of the communities of your project, the program of the brief, the local users, national and international like-minded people and institutions. It also exists in the interaction between the different scales within the site, the ecosystems in its landscape and humans and species between and inside buildings. Spend time sensing the place you are designing, walk through it, look, listen, smell, touch, taste, and record in drawings, photographs and videos. Go to the site many times.

This equally applies to your own communities of practice, those that will support you, that you will learn from, and that you will contribute to. Your capacity to design relies on the different collectives you belong to, within the design studio and beyond, friends, like-minded people, as well as other-than-human species, ecosystems, and technology. Draw these various contextual scales, the territories and constellations. Connect, ask questions, share ideas, and listen to those around you; they have much to communicate and may need your help.

The best way to assemble a group is to collaborate

around a sense of purpose, a shared direction, however vague this might be at the beginning.

Your community of practice is also formed of people you may never meet, the practices of others experienced through the places or artefacts they have created. These you need to experience, whenever possible in the flesh, visit buildings, landscapes, exhibitions, archives… Slow down and sense the world with avid curiosity. Research them rigorously and critically. Over time, you will develop your own library of precedents and your pantheon of creators; this is how you will shape the designer you will be.

Be careful not to be drowned in too much information, but do go and see a few things each week on average.

Whenever you are lacking confidence or clarity in order to make architectural decisions, think of and connect to the project's and your own communities. The answer is usually there.

4. ANALYSE AND DESIGN WITH RHYTHMS

Architectural design is equally about time as it is about space. Different activities happen at different times, following different rhythms. An understanding of these rhythms is necessary to design for economic flexibility and with the rhythms of nature. Define and draw the key rhythms of your project, and synchronise their patterns, their beat. There are multiple timeframes from the day, to seasons, to years, decades and beyond.

These rhythms also apply to your own work. Rhythms of events to bring your communities together. Regular rhythms of making, drawings, writing. Each of us is more effective at different times of day for different things. Produce constantly but thoughtfully.

5. IMAGINE SCENARIOS OF OTHER-THAN-HUMAN AND HUMAN INHABITATIONS

Regenerative design is primarily about life. Its qualities, benefits and aesthetics are based on relations between building, landscape, ecosystems, beings, humans, and climate. Always design, draw, model the building with the inhabitation of some of these living, or life-like, elements. Draw activities on plans and sections, model inhabitations with buildings. Buildings are never beautiful by themselves, unless they are monuments or tombs, maybe. Draw nature recovery frameworks at all connected scales, integrate habitats and wildlife connectivity from the very fabric of the building to the site, surroundings, region and beyond.

This is not to define exactly what will happen, as it is impossible. It is to define the affordance of the buildings through scenarios. And it also communicates this affordance as it makes such drawings and models inhabitable for the viewer, approachable. They can imagine how they might inhabit.

Regenerative architecture is performative; its quality is about what could take place inside it, what happens, or could happen, to materials, to living beings, to systems. Its qualities are often intangible – flexibility, change, growth, decay, generosity, climatic conditions – yet they are concrete, material.

6. TELL STORIES TO MAKE SENSE OF THE COMPLEXITY OF SOCIAL ECOSYSTEMS

Living systems are complex; they include other-than-human and humans, climatic elements, and materials. They need a multitude of media to analyse different layers. These different layers connect in action, in the performance of the architecture by life. This is best conceived and conveyed as narratives.

The artefacts you produce need to be composed in constellations and groupings, in the form of books, exhibitions, guides, and maps. Within these settings, narratives are told to make sense of this complexity and connect to our human empathy and subjectivity, to convey their meaning.

7. NURTURE EMERGENCE WITH STRONG, OPEN, AND MEANINGFUL SCAFFOLDINGS

Regenerative design is equally bottom-up and top-down. The bottom-up quality of emergence needs the safety and efficiency of strong yet open scaffolding and frameworks. Projects need structures of buildings as support systems, and landscape structure as mosaics of ecosystems. Learning and design require the scaffolding of pedagogical and design processes, composed of scores and collective events.

Be open yourself, but organised and regularly working. Ecological and creative emergence is unpredictable and needs space, and time. Give space to allow unpredictability and chance. Use media you cannot entirely control. Embrace what may first appear like mistakes, as they often are key opportunities. Be open to your own intuition; let it take form as you make and draw, especially, yet not only, by hand, trust that it can think in more complex ways, and faster, than conscious rationality. Your intuition knows, as long as you are engaged with the world. You must also set yourself a scaffolding of deliverables each week, your best creativity will not appear suddenly a few days before a deadline.

8. BECOME AWARE OF AND REGULARLY SHIFT BETWEEN PARADIGMS

Whether we are conscious of it or not, we always think and design from a position. We might see nature as something separate from us and controllable, something that only humans can save, or nature as a condition we belong to, as systems able to create, provide, support, collectives that we humans are part of, always, but that don't need us, apart from our respect and letting them be, enough.

Our position changes with the context and purpose or task at hand. It is usually difficult to be aware of this at that point. Awareness usually comes from reading or experiencing something that challenges one's own paradigm. Read, experience, and discuss with those who disagree.

No paradigm is entirely true; they are more or less useful, and this can evolve fast. Shift between paradigms as needed through the design process. Between understanding architecture as a mosaic of ecosystems and building as a living being. Between systemic and biological, or even mechanical (yes, you will at times need a mechanical mindset to develop your project).

9. CREATE THROUGH YOUR BODY AS MUCH AS DIGITALLY

Use your body as much as digital tools, one after the other or together. The body connects to embodied memory of space, to intuition, to meaning, empathy, in ways that we cannot be rationally aware at that point. We can only experience intuition while we design emotionally and physically, through a sense of purpose, a warm tension, an energised fascination. The complexity of this thinking is only revealed rationally later, often at the end. Sketching, as drawing or modelling, has the fluidity needed for this empathetic creativity (this includes with a stylus on a tablet). The digital brings precision and speed, especially CAD softwares, but this is more useful at the later stages as they render our mind rigid. Maybe new digital tools will be intuitive, as long as they afford the fluid dialogue, the conversation between our mind and the medium that all design process relies on.

10. NURTURE DIVERSITY

Regeneration and resilience necessitate systemic, biological and cultural diversities. Wherever you go, nurture and champion diversity, of opinion, of ecologies, knowledge, biological, social, cultural, and philosophical.

Design is a conversation with the self through a medium. It never takes place solely in the head; it needs a movement between body and media. Designing regeneratively requires a multitude of media to think through the multitude of layers, space and time, and paradigms. Work, produce, make, test, especially if you have no idea where it is going. You can't at the beginning, as it is the making itself that brings clarity and confidence. Trust that your instinct will take you on a productive journey; it always does, as long as you work regularly.

And always remember to surround yourself with a diversity of people; belong to different groups. It is through the discussions with this cultural diversity that you will gain conviction, nuance, and develop your own creativity.

CO-CREATING 'ECOLOGIES OF FREEDOM'

As I am summarising the above principles, I am realising how regenerative design, as practised in our studio at least, resonates with the libertarian ecological principles described by the American social theorist and political philosopher Murray Bookchin in *The Ecology of Freedom*. His position is that ecosystems and anarchist/libertarian political systems share many qualities and principles, and that only such a horizontal political system can lead to a resilient relationship between humans and other living beings and systems. It is fitting to end this book with his summary of the key characteristics of an ecological society as one where:

'mutualism, self-organization, freedom, and subjectivity, cohered by social ecology's principles of unity in diversity, spontaneity, and non-hierarchical relationships, are thus ends in themselves [where humans have a responsibility as] the self-reflexive voice of nature' (4)

And maybe this self-organising creative spontaneity benefits from an open, yet strong, top-down scaffolding, as our studio does.

Endnotes

(1) Sister Corita Kent, Immaculate Heart College Art Department Ten Rules (1967-68) https://www.corita.org/tenrules [accessed on 07-08-2025]

(2) Brian Eno, Oblique Strategies (1975, 1978 1979) https://stoney.sb.org/eno/oblique.html [accessed on 07-08-2025]

(3) Michel Corajoud, A letter to Students (2000), in the video by Ila Bêka & Louise Lemoine Sur les traces de Michel Corajoud/Learning from Michel Corajoud (Voyage Autour de la Lune, IFLA EU, 2016) https://www.youtube.com/watch?v=h3nVqxQRsaY [accessed on 07-08-2025], also found, with the previous two texts, in this brief to landscape architecture students, Mark R. Eischeid, The Oregon Sequence: Vanport (2020) https://bpb-us-e1.wpmucdn.com/blogs.uoregon.edu/dist/e/14815/files/2020/10/LA-4589_2020_OR-Sequence-Vanport_syllabus1.pdf [accessed on 07-08-2025]

(4) Murray Bookchin, The Ecology of Freedom: The Emergence and Dissolution of Hierarchy (AK Press, 2005) p.365

ACKNOWLEDGEMENTS

The studio is connected to many communities and individuals, without whom these scores would not have developed.

Firstly, I wish to thank all the amazingly committed students who have taken the chance to join us on this regenerative journey. All the students who have embraced our methods, especially at the beginning when we were developing them, including those who have contributed to their development, most of whom are present in the book. This pedagogical and design method research would not have developed without your creative use of our prompts.

I am hugely grateful for the four brilliant co-tutors who have taught the studio with me and who have each contributed in their own way. My now good friend Anthony Powis who was involved with the first epoch of the studio and helped develop its methods (2018-21), Michael Spooner with whom we taught the first year on rewilding, in particular for the walks and housing typologies that he developed for the collective masterplan project (2021-22), Bruce Irwin and his sharp eye for representation (2022-23), Christopher Daniel for the productive nerdy conversations we have had with and without students on systemic design, long temporalities, and rituals of care (since 2023). I am so thankful for the generosity you have demonstrated towards the students and studio.

Much gratitude goes towards Camilla Wilkinson, with whom we created a previous studio looking at spatial agency and intangible architectural qualities. This studio would not have been successful without learning from your ethical stance, design methods, attention to detail, and curation. Our collaboration, combined with the insights of my PhD, formed the foundation for this studio.

The studio has benefited from the insights of many reviewers who have generously commented on the students' work and shared precedents and references that have been key to the development of the studio.

- *Melody Akanji (Croydon Urban Room)*
- *Edmund Alcock (KSR)*
- *Daniel Berende*
- *Adam Cossey (Hawkins\Brown Architects)*
- *Esther Calinawan*
- *Pereen d'Avoine (Russian for Fish)*
- *Jenny Dunn (social practice artist)*
- *Karen Fitzsimon (landscape architect and historian)*
- *Keb Garavito Bruhn (Pilbrow and Partners Architects),*
- *Christina Geros (RCA)*
- *Chloe Harrison (Wilder Horsham District, and Sussex Wildlife Trust)*

- *Hwei Fan Liang (ACAN, Ravensbourne University, UEL)*
- *Lee Jesson (Ash Sakula and Thursday Works)*
- *Kate Jordan*
- *Krystallia Kamvasinou*
- *Jenny Kingston (muf architecture/art)*
- *Ben Leathes (Aukett Swanke)*
- *Philip Longman*
- *Guy Mannes-Abbott (writer and activist)*
- *Oscar Mather (Lynch Architects)*
- *Inês Neto dos Santos (multidisciplinary artist working with food fermentation)*
- *Natalie Newey*
- *Andrew Ó Murchú (Both And Group)*
- *Mette Pedersen (Kraaijvanger Architects)*
- *Anthony Powis (Sheffield School of Architecture & Landscape, and Central Saint Martins)*
- *Kester Rattenbury (London School of Architecture and writer)*
- *Carl Reid (Pilbrow and Partners Architects)*
- *Dain Son Robinson (Sustainable Development Goal Coordinator, UoW)*
- *Caspar Rodgers (alma-nac)*
- *Jeremy Rye (Jeremy Rye Studio)*
- *Shahed Saleem*
- *Duarte Santo (Cornell University)*
- *Kacper Sehnke (Falconer Chester Hall Architects)*
- *Finola Simpson (Gollifer Langston Architects, RCA)*
- *Urna Sodnomjamts*
- *Anna-Marie Versteeg (Ivanov Versteeg Architecture)*
- *Lourenço Viveiros (Pilbrow and Partners Architects)*
- *Ed Wall (University of Greenwich)*
- *Tim Waterman (The Bartlett, UCL)*
- *Victoria Watson*
- *Camilla Wilkinson*
- *Julian Williams*
- *Paolo Zaide*

Special thanks go to the many who have shared their knowledge of our sites and study trip destinations:

- *Richard Black (Wilder Horsham District and Sussex Wildlife Trust)*
- *Brandlhuber+ Architects and Urban Planners*
- *Fabien Gantois (Fabien Gantois Architecture)*
- *Chloe Harrison (Wilder Horsham District and Sussex Wildlife Trust)*
- *Sandra Jasper (Humboldt-Universität, Berlin)*
- *Colleen Myles (editor and co-author of Fermented Landscapes)*

- Inês Neto dos Santos (multidisciplinary artist working with food fermentation)
- John Phillips (Grazing and Landscape Project Officer, City of London)
- Poligonal Office for Urban Communication

The team at the University of Westminster, where this studio is located, was essential in supporting the studio. Kate Heron, the head of our then Architecture Department, who encouraged me to do a PhD, and first employed me at the University of Westminster. The following head of school, Harry Charrington, and Julian Williams, the previous head of BA, who gave us the opportunity to create the studio in the Bachelor's in Architecture course in September 2018. Paolo Zaide, the head of BA, who nurtured a positive and creative culture, championed speculative architecture, and allowed us to pursue our enquiries in 3rd year.

Natalie Newey, whose professional and generous leadership of the 2nd year created a perfect environment for the first 4 years of the development of our pedagogies. Will McLean and Scott Batty, who head the technical modules with a strong environmental and circularity agenda, have been instrumental in nurturing a synergy between their teaching and the studio's focus on regenerative materiality and nature-based solutions. We thank their entire team, including Urna Sodnomjamts, who has brought a high level of creativity to our regenerative tectonics in recent years. François Girardin for his recommendion of Theresa Sauer's book Notations 21 [1], as well as his yearly support during the setting up of the summer show exhibitions.

A special thank you goes to Benjamin Grafham, an ex-student of our studio who has brilliantly and elegantly laid out this book.

We are also indebted to those who have inspired us and have not met, most of whom are mentioned in the chapters. We are connected to many others, of course; there isn't the space to thank you all in writing, and my brain might be failing me. Please excuse us. We send a heartfelt thank you to you all.

Endnotes

[1] Theresa Sauer, Notations 21 (Mark Batty Publisher, 2009)

LIST OF PROJECTS

NONDITA JESSICA ABDUL MATIN — 244
Waste to Energy Hub

MELODY AKANJI — 245
Emi's (Cosmic) Archipelago

EDMUND ALCOCK — 246
The Cycle of Pannage

SYAFIQAH AZIZ — 247
For Rest

ALEXANDRA BERCULEAN — 248
Epping Forrest Institute on Animal Behaviour

DANIEL BERENDE — 249
Grow.Kill.Eat.Repeat: Aquaponics and the Architecture of Self-Sustaining Ecologies

GEORGIA BRESCIANI — 250
A (Raw)dical Cheese Factory

GEORGE DARLINGTON — 251
Communal Meadery

MERLA ELAKKAD — 252
Demolition Factory

DANIELLE ELEFANTE — 253
The Department of Wasted Energy and Circularity

DIEGO GALLARDO — 254
Botanical Co(w)lisium

BENJAMIN GRAFHAM — 255
"there's something in the walls," The Unseen Labyrinth

JULIA LASSOTA — 256
Botanical Co(w)lisium

EUNSEO LEE — 257
The Silvaeseum

BEN LEATHES — 258
The Silvaeseum

BEN LEATHES — 259
Anthropic Tropism

HARRY MELLOR — 260
Anthropic Tropism

DARYA PROKOPETS — 261
Sanctuary for the Dispossessed

FLORENTINE ROCKENBAUER — 262
Nature and Humanity Council

THAIS RIBEIRO RODRIGUES — 263
The Institute for Sympoiesis

KACPER SEHNKE — 264
The Council for Econimic Restoration

FINOLA SIMPSON — 265
The Purple Emporer

FINOLA SIMPSON — 266
Ritual Rewilding

DAWOUD SOHAIL — 267
A Systems Directorate

SHAH-REE TASSADIQ — 268
Nakshi Kanthar Math – The Field of Embroidery Quilt

REBECCA THOMPSON — 269
Department of Half-Earth Socialism

ISABELLA TORRESAN TESTOLIN — 270
Forging Utopia

YOHEI YAMANE — 271
Deadwood Villas

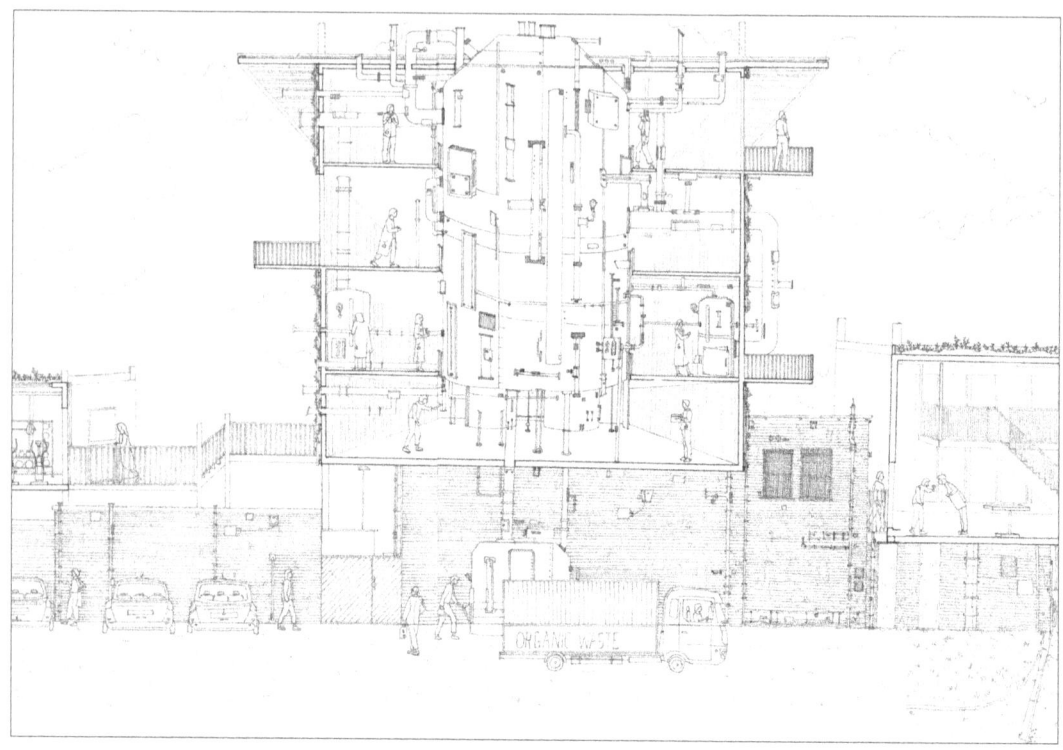

Section through energy centre

NONDITA JESSICA ABDUL MATIN

WASTE-TO-ENERGY HUB

The regenerative waste-to-energy hub bridges the connection between architecture and living ecosystems. Buildings serve as mediators between people and nature, managing flows of energy and materials. A biodigester converts organic waste into renewable heat and electricity that powers the entire facility.

The design integrates community spaces where sustainability meets daily life, from a gym and tennis courts to a pub with sunset views. Structures built with cross-laminated timber support climbing plants, creating living walls that purify air and support biodiversity. Bridges link facilities, framing forest views and reinforcing connectivity.

Rather than disrupting the environment, the project strengthens ecological connections. Waste becomes energy, buildings nurture plants, and community spaces create appreciation for nature. This actively regenerates its surroundings while serving human needs.

Temple for Yemoja (Still)

MELODY AKANJI

EMI'S (COSMIC) ARCHIPELAGO

Emi meaning (souls) in Yoruba refers to all living things. Emi's archipelago is an afro-futuristic attempt to diversify the voices of parliament in 2030.

Exploring the rituals of Egungun, masquerades and Orisha in Yoruba animistic culture, this brief speculates a London in which ecology becomes embodied in space, time and material. An archipelago for all living things attempts to redefine and reflect on what we understand as the flow of life; what it really means to find ecological unity and equity and how democratic processes can become diversified. The project focuses on 3 deities within Yoruba culture, Oshun for the water, Aja for earth and Yemoja for air; and frames the programme around microclimatic temples for each god. There is a main space for ritual and points of arrival - a walkway connects all of these moments (islands) - unifying the archipelago, which sits on the Thames next to the Houses of Parliament.

Human and Pig dwelling

EDMUND ALCOCK

THE CYCLE OF PANNAGE

The proposal's client is a "custodian of wild pigs" in the countryside near Southwater, Sussex. The client is a master of 'Pannage' an ancient process of managing pigs' movement and consumption across the land in the Autumn months consuming acorns, chestnuts and beech mast from the fallen trees. This is not only good for the pigs welfare, but also the soil of the land as it is turned by the pigs as they root for their food. The pig keeper will also smoke his pigs to create high-quality cured meats for their and their neighbours' consumption - akin to the Iberico process originating in Catalonia, Spain.

The building and client's programme relates to the wider community through its preservation of the local ecology by managing the pigs' movement and their interaction with the soil. The building itself is made from locally sourced materials such as clay of the Sussex Weald, fallen Oak trees, and Water Reed and Straw. By ensuring the wild pigs 'root' for a certain time, the topsoil's organic matter improves, and ecologies can thrive. Too long and the roots of trees where the pigs forage become depleted and damaging the old oak trees. And these oak trees are linked to other ecologies, such as butterflies. The pigs also provide food for the local community in the form of delicious cured meats.

Page from the graphic novel portfolio with isometric views

SYAFIQAH AZIZ

FOR REST

For Rest is a conceptual proposal crafted for the worn-out and weary, offering a sanctuary where nature becomes the cure. Rooted in Jane Bennett's Vibrant Matter, the project draws from her idea that food holds political power—an agent that shapes public behaviour and morality. Translating this into today's world, the metaphor of a gluttonous king emerges, symbolising corrupt governance driven by excess, greed, and blind consumption. His unchecked appetite leads to societal decay, breeding chaos and a mental health crisis among the people. Set in the quiet heart of Stewardstone near Barn Hill, For Rest responds by carving out a contemplative space—a poetic pause from the noise. It's a call to slow down, reset, and return to clarity.

Model

ALEXANDRA BERCULEAN

EPPING FOREST INSTITUTE ON ANIMAL BEHAVIOUR

The proposed project leverages advanced AI to collect and analyse data from satellite imagery, drones, acoustic sensors, and remote cameras. This technology will offer deep insights into animal populations, habitats, and the factors affecting their survival. The resulting knowledge will support Epping Forest conservators, City of London staff, and national groups in protecting and managing the forest's unique ecosystem. Sustainability is central to the design. The structure will be built using rammed earth, utilizing local clay to minimize environmental impact and blend seamlessly with the landscape. To further enhance biodiversity, the façade is made from terracotta—a deliberate choice to attract birds and insects, fostering cohabitation between wildlife and the built environment.

Inhabited model

DANIEL BERENDE

GROW.KILL.EAT.REPEAT, AQUAPONICS AND THE ARCHITECTURE OF SELF-SUSTAINING ECOLOGIES

This project proposes an inhabited ecology — an integrated architectural system where aquaponic farming, seasonal dining, and student accommodation form a closed loop of exchange. Set within the suburban fabric of London, it reimagines relationships between food, labor, and living through reciprocal infrastructure. Fish and plants are cultivated in tandem; the produce sustains a restaurant staffed by students who live on-site in exchange for their labor. At its core, the project acts as a counterculture — resisting the systemic suppression of the realities behind food production and consumption. In a society that hides death, labor, and sacrifice behind packaging and convenience, this architecture restores ethical visibility. The killing and preparation of fish is made visible — not as spectacle, but as ritual. This is not merely a sustainable system, but a ritual architecture: one that confronts the cycles of life and death, exchange and responsibility. It offers a critical alternative to passive consumerism, proposing instead a model of active, honest inhabitation within self-sustaining urban ecologies.

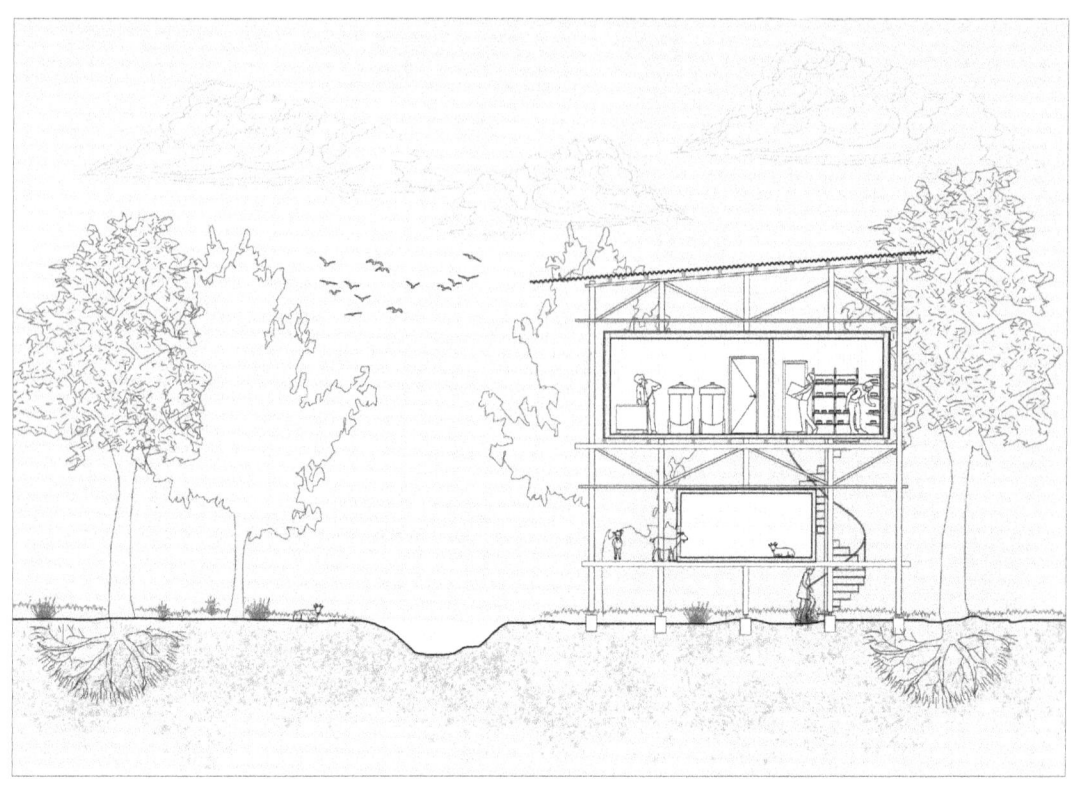

Section through the Cheese Making

GIORGIA BRESCIANI

A (RAW)DICAL CHEESE FACTORY

With the desire to escape homogenization of production and consumption and bring back a sense of identity and authenticity, the (Raw)dical Cheese Factory aims to establish rawness as a biopolitical act. Post-Pasteurian culture solidified microbes' relation to humans only in terms of harm, making them seen by society as something to eliminate, growing a sense of hyper attention to sterility. This project has an objective to exorcise the fear of microbes, emphasizing the clear symbiosis and entangling that they share with humans. The slogan can be identified as "What protects the cheese protects us". The (Raw)dical Cheese Factory aims to produce raw goat cheese, as its rawness can be seen as a guarantee of safety. As a provocation to understand safety and contamination, the cheese will be made by adding to the raw milk different kinds of cultures of bacteria, taken from distinct unusual places, such as old trees, but also human bacteria, taking swabs directly from parts of the human body.

Overview of Project 10 years after its construction

GEORGE DARLINGTON

COMMUNAL MEADERY

The project focuses on the production of mead through the fermentation of honey. Located in North London's greenbelt, the Lee Valley, it neighbours Epping Forest but also many plant nurseries and agricultural land. It aims to challenge modern production methods and be entirely self sustaining. It achieves this thanks to the symbiotic relationship of agroforestry, permaculture and natural beekeeping. Its ethos is also affected, it is a communal meadery that does not prioritise profits or production but community.

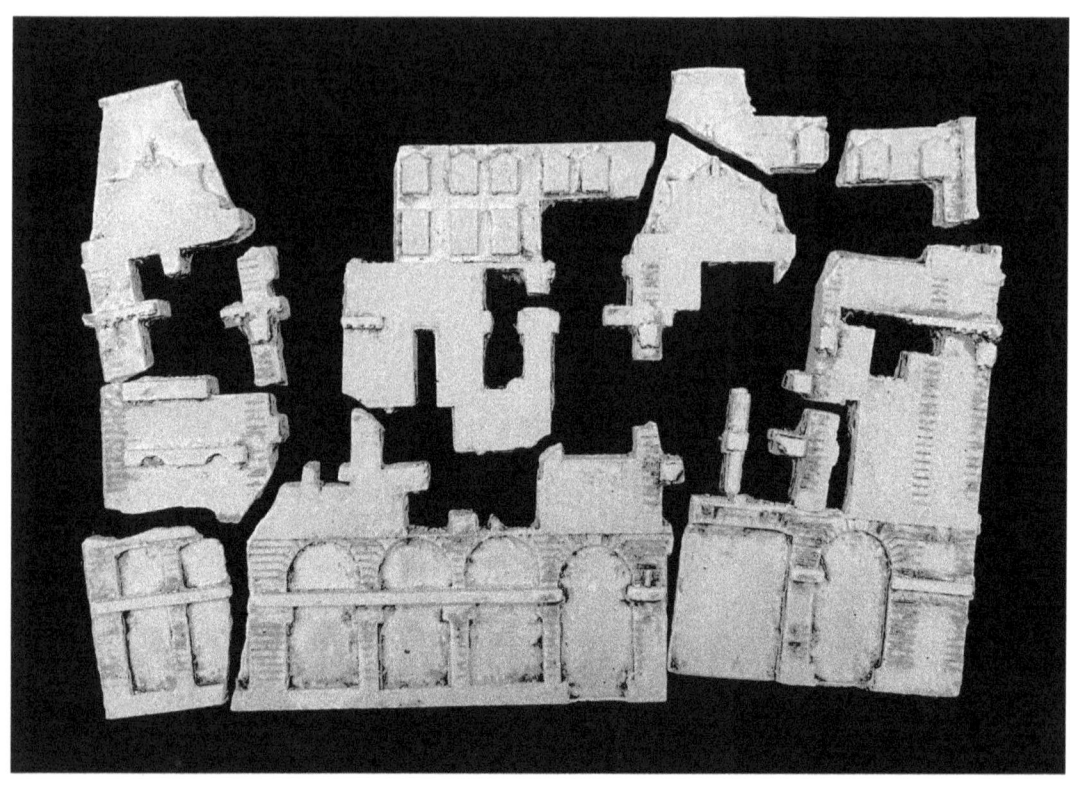

Facade model

MERLA ELAKKAD

DEMOLITION FACTORY

An anarchist social club located in Whitehall, a protest both within and against a system that inherently exacerbates hierarchy. In pursuit of a horizontal society, this project establishes a framework and acts as a cooperative, encouraging other autonomous social centres to join. increasing their longevity and creating a hub for Anarchy in the UK.

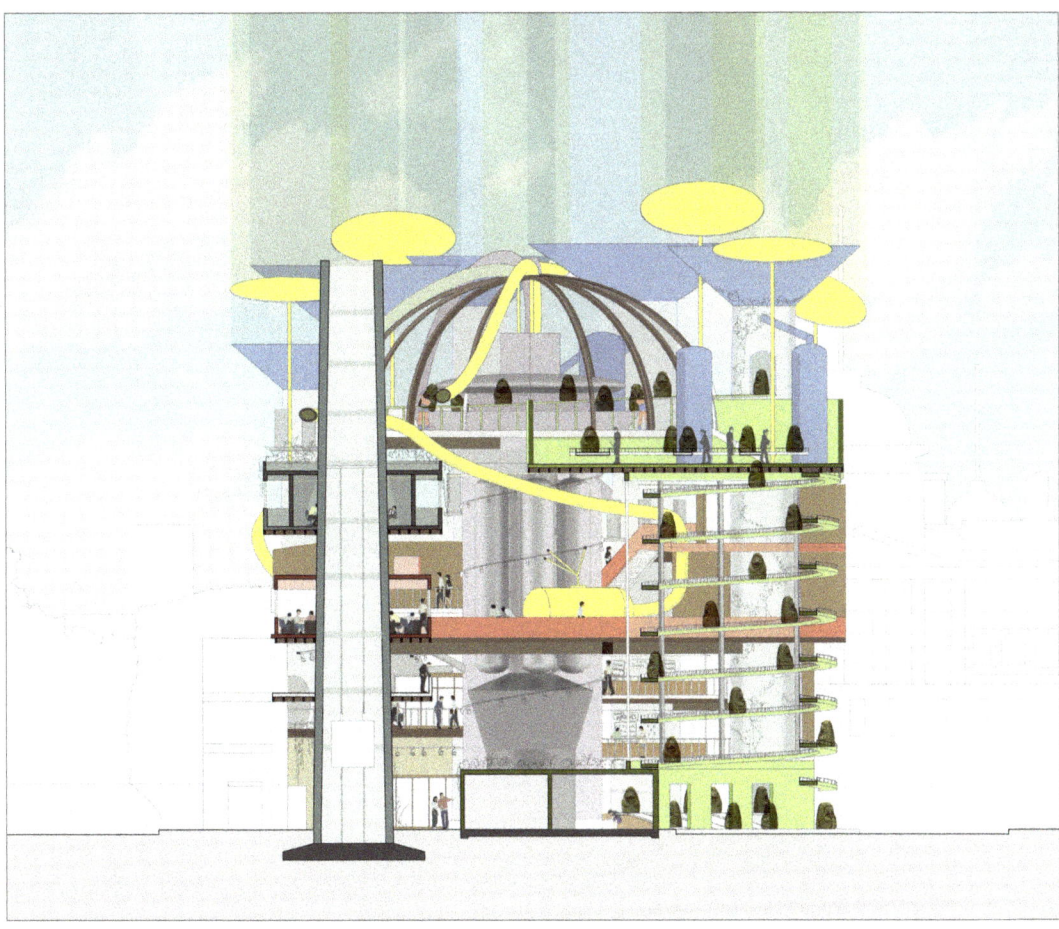

Section

DANIELLE ELEFANTE

THE DEPARTMENT OF WASTED ENERGY AND CIRCULARITY

In this apocalyptic story- one that may be closer than we think- we depict a future where nonrenewable energies have been depleted, and both human and nonhuman beings must find new ways to achieve a life of vibrancy again. The Department of Wasted Energy and Circularity rises as a beacon of hope, bringing power back to matter and materiality by creating Biogas through anaerobic digestion tanks, to rebuild and power the entire city. This process cleans the landfill through small automated bins, converting waste into much-needed energy. The Department stands tall beside now powerless governmental buildings, exposing raw matter to politicians in an uncomfortable, confrontational, and unavoidable way. Here, scientists, politicians, humans, and materials collaborate toward a future rooted in regeneration and cyclical systems. Embedded within its raw infrastructure lies a powerful message: the future must be regenerative. What was once discarded now fuels resistance, creativity, and survival. From the ruins, we imagine not just recovery, but radical renewal and transformation.

Inside the exhibition

DIEGO GALLARDO

BOTANICAL CO[W]LISEUM

Botanical Co[w]liseum is a call for action. This project consists of a monumental design, in the shape of a cow and a tree, to address the disruptions to the farming industry and the conflicts between farmers and governments through the implementation of regenerative agriculture. The cow hosts the headquarters for NFU, and its shape is a form of protest placed in front of the Prime Minister's residence, for him to raise awareness in parliament. This cow would expand into St. James Park, where a second monumental building would be constructed. A tree would rise up from the ground to house the Department of Regenerative Agriculture, a political institution implemented to strengthen this practice across the UK and Europe, and it will showcase examples of regenerative agriculture across St James Park, in the form of plots of land. Visitors will have an immersive experience through the entire building, where they will enjoy an exhibition about regenerative agriculture, a restaurant, and the attraction of going from the bottom to the top of the tree.

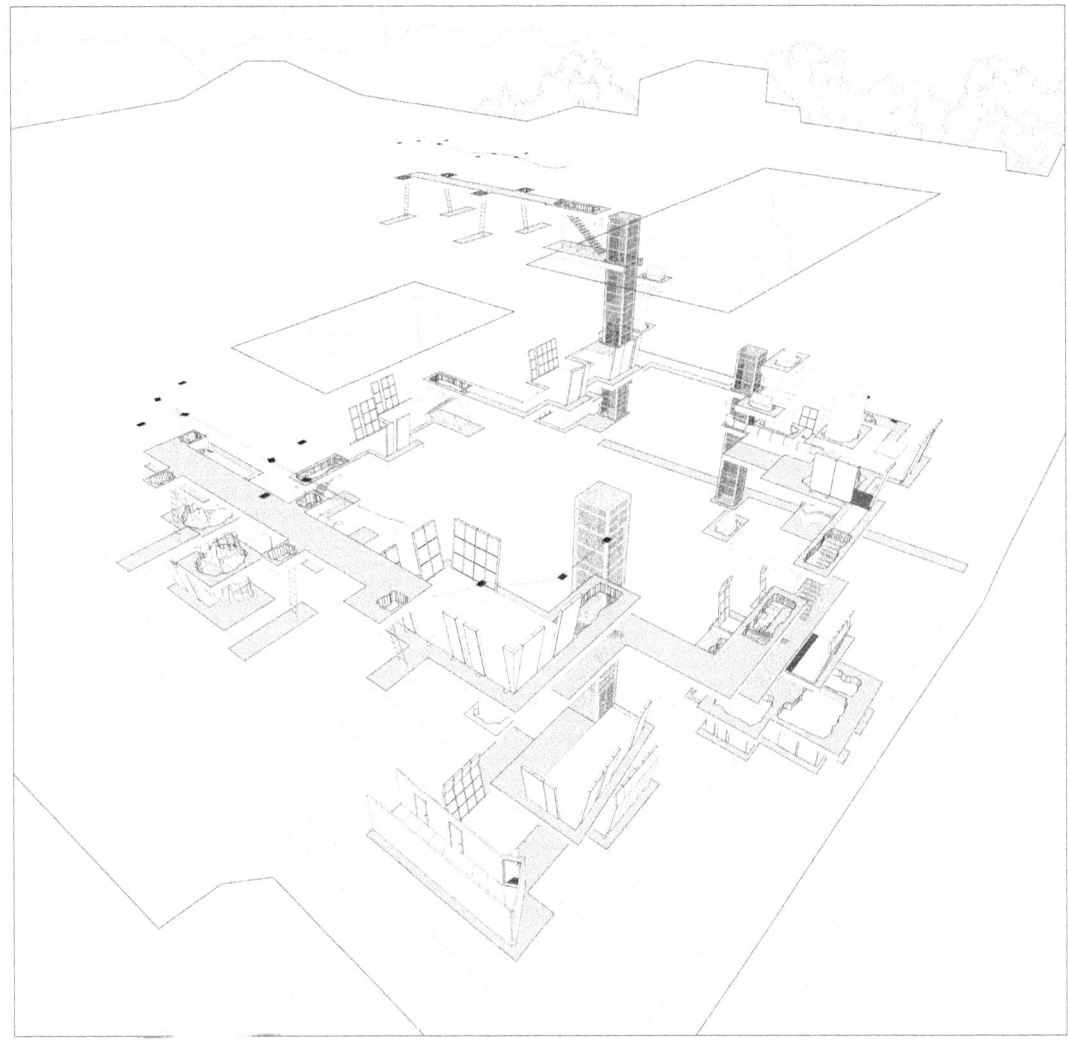

Aerial Perspective View

BENJAMIN GRAFHAM

THE UNSEEN LABYRINTH

Tensions peak thanks to the criminalisation of protesters and governmental inertia on climate issues.

A climate-crisis body is formed, kin to Kim Stanley Robinson's 'Ministry for the Future,' within which a covert faction is quietly created. One that embraces the seemingly inescapable negative public perception of climate activism, using secretive and violent methods historically mirrored by our government, to force change.

'The Unseen Labyrinth' uses this narrative to explore deceptive Architecture, serving two programs in the same building, concealing one from the other.

Ground Floor Plan

JULIA LASSOTA

(DE)COMPOSITION OF THE LANDSCAPE

This project explores a regenerative approach to architecture and material use, centred around a forest management practice known as thinning — selectively removing trees to support the health of the wider ecosystem. The harvested wood is transported to the site, where it is carefully sorted and processed. Higher-quality timber is used in a furniture-making workshop, allowing for skilled, craft-based production, while the smaller offcuts and scraps are directed to a second, more community-oriented workshop. Here, local residents and visitors can learn woodworking skills and create small objects or trinkets, extending the material's lifecycle and accessibility. The building itself is constructed using the same timber from the forest, grounding the architecture in its local ecology. Integrated residential flats provide housing for people who work on-site, encouraging a self-sustaining community model that blends living, making, and learning in close proximity. The result is a holistic, circular system rooted in collaboration and care.

Progression of living facade growth

EUNSEO LEE

DEPARTMENT OF PLANTS

The creation of an ecological government building housing the 'Department of Plants' stands as a beacon of biophilic architecture within London's political landscape. Situated at the heart of London, this innovative structure challenges the conventional notion that urban development must come at the expense of nature. Instead, it boldly asserts that buildings can thrive in harmony with the natural world. By integrating lush greenery and sustainable design features throughout its architecture, the building serves as a powerful testament to the intrinsic value and benefits of nature in the built environment. As people interact with the building and experience its biophilic elements, they are likely to develop a deeper appreciation for the beauty and benefits of nature. Moreover, the presence of the 'Department of Plants/ within this eco-friendly building sends a clear message to London's political powers about the importance of prioritising nature in policy making and urban planning. In essence, this ecological government building represents a paradigm shift in how we perceive and interact with the built environment. It demonstrates that sustainability and aesthetics can coexist, and that a thriving city is one where nature thrives alongside its residents.

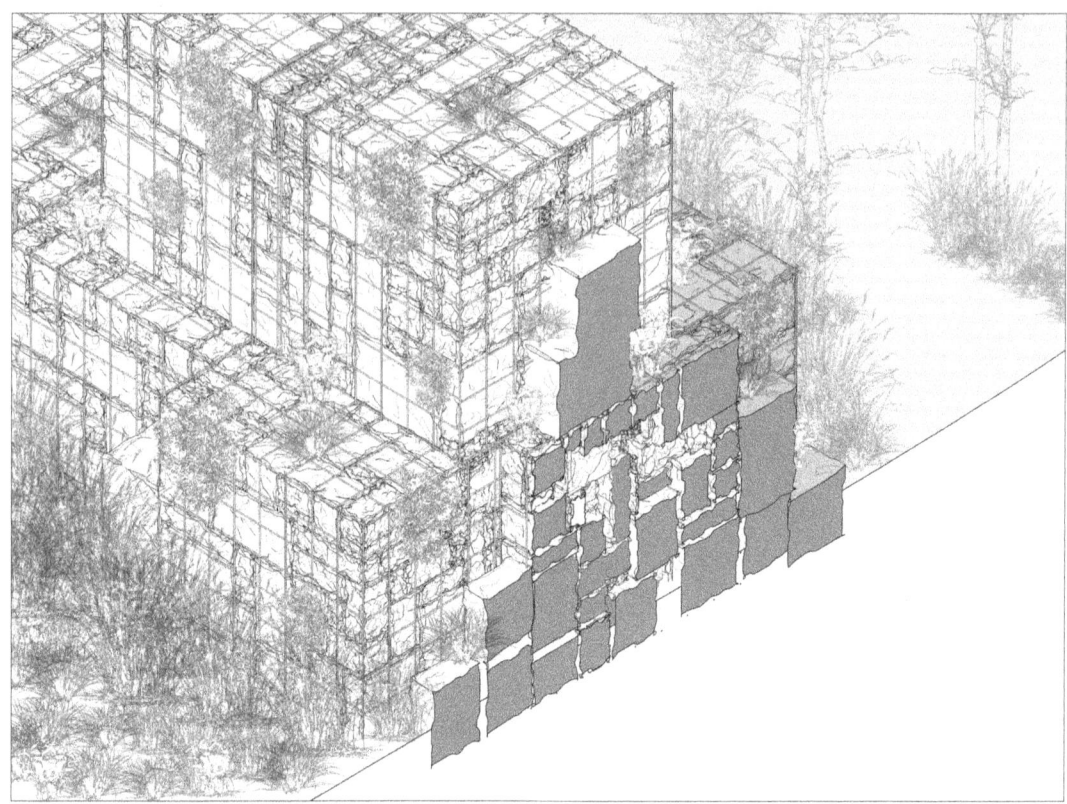

Gabion ecological section

BEN LEATHES

THE SILVAESIUM

The Silvaesium is a facility located in Epping Forest that aims to increase biodiversity and educate the public about their local forest biome. Its design integrates habitats and fosters biodiversity in an effort to restore what the Anthropocene has paved over and, through new technologies and public collaboration, strives to unite people and nature. Strategically placed throughout the forest, EcoNodes function as mobile data hubs that rely on public involvement to collect samples, alongside an app where the forest can be documented. This encourages people to take a closer look at areas they might not have ventured into before, bringing the community together to enjoy nature and contribute to its revival. The Ecotone façade employs deciduous foliage, serving both as a protective barrier against the elements and as a habitat for wildlife. The Silvaesium aims to reconnect the public with nature by encouraging data collection while being present in the forest. Its mission is to understand and support the forest and to further our research into how ecosystems function.

Rave night render

BEN LEATHES

ANTHROPIC TROPISM

Modern ecosystems have suffered degradation due to human activities, and most have lost some of their most valuable keystone species. This project proposes that humans step in to fill the void left by the loss of megafauna in Epping Forest. Through a series of events held within the forest, this Anthropic Tropism aims to recreate the ecological benefits that large animals once provided within ecosystems. These events, including small-scale raves, would utilise emerging technologies such as augmented reality to guide participants through the forest, creating immersive gatherings that bring together local people. To support these events, infrastructure would be implemented to aid users in navigating the landscape while also creating micro-biomes of their own. This infrastructure would operate off-grid and be constructed using sustainable materials that can be returned to the forest at the end of their useful life.

CAD drawn proposal axonometric
painted by hand with watercolours

HARRY MELLOR

LEGIBLE LANDSCAPES FOR LOCAL LEARNING

We are living in a version of modernity with no character or charm, destroying greenery and vegetation to satisfy stakeholders with no regard for the environment. An empty field in Southwater, West Sussex is being developed into a standard bland housing estate which would remove habitats and alter the eco system of the area. The aim was to design a proposal which catered for the same number of residents, but on half the site area; leaving the rest for nature to thrive once more. Legible Landscapes for Local Learning is a mixed-use research lab and housing complex for measuring various aspects of the environment, informing relevant local parties on what should happen, can happen and needs to happen to the environment around them. As part of a wider studio masterplan, the proposal seeks to enhance knowledge of local residents on environmental and sustainably matters. The project brings together the urban and natural worlds into a co-inhabited scheme with the proposal becoming wilder towards the existing hedgerow.

Meadow Ecological Section

DARYA PROKOPETS

SANCTUARY FOR THE DISPOSSESSED

This project proposes an architectural scheme for a research centre that works in close relationship with the surrounding wild landscape. It is designed not only for human use but as part of a broader ecological system where humans and nonhuman species are equally valued. The client is understood as the ecosystem itself: species, scientists, volunteers, and local communities all participating in mutual care and restoration.

The permanent research centre operates year-round, addressing local environmental challenges through ongoing investigations. Once a year, a two-week summer festival invites volunteers, researchers, and visitors to collaborate, apply research findings, and actively restore habitats. The festival also offers lectures, communal dining, social spaces, and forest bathing, fostering the exchange of knowledge and connection with nature.

Additional site elements: camping areas, cafés, bars, and bathing facilities are designed to have minimal environmental impact while encouraging meaningful interactions with the land. A water harvesting system and other low-impact strategies support self-sufficiency. The project aims not only to offer comfort and recreation, but to encourage a long-term relationship of care between people and place. It becomes a dynamic, restorative sanctuary embedded in the landscape.

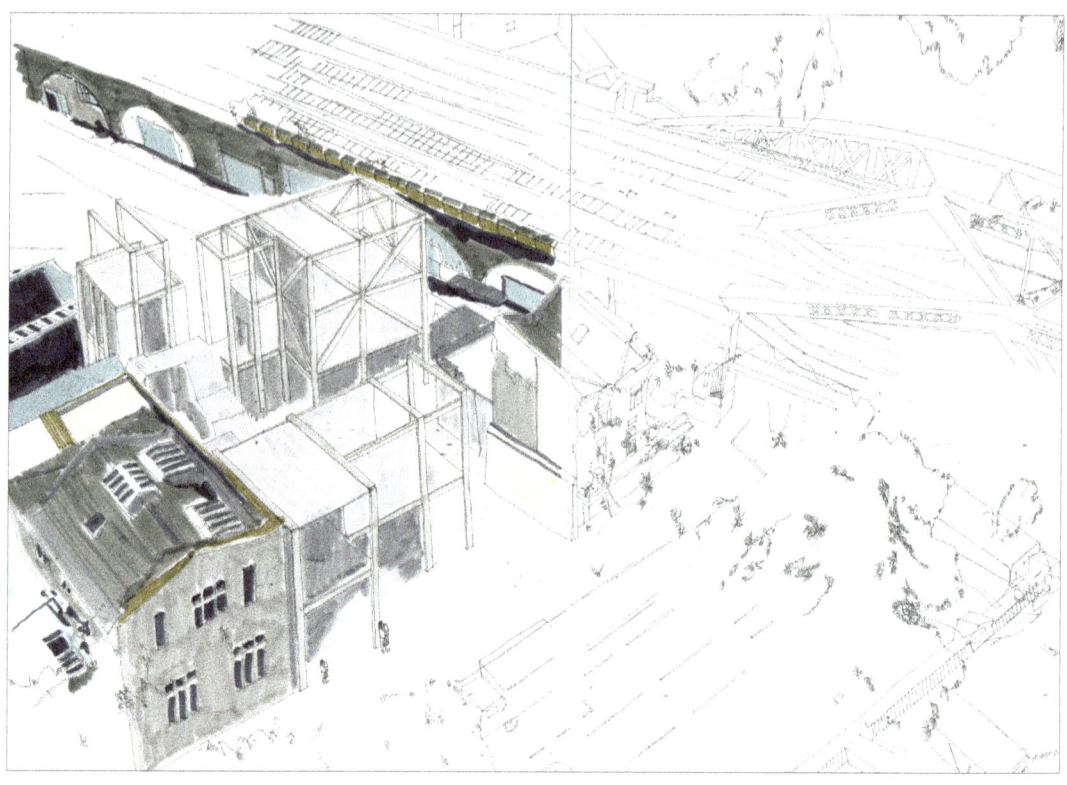

Aerial Perspective

FLORENTINE ROCKENBAUER

NATURE AND HUMANITY COUNCIL

The Nature and Humanity Council is a proposition for a civic architecture rooted in ecological reciprocity. Set within Epping Forest, the project establishes a space where governance extends beyond the human; a place in which natural systems are not just protected but actively included. Rather than inserting a structure onto the site, the design unfolds with it and its users.

The spatial configuration is a deliberate 50/50 split between enclosed chambers and open yet shielded volumes. This balance reflects not only programmatic need but a deeper ethic of coexistence. Materials, including netted wire, are chosen to accommodate slow habitation by vegetation, insects, and mosses over time. The building is porous by design, inviting occupation across seasons and species.

Part council chamber, part field station, part community platform, the project resists typological fixity. Researchers, students, and local residents are all called into relation, not to dominate nature but to learn from it. In this modest, site-specific proposal lies a larger argument: that architecture, if conceived with care, can mediate new forms of collective life: attentive, plural, and regenerative.

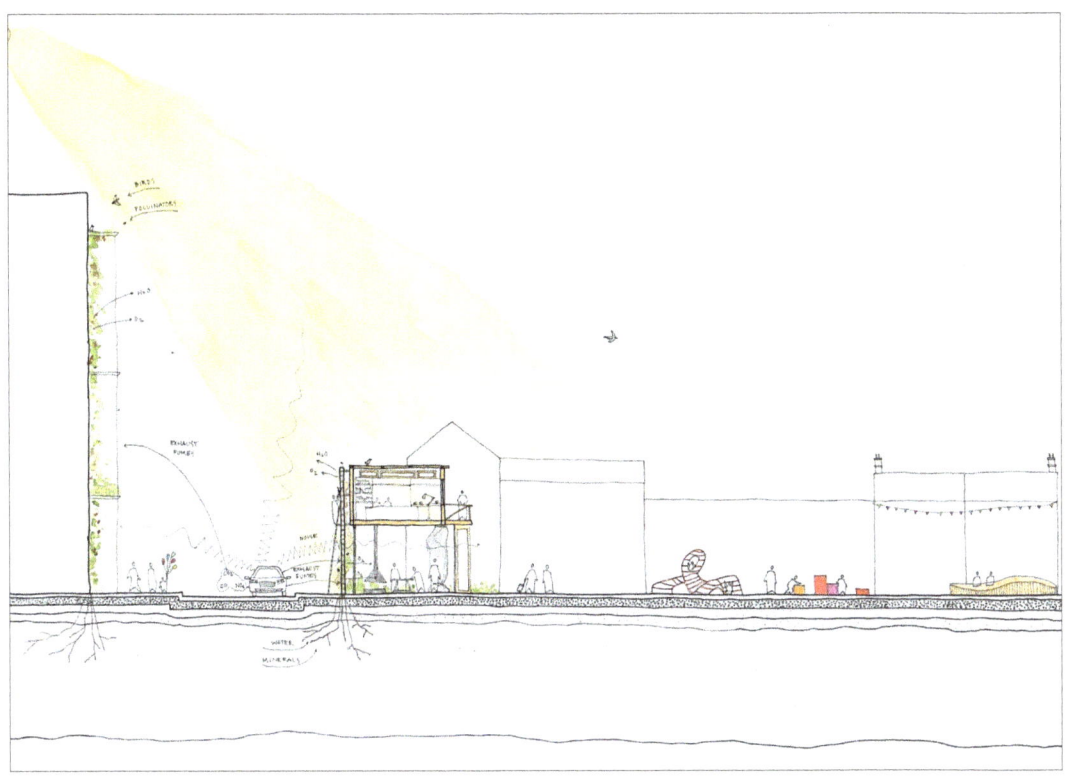

Ecological Section of The Centre for
Co-Design Processes

THAIS RIBEIRO RODRIGUES

THE INSTITUTE FOR SYMPOIESIS

Inspired by Donna Haraway's book "Staying with the Trouble: Making Kin in the Chthulucene", The Institute for Sympoiesis is an interdisciplinary organisation where artists, architects and scientists come together to explore new responses to the ecological challenges of the Anthropocene. Through annual residencies, the Institute fosters collaboration across different species and disciplines, encouraging "response-ability" and symbiotic ways of living. A layered façade with inner and outer rows of columns acts as a sheltering "membrane", akin to a living organism. This in-between space houses circulation and more permanent infrastructure, while the interior of the building consists of a vast open-plan area, divided by curtains and ephemeral partitions to allow for maximum flexibility of uses and activities.

The starting point for this project was my research into architect Lina Bo Bardi, her design process and projects, more specifically the SESC Pompeia in São Paulo, Brazil. Having Lina herself as my client, the brief was to provide an open plan design studio and meeting/consultation area, which would facilitate her work as a designer for the regeneration project of Greenhill Way, in the borough of Harrow, as well as a flexible public space which could be occupied and used in a variety of ways - encouraging a diverse group of people to gather and engage as a community and, on a wider scale, enabling the entanglement of humans, plants and animals.

Isometric render

RIBA PRESIDENT BRONZE MEDAL WINNER + RIBA AWARD FOR SUSTAINABLE DESIGN – 2023

KACPER SEHNKE

THE COUNCIL FOR ECOLOGICAL RESTORATION

The Council for Ecological Restoration is a global and national initiative focused on regenerating ecosystems by integrating natural processes into architecture, particularly through sustainable timber use. Hosting the United Nations Decade for Ecosystem Restoration, the building serves as a hub for political discourse, research, and advocacy aimed at protecting biodiversity.

Located near Chingford tube station in Epping Forest, the project reclaims the concrete-covered site of the former Connaught Tennis Club. Its core aim is to remediate the land by breaking down existing concrete to encourage native plant regrowth and ecological restoration. Recycled and upcycled timber from consumer goods and deconstructed buildings form part of the structure, while timber harvested through Epping Forest's sustainable pollarding practices is used for the envelope.

The design supports vertical plant growth and provides nesting spaces for wildlife, enhancing biodiversity without contributing to deforestation. As the building naturally decays, it transforms into habitat, with its materials decomposing into the soil and merging with the landscape. Embracing regenerative design principles, the project uses circular strategies through both technical and biological systems to restore habitats, foster biodiversity, and illustrate a long-term, sustainable vision for architectural and ecological integration.

Elevation

FINOLA SIMPSON

THE PURPLE EMPEROR

This project proposes a lightweight, elevated research and living structure for a lepidopterist studying and conserving the endangered Purple Emperor butterfly. Located in Southwater, Sussex—adjacent to the Knepp Estate and protected wildlife corridors—the design is sited within an existing oak woodland, elevating the structure to the tree canopy where the butterfly dwells, while minimising disturbance to the fragile ground ecology below.

Inspired by the form of the butterfly's pupa, the building's massing follows a tapering logic: the lower levels house insulated research and living spaces, while the upper levels open into netted, semi-permeable structures that foster coexistence between human and butterfly. A tensile terrace extends into the treetops, allowing close observation of the butterfly's breeding behaviours.

The project adopts regenerative principles by incorporating short-rotation pollarding and coppicing of willow trees, enhancing habitat while supplying renewable material for wattle and daub cladding and biomass heating. The lifecycle of the butterfly shapes both the programme and the seasonal use of the space—supporting scientific study in summer and habitat maintenance in winter. Through spatial sequencing, material logic, and ecological integration, the proposal celebrates the delicate relationship between species, season, and structure.

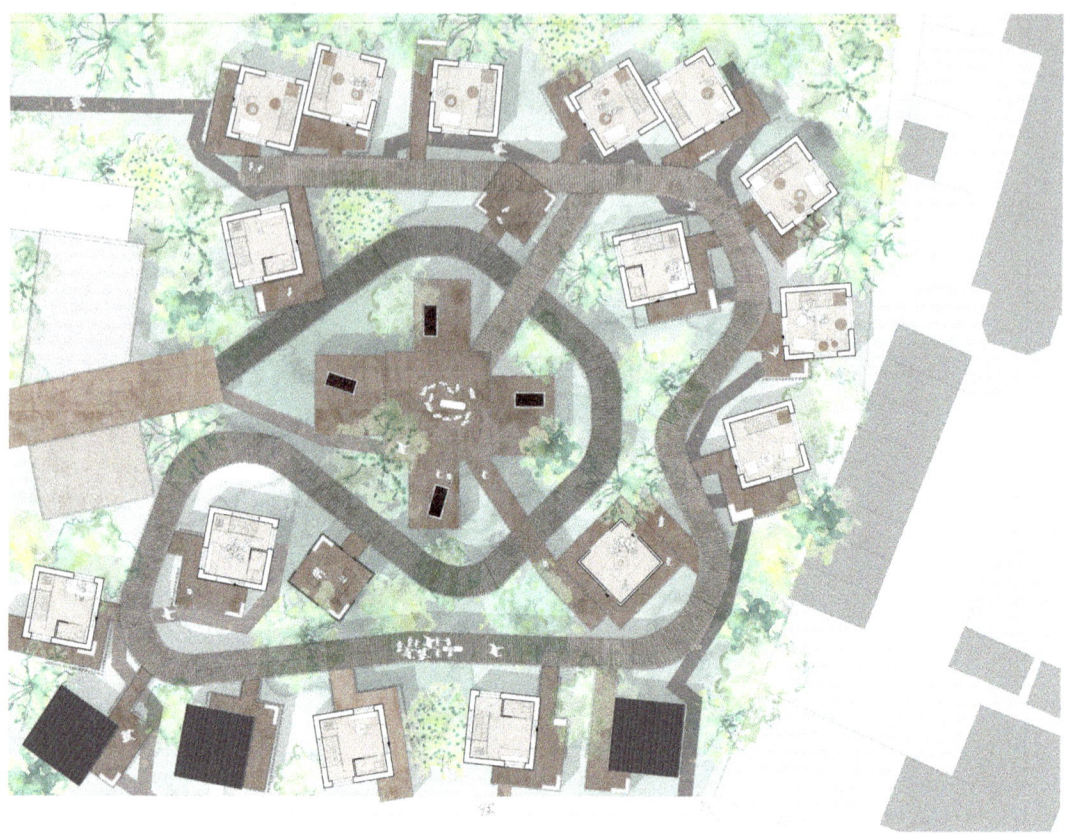

Elevation

FINOLA SIMPSON

THE PURPLE EMPEROR

Ritual Rewilding is a mixed-use residential scheme set in Southwater, Sussex, comprising 17 compact timber-clad homes and a human body composting facility. The project reframes death as part of an ecological cycle, offering a sustainable alternative to traditional burial and cremation methods. Through natural organic reduction, human remains are transformed into nutrient-rich soil over six weeks. This soil can be used by families to plant memorial trees in rewilded zones or donated to sites degraded by over-farming—creating a vertical cemetery of living memorials.

The design is structured around a central ritual walkway, guiding mourners in a ceremonial procession to place their loved one into decomposition towers. The housing is arranged around this space, creating a mourning community embedded within nature. Tall, slender units allow permeability for wildlife, while green façades and timber construction minimise environmental impact.

Inspired by Semiosis by Sue Burke, the proposal imagines the human body as a source of ecological value. It challenges Western attitudes towards death by integrating ritual, regeneration, and environmental responsibility. The project incorporates passive environmental strategies, a closed-loop heating system powered by decomposition, and landscape design that supports biodiversity, mental well-being, and long-term ecological restoration.

Enter the directorate unaware of loss
nor aware of gain

DAWOUD SOHAIL

A SYSTEMS DIRECTORATE

A history of human conflict & political deviation has led us into a crisis built on environmental issues. The directorate, stems as a new found hybrid between data centres, ecological repositories & debate chambers initiated by predictive modelling systems as an uncanny siege over existing departmental bodies. Contemporary machine systems monitor ecological parameters (physical, chemical, biological). Kin to organic machine concepts in James Bridle's 'Ways of being' integration into the surrounding context to monitor, facilitate & enhance relays at a primary level.

The Directorate uses this narrative to explore reclaimed metabolic architecture, serving multiple staged program levels in a single structure with divided opportunistic inhabitants in mind.

Original concepts for the 'Uncanny Panopticon' and relevant servant spaces innovate cognitive research from Katherine Hayles 'Unthought' utilising encapsulation of physical bodies to maintain a baseline for debate, controversially separating thought from the body.

Perspective view of the ritual entrance

SHAH-REE TASADDIQ

NAKSHI KANTHAR MATH – THE FIELD OF EMBROIDERY QUILT

My approach to the Cosmopolitical Parliament is deeply inspired by the concept of giving 'voices to ecosystems'. Drawing from Christina Cogdell's 'Toward a Living Architecture?' and the ritual of Black Rod, I developed a vision to create an ecological assembly for members of parliament and other professionals. The Bengali folktale 'Nakshi Kanthar Math' pro-foundly shaped this project. It narrates the journey of Saju, who, after being separated from her husband, found solace and enlightenment by crafting a quilt adorned with ecological motifs, symbolising her connection to nature. This powerful narrative inspired me to design a platform for ecology to voice its struggles, benefiting society. The biomorphic shell, acting as the ecotone façade, facilitates circulation throughout the towers and houses of parliament, protects the interior from the elements, and stands as a testament to ecological power. Additionally, the tapestries form the tent-like structures that define the various spaces within the biomorphic shell. These tapestries not only serve a functional purpose but also resonate with the narrative of Saju's quilt, embodying a deep connection to nature and ecological awareness.

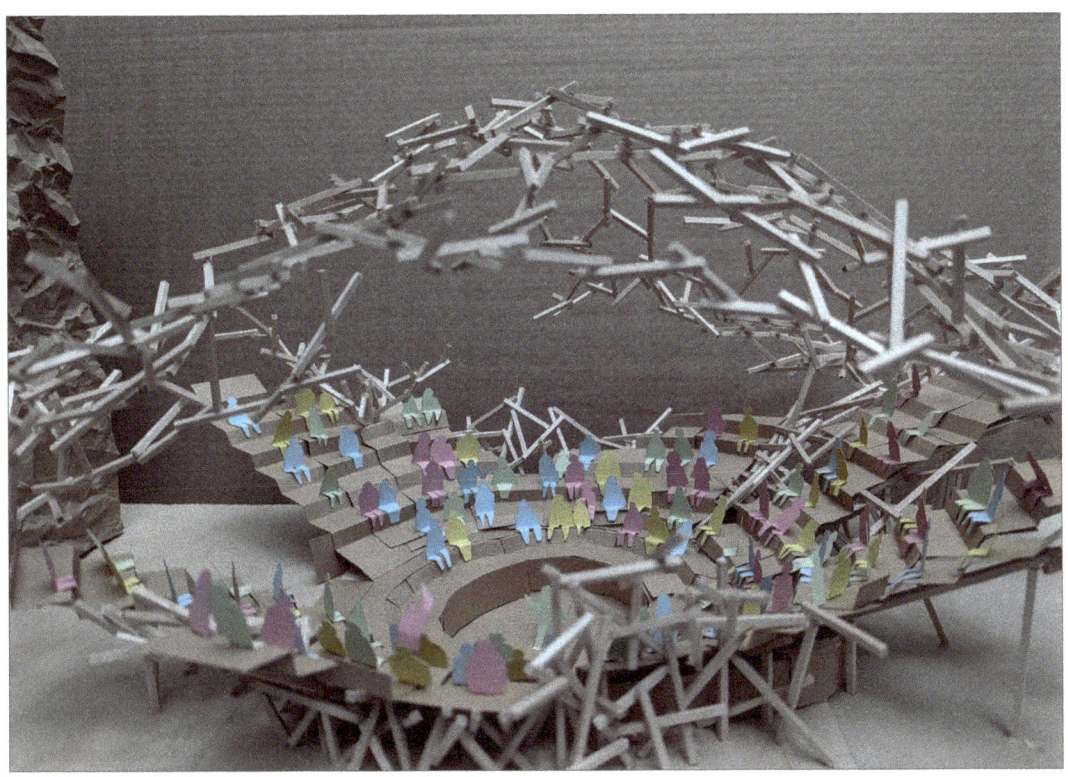

Model of the deliberation amphitheatre

REBECCA THOMPSON

DEPARTMENT OF HALF-EARTH SOCIALISM

The Department of Half-Earth Socialism is a speculative architectural proposal responding to the ecological crisis of the Sixth Mass Extinction. Inspired by the work of Drew Pendergrass and Troy Vettese, this project explores how architecture can serve as a political, ecological, and educational tool to reshape our relationship with the natural world. Situated between St. James's Park and 10 Downing Street, the project symbolically and physically bridges environment and politics.

The proposal calls for the rewilding of 50% of UK land, a shift toward eco-centric living, and the removal of excess impermeable surfaces in cities. The architecture reflects this vision: a circular amphitheatre anchors the site, surrounded by distinct programmes including a library, studios, and planning offices, all nestled within a landscape reformed through depaving and replanting. A green roof supported by tree-like timber columns provides habitat for birds and insects, while acting as a visual reminder of human-nature interconnectedness.

This project challenges the boundaries of architecture, positioning it as a vehicle for ecological stewardship, systemic change, and collective imagination. It argues that design is never neutral. Every decision is political, and every plan is a step toward or away from planetary survival.

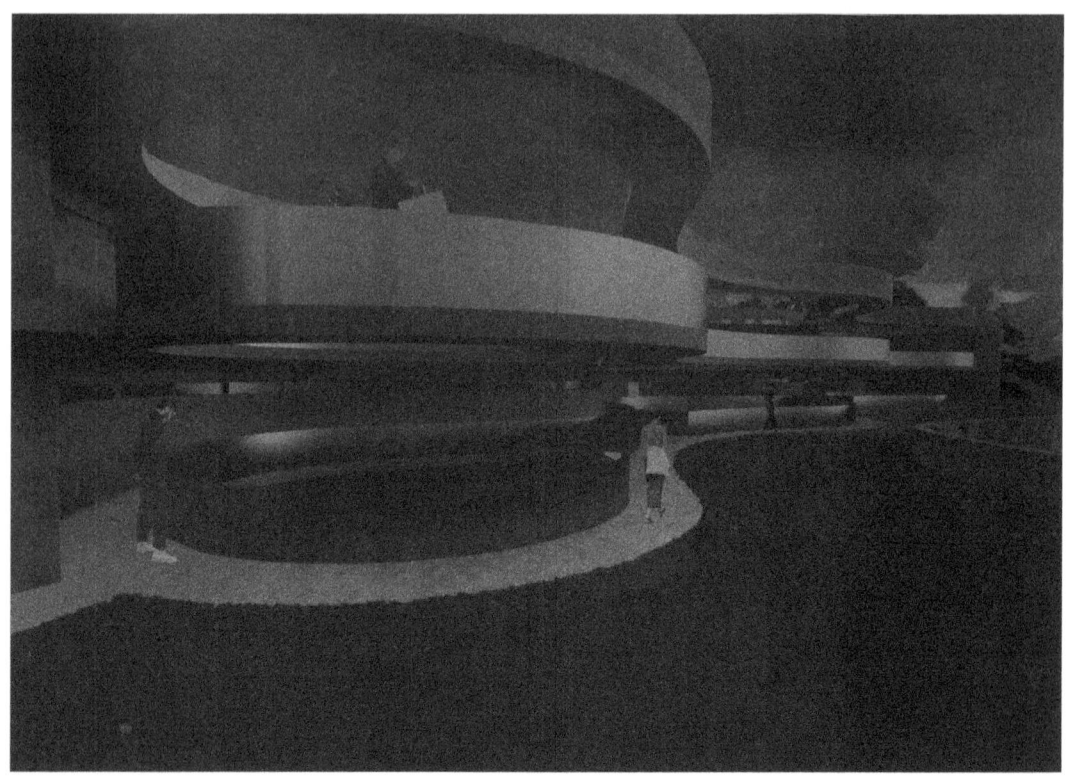

Internal view showing the second-floor terrace

ISABELLA TORRESAN TESTOLIN

FORGING UTOPIA

As climate change accelerates beyond the point of reversal, adaptation becomes our most urgent response. This project proposes a speculative commune and research facility in Southwater, Horsham, where scientists and CRISPR pioneers live and work collaboratively to redesign local flora and fauna for survival in disrupted ecologies.

At its heart are three sealed biomes simulating extreme environmental conditions, serving as incubators to test genetic adaptations in real time. Inspired by the natural landscape, the architecture embraces an organic form that harmonises with its surroundings. Residences and laboratories wrap around the central biomes, with open walkways providing constant visual and conceptual connection to the research core. The building is constructed from bio-receptive concrete, which encourages the growth of mosses, fungi, and lichens, offering ecological benefits like CO_2 absorption, air purification, and reduction of the urban heat island effect.

This project is both a response to climate anxiety and a provocation: how might architecture support radical new ways of living, working, and evolving in the face of environmental collapse?

Multispecies perspective section

YOHEI YAMANE

DEADWOOD VILLAS

Deadwood Villas proposes an ecological prototype that redefines architecture as part of a living, decomposing habitat. In response to biodiversity loss driven by climate change, the project focuses on preserving species that inhabit decaying wood, such as fungi, lichens, and insects often overlooked but vital at the lowest tropic levels. These organisms not only consume deadwood as a food source but are also consumed by other animals, making them essential to the broader ecosystem. The proposal mimics this relationship by creating modular, deadwood-based micro-habitats distributed throughout Epping Forest.

As the structure decays naturally over time, it supports ecological succession and invites continuous renewal, suggesting that architecture can be designed for decomposition, not permanence. The form is lightweight, repeatable, and potentially fabricable via 3D printing. The Villas create an evolving microcosm of species interactions, challenging the human-centric view of shelter and offering a regenerative, species-inclusive approach to inhabitation.

STUDIO STUDENTS

DS(2)4: ENVISIONING ARCHITECTURAL ECOLOGIES

2018-2019

- *Adejoke Adewunmi*
- *Daniel Berende*
- *Shivani Bhawnani*
- *Esther Calinawan*
- *Barbara Cellario*
- *Hannah Clarke*
- *Bryan Cotta*
- *Maryam Daoudi*
- *Georgia Dunmore*
- *Angeliki Giannakodimou*
- *Paul Greaves*
- *Wojciech Hoffmann*
- *Georgiana Ilie*
- *Anastazja Jankowska*
- *Niamh Lenderyou*
- *Kyungsoo Min*
- *Billy Nguyen*
- *Georgia Papadopoulou*
- *Casian Podianu*
- *Jacqueline Rosales Quezada*

DS(2)4: THE INSTITUTE FOR LIVING SYSTEMS DESIGN

2019-2020

- *Mohamed Alkhaja*
- *Jehaan Bhoyroo*
- *Erika Boguckaite*
- *Ugne Boskaite*
- *Erin David Rae Camagay*
- *Filippo Cocca*
- *Maik Fischer*
- *Jakub Jazdzynski*
- *Noor Kassem (S2)*
- *Soraya Mohajeri*
- *Giovanni Musumeci*
- *Melissa Nese*
- *Leticia Ramirez*
- *Thais Ribeiro Rodrigues*
- *Yael Schreiber (S1)*
- *Anastasia Shepel*
- *Shani Warshawsky*
- *Nicholas Wood*

DS(2)4: FERMENTED ARCHITECTURES

2020-2021

- Zamzam Al-Rubaye
- Syafiqah Aziz
- Wiame Azzouzi
- Arjun Bansal
- Rbiya Bashir
- Giorgia Bresciani
- Nina Busz
- Iman Dagnoko
- George Darlington,
- Mateusz Gliniewicz
- Joe Harding
- Mihna Landin Johansson
- Jessica Leach
- Betina Menescal
- Julia Pastor
- Aleyna Pekshen
- Jenan Rachid
- Changsoo Yoo

DS(2)4: FERAL ARCHITECTURES

2021-2022

- Edmund Alcock
- Monica Basta
- Lilia Beha
- Victorino De Castro
- Roza Hassan
- Param Hirani
- Alejandra Iglesias Garcia
- Ana Ivaschescu
- Julia Lassota
- Benjamin Leathes
- Nausheen Mahmood
- Harry Mellor
- Darya Prokopets
- Yasmin Satter
- Finola Simpson
- Magdalena Swiech
- Maryam Syed
- Karolina Szymczak
- Isabella Testolin

DS(3)2: ARCHITECTURAL ANIMISM

2022-2023

- Nondita Abdul Matin
- Alexandra Berculean
- Ariane Canet
- Dominik Figurski
- Luke Harvey
- Benjamin Leathes
- Ioana Macovei
- Farah Mazloum
- Erphan Mohammadkhani
- Yusufi Nimuchwala Aziz
- Florentine Rockenbauer
- Kacper Sehnke
- Saleh Shesha
- Nikhil Shetty
- Karen Silva Cardoso
- Christian Thunick
- Yohei Yamane

DS(3)2: THE COSMOPOLITICAL PARLIAMENT

2023-2024

- Mahmudul Ahsan
- Melody Akanji
- Merla Elakkad
- Danielle Elefante
- Sana Esmat
- Gabrielle Ferreira Silva
- Diego Gallardo
- Benjamin Grafham
- Emily Guacho Espinosa
- Malak Halibi
- Luke Harvey
- Jameelah Hussain
- Eunseo Lee
- Caroline Moisa
- Vanessa Muamba
- Raiyan Rizwan
- Linda Salihu
- Dawoud Sohail
- Shah-Ree Tasaddiq

A Carrier Bag of Regenerative Design Scores: Design Methods and Media for Regenerative Architecture

DS.3(2): 2022-2024, DS.2(4): 2018-2022
Edited by Eric Guibert

A University of Westminster, School of Architecture + Cities Publication

Book design and template by Mark Boyce & layout by Benjamin Grafham

All texts ©2025 the authors

A Carrier Bag of Regenerative Design Scores © 2025 by Eric Guibert is licensed under CC BY-NC 4.0. To view a copy of this license, visit https://creativecommons.org/licenses/by-nc/4.0/

ISBN 978-1-8383870-8-2

Books in the Studio as Book series are available to purchase via OpenStudioWestminster here: *http://www.openstudiowestminster.org/studio-as-book/ or from online book stores.*
The editors have attempted to acknowledge all sources of images used and apologise for any errors or omissions.

School of Architecture + Cities

University of Westminster
35 Marylebone Road
London
NW1 5LS

www.ingramcontent.com/pod-product-compliance
Lightning Source LLC
Chambersburg PA
CBHW040311240426
43666CB00022B/2925